THE
PROGRESS OF DOGMA

The
Progress of Dogma

BEING
THE ELLIOT LECTURES, DELIVERED AT THE
WESTERN THEOLOGICAL SEMINARY,
ALLEGHENY, PENNYSLVANIA, U.S.A.
1897

BY

James Orr

A REGENT REPRINT
INTRODUCED BY

Stephen N. Williams

REGENT COLLEGE PUBLISHING
Vancouver, British Columbia

The Progress of Dogma
Foreword by Stephen Williams © 2000 by Regent College Publishing

Originally published in England by Hodder & Stoughton

Reprinted 2000 by Regent College Publishing, an imprint of the
Regent Bookstore, 5800 University Blvd., Vancouver, B.C. V6T 2E4 Canada
www.regentpublishing.com

Printed in the United States of America

A catalogue record for this publication is available from the National Library
of Canada.

Foreword

James Orr (1844-1913) was one of the most vigorous, learned and level-headed theologians of his time. His authorship spanned the closing years of the nineteenth and opening years of the twentieth century. He was initially appointed to the Chair of Church History at the United Presbyterian College in Edinburgh, Scotland, but by the time that *The Progress of Dogma* was actually in print, he had moved to the Chair of Apologetics and Systematic Theology at the College of the newly-founded United Free Church in Glasgow. Although he was a constructive and positive thinker, his works were characteristically defences of evangelical orthodoxy against what he saw as serious threats, but they were marked not by sheer stubborn traditionalism but by an appreciation of all that was good and true in the thought of his day and by willingness to subject conservative positions to independent scrutiny. He ranged over the whole field of theology in a way that would be impossible today and was difficult enough in his time. We might spare a thought for James Orr whenever we sing the line from the hymn "Stand up, Stand up for Jesus" which goes: "Where duty calls or danger, be never wanting there."

The reprinting of this major work by Orr is indeed a welcome event. Its argument, presented in lectures given at Western Theological Seminary, Allegheny, Pennsylvania in 1897, often intrigues those who encounter it for the first time and those who wrestle with it for a second or third time. Its essence can be stated quite straightforwardly: Over the centuries, theological thought has concentrated on and clarified different doctrines in a logical and not a random order, an order that reflects a standard text-book treatment of the themes of systematic theology. So a well-organized text would proceed by discussing foundations, then the doctrines of God, humanity, Christ, atonement, the subjective appropriation of the work of Christ (faith; regeneration) and eschatology. Now when we survey the history of doctrine, we find that this was precisely the order in which the Church worked through its theological themes from the days of the second-century Apologists through trinitarian, then Pelagian, then christological controversies and definitions to the medieval and Reformation advances in the understanding of atonement and of faith. Eschatology, Orr suggested, is the task of our day. One imagines that this notion sent a shiver of excited aspiration down the spines of sympathetic younger theologians who heard it proposed.

Of course, this scheme was then, and is now, open to serious challenge. Firstly, readers of Orr's introductory chapter will often feel that the author presses too far any kinship between the methods and approaches of theology and natural science, to say the very least. Secondly, both logically and historically one can challenge Orr's claim that the question of humanity and sin must be dealt with before moving on from the doctrine of God (the dogma of the Trinity) to the christological decisions of Chalcedon. Thirdly, Augustine, the key figure in the development of theological anthropology, was engaged in the Donatist along with the Pelagian controversy, but the doctrine of church and sacraments does not enter into Orr's systematic or historical scheme. We should also add—whether or not this much affects the argument of his volume—that the twenty-first century reader will bear in mind that scholarship has moved on since it was written, so that, for example, portrayals of fourth-century Arianism or the Lutheran view of justification against its medieval past, will now look different. And doubtless one could cast a few more stones.

Yet there are those who emerge now, as emerged then, from a reading of Orr's work with a strong feeling that even if its detailed arguments are questionable, it is propounding something of great importance. But what? The problem of trying to put one's finger on what that might be generates plenty of theological excitement, for those who go in for such things. There is no denying that there have been marked phases in the history of theological thought, and the logical relations of themes do seem broadly, if not exactly, as Orr describes them. Of course, if we write textbooks of systematic theology, there are different ways of ordering the exposition, and it crosses one's mind that Orr might be wielding a saw that could cut off the branch he is sitting on when he announces, towards the end of the book: "Whether the Person of Christ can properly be made the governing principle of a theological system—which, as I said at the beginning, must follow the order of the logical dependence of doctrines —is another matter" (p. 336). Or does it just show that if Orr cared to modify his own scheme, the result would be even more arresting? Anyway, let the reader, to his or her considerable profit, read the volume and figure out what its achievement is and what is perennially important about the achievement.

However, there is something else going on in *The Progress of Dogma,* of considerable interest and of greater importance still.

Up to the final chapter of the book, at least after negotiating Orr's general allusions to science and evolution in the first chapter, the reader will have safely docketed the author away as a conservative Protestant, neither obscurantist nor uncritical of the tradition, yet a solid and convinced defender of its main lines. Now, as he comes to his finale, a new light is cast on the whole. For most of that last chapter, Orr does not deal directly with eschatology, which is explicitly treated in fewer than seven pages. What he does instead is to celebrate attainments in nineteenth-century theology amidst the deep and wide intellectual currents that it navigated. Of course, he is seriously at odds with much in it but maintains that the conservation of older doctrine can go hand in hand with a reconceiving of the Christian faith along lines which enrich and expand Christian thought, its traditional substance embedded in a new form. But Orr does this in such a way as to make one ask the question whether significant theological modifications are being permitted entry. It is as though, having safely secured the old, he is now free to embrace the new and, in embracing the new, generates in the readers mind just the hint of a suspicion about his fidelity to the old.

Now it is a suspicion that we should swiftly banish. Many of us will believe that on a proper reading of this volume, Orr emerges as consistent and remains conservative, and the course of Orr's writing subsequent to *The Progress of Dogma* will in any case dispel any lingering doubts in those disposed to worry about these matters. Later, in

1910, when the famous series of pamphlets known as *The Fundamentals* was launched, the first volume featured a contribution by none other than James Orr. Three others followed in subsequent numbers, though they were all actually reprints of essays previously published by their author. Orr's credentials as an early 'fundamentalist' were well-earned in the first decade of the new century, with publications on the Old Testament, the Virgin Birth and the resurrection of Jesus Christ. (The term 'fundamentalism' is misleading, though, for fundamentalism later took a sharper conservative turn and spawned a different intellectual attitude than his contributions portended.) His academic credentials had been well and publicly established in the previous decade, with his major work, *The Christian View of God and the World* and an exposition of Ritschl's theology, published in 1897. Learned and sharply critical, this latter volume introduced the British theological public to Ritschl with thorough reference to the actual text of that distinguished German theologian's writings. In his heyday, Ritschl was the greatest force in German theological liberalism and, indeed, *The Progress of Dogma* was explicitly pitted against the magisterial history of dogma produced by one commonly associated with Ritschl, namely Adolf von Harnack.

Nevertheless, in the last chapter of this work, Orr turned out to be relatively optimistic about the nineteenth century. His remarks on Kant, both here and in his earlier work, deserve attention. Kant had made his mistakes and these were by no means trivial, but he had also rendered theology a great service.

> [Kant's] nobler service to theology undeniably lay in his exaltation of the place of practical reason, and in his conception, based on *its* postulates, of the world as

a teleological moral system, with God as its author, and the kingdom of God as its end. (p.313)

"Teleology"; "morality"; "kingdom": important words. *Teleology*: the world has a destiny as well as an order. *Morality*: the practical consciousness of the moral law within us is a datum about humanity which we must never deny or denigrate. *Kingdom*: at intervals during *The Progress of Dogma,* Orr criticises the inadequacy of the Augustinian-Calvinist view of the election of the individual and advertises the need for an eschatological outlook on the promises and purposes of God which envision a mighty comprehensive kingdom. And now we've said it—*eschatology.* One thing that Orr seems to be doing in this work, though he leaves the reader to pull the strands together, is contemplating revising the system of theology from within an eschatological perspective. By "eschatology" is meant not just the doctrine of the last things that close or follow the close of history as we know it. Rather, we are to keep in mind the entire cosmos as a vast, embracing unity, moving towards a God-appointed goal. If readers care to pick up the vocabulary in this volume which relates to the organic; the unity of natural and supernatural, physical and moral; election; kingdom of God, they will come away with the sense that Orr's theology encompasses a great visionary breadth which in principle greatly enhances and in potency significantly modifies, the systematic theology hitherto outlined, espoused and defended. The nineteenth century has opened a window.

Readers must not be robbed of the pleasure of seeking out just whether or how these things are so. An allusion to *The Christian View of God and the World* should spice the investigation further. This work contained an appendix on "The Idea of the Kingdom of God." Originally, says the author, he had planned to incorporate a lecture on this subject in the body of the book, but eventually he did not do so. Why not? Different reasons are given but the most striking, which arrests us straight in our tracks, is found in the second part of a sentence which almost slides past us unobtrusively: "...The time is not yet ripe for making it [the kingdom of God] the one and all-inclusive notion in theology" (p. 404). Now Ritschl had in his fashion made it so. In his expositions of Ritschl, it is clear that the main point on which Orr could see virtue in Ritschl's contribution, was the attention he gave to the concept of the kingdom. Orr is not yet ready to be persuaded, but he implies that possibly the notion of the kingdom can be used to re-order one's grand theological scheme. In Orr's hands, this would not mean abandoning any building-block that is important in the constructive history of theological dogma. But it surely might alter the entire look of the construction. Orr never developed these possibilities.

I believe that James Orr has a great deal to teach us and this reprinted volume affords us an opportunity to meet him. It seems to me that the cumulative effect of his corpus is to make a case for an open orthodoxy: a steady conviction that foundational, trinitarian and soteriological essentials should remain intact, combined with openness to new light from any quarter, suitably traced to its source and tested for its illuminating power. One wonders whether Orr has bequeathed to us a theological task that no one so far has undertaken with signal success. Certainly he has left us an enduring legacy in spirit and attitude. It is true that he has sometimes been regarded as having grown more rigid in his conservatism as he went on, whether for better or for worse. It is also true that he opined that future advances in Christian thinking would be more in the realm of Christian Ethics than Christian Theology, to use his words. Be all this as it may, the voice of James Orr is one that we neglect at our peril in today's church, for more reasons than one. It is much to be hoped that the reprinting of this volume will help to re-open channels of communication between those who, separated by time and death, nonetheless abide together in fellowship in the one Church of Jesus Christ. It is good and right that we so abide until, in words Orr liked to quote, "we all reach unity in the faith and in the knowledge of the Son of God and become mature, attaining to the whole measure of the fullness of Christ" (Eph 4:13).

—Stephen N. Williams
Union Theological College
Belfast
February, 2000

PREFACE

THE lectures in this volume were delivered in the autumn of 1897, before the Western Theological Seminary, Allegheny, Pennsylvania, U.S.A., and the Christian public, as the fourth course in a series of lectures provided for by the Elliot Lectureship Fund. They are now published, at request of the Faculty, practically as delivered, any slight changes being on the form, not on the substance. It need not be said that no attempt is made to deal exhaustively with the History of Doctrine. The design of the lectures goes no further than to provide broad outlines, which may suffice to illustrate the principles expounded at the commencement, and serve as an introduction to the subject. The lectures met with acceptance at the time of their delivery, and the author is not without hope that they may be found useful to some who, without being professed scholars, feel an intelligent interest in the trend of theological thought through the centuries. Their object will be gained if the conviction is implanted that here also "an increasing purpose" runs "through the ages," and that the labour spent by myriads of minds on the fashioning of dogma, has not, as so many in our day seem to think, been utterly fatuous, and the mere forging of fetters for the human spirit.

The literature on the subject treated of is enormous, and valuable additions have been made to it even since the lectures were delivered. The material of the lectures is so much the accumulation of years of thought and study, that acknowledgment of obligation in detail is out of the question, and has not been attempted. The course, in any case, was not intended for proficients, but for learners, and elaborate references to literature would not have been in place. For the same reason notes have been sparingly employed, and the greater part of the references are to works in English, or of which translations into English exist. Quotations also, for convenience, are invariably given in translation, though the temptation was strong sometimes to give the pithier words of the original. Greater freedom has been used in the references to such works as Harnack's *History of Dogma*, for the obvious reason that one object of the lectures is to combat certain of the positions of that brilliant author.

In dealing with so wide a field, involving so large a mass of historical and literary detail, the author cannot hope to have escaped falling into errors which the eyes of experts will readily detect. He can only trust that they do not relate to other than minor points. That his general standpoint is out of harmony with prevalent tendencies, he is well aware, and he is prepared for wide dissent from many of his statements and conclusions. But it is because of this difference of view the lectures were written. They must rely on their own power to produce conviction.

For a fuller treatment of some of the theological

points, the author may refer to his volume on *The Christian View of God and the World* (5th edition, Andrew Elliot, Edinburgh); and for a sketch of the history and literature of the earlier period, to a Primer just published by Messrs. Hodder and Stoughton, on *The Early Church : Its History and Literature*, between which and the present lectures, as proceeding on similar lines, a general agreement will be traced.

I am indebted to the Rev. J. M. Wilson, B.D. Glasgow, for kind assistance in the revision of the proofs.

JAMES ORR.

Glasgow, 1901.

" Till we all attain unto the unity of the faith, and of the knowledge of the Son of God, unto a full-grown man, unto the measure of the stature of the fulness of Christ."—EPH. iv. 1 .

CONTENTS

LECTURE I

Introduction.

 Unity of nations in Christ.

 Fundamental Problem—Is there a recognisable law in the
  progress of dogma, and, if so, what aid does it afford in
  determining our attitude to theological system ?

 Is there dogmatic truth ? Objections :—

  (1) Dogma wholly excluded from Christianity.

  (2) Dogma a work of the Greek spirit.

  (3) The foundation of dogma in Scripture destroyed by
   criticism.

 View of the lectures : there is a doctrinal content in Christianity, which it is the duty of the Church to ascertain
  and witness for.

I. Dogma as an evolution in history.

 Stability of dogmatic products implied in the claim of theology
  to be a " science."

 What *is* dogma ? Distinction of " doctrine," " dogma," and
  " theology."

 Need of *criteria* of dogmatic products.

  (1) Scripture the ultimate test.

   Secondary tests : organic unity, correlation with experience, verification by practical results.

LECTURE II

Double conflict of the Church of the second century with Pagan-
    ism and with Gnosticism.
Fundamental identity of the conflicts.
    In both the Church fighting for its existence.
    In both driven back on fundamental ideas.
I. The conflict of the Church with Paganism—Early *apologetic*.
    Relation of apology to the literary character of the age.
    Bulk and range of the apologetic literature.
    Comparison of ancient with modern apology—difficult task of
        the former.
    The literary attack on Christianity : Celsus as type.
        Character of the *True Word* of Celsus.
        Causes of its failure to arrest the progress of Christianity.
    Three-fold task of the Christian apology as defensive, aggressive,
        and positive.
        (1) Its *defensive* task in relation to Jews and Gentiles.
            Its refutation of calumnies and plea for toleration.
        (2) Its *aggressive* task.
            Common ground with *Jews* in acknowledgment of Old
                Testament revelation.
            Polemical attitude towards *pagan* idolatry.
            Vindication, in opposition thereto, of truths of natural
                religion.
        (3) Its *positive* task—Evidences of revelation. Prophecy,
            miracles, spread of Gospel, spiritual fruits.
    The apologists and natural theology—charges of misappre-
        hending Christianity (Harnack).
        (1) Their works are *apologies*, not doctrinal treatises.
        (2) Their task called on them to give prominence to the
            truths of natural religion (Being, Unity, Spirituality
            of God ; Providence ; Judgment, etc.).
        (3) The doctrines in question real parts of the Christian
            system, and treated as such.

LECTURE IV

The Monarchian Controversies in the Third Century a prelude to
  the Arian Controversy in the Fourth.

LECTURE V

Transition to problems of man and freedom in relation to
  divine grace.
Place and importance of the Augustinian theology—Contrast of
  Greek and Latin theology.
I. Augustine's experience the key to his theology.
    His personal history as mirrored in the *Confessions.*
    Is his theology influenced by Manichæism?
    Two sides of his theology.
        (1) Its *churchly* or Old Catholic side.
            Catholicism here rightly claims Augustine.
        (2) Its *doctrinal* side.
            Here Protestantism shows more affinity.
    Two differences from Protestantism—results of sacramentarian
        principle.
        (1) Wide sense given to "justification."
        (2) Test of predestination not *regeneration,* but *persever-
            ance.*
            Inconsistencies of his scheme.
II. Positive exhibition of Augustine's theology.
        (1) Doctrine of *God* and of *the soul's relation to Him.*
        (2) Doctrine of *sin*—its nature as *privation* and results.
            Hereditary sin and the organic constitution of the race.
        (3) Doctrine of *grace*—grace and freedom.
        (4) Doctrine of *predestination*—Salvation of the individual
            viewed *sub specie æternitatis.*
            Religious interest of this doctrine.
III. The Pelagian opposition.
    Place of the Pelagian controversy in history of doctrine.
    Rise of the Pelagian opposition—the Pelagian doctrine in its
        antithesis to the Augustinian.
        (1) Contrast on the *nature of God and man.*
        (2) Contrast on the *nature of the will and freedom.*
        (3) Contrast on the *nature of virtue and vice.*
            Are there evil hereditary dispositions?

LECTURE VI

THE DOCTRINE OF THE PERSON OF CHRIST — THE
CHRISTOLOGICAL CONTROVERSIES : APOLLINARIAN,
NESTORIAN, EUTYCHIAN, MONOPHYSITE, MONO-
THELITE (FIFTH TO SEVENTH CENTURIES)   .

Relation of Christology to theology and soteriology.

Unlovely character of controversies, yet doctrinally inevitable.

LECTURE VII

Relation to previous developments.
    Epoch-making importance of Anselm.
I. Earlier development of the doctrine of Atonement.
    The Church always knew itself redeemed by Christ, and attri-
        buted a propitiatory efficacy to His death.
    Views of the *Apostolic Fathers.*
    Beginnings of theology of atonement in the *Old Catholic
        Fathers.*
        The " recapitulation" doctrine of Irenæus.
        Many-sidedness of Origen—germ of " ransom to Satan "
        theory.
    The *Nicene* period—*The Incarnation of the Word* of Athanasius.
        Remarkable development of idea of atonement as en-
        durance of penalty of sin.
    Repudiation of " ransom to Satan " view by Gregory of
        Nazianzus.
    Juristic development in *Western* theology from Tertullian.
        Emphasis on idea that atonement not the cause but the
        effect of love of God.
    Witness to belief in propitiatory aspect of Christ's death in the
        doctrine of the Mass.
II. First systematic attempt at theology of the atonement in
        Anselm's *Cur Deus Homo.*
    Question mooted in his day of the necessity of the sufferings of
        the Son of God for forgiveness of sins.
    The atonement no mere *preferential* scheme of the divine
        wisdom : must have its ground in deep principles of the
        divine character and government.
    Analysis of Anselm's positions : —
        Idea of sin as that which robs God of His honour.
        Necessity of punishment of sin.
        Impossibility of man rendering satisfaction.
        The Redeemer must be both God and man.

Nature of the satisfaction—not in mere obedience, for that already due from Christ.

Not in endurance of penalty.

But in voluntary surrender of Himself to suffering and death for His Father's honour.

Merit of this infinite sacrifice counterbalances all the demerit of human sin.

Strength and weakness of the theory.

Does not bring atonement into relation with punitive will of God.

Moves in forms of Catholic doctrine of merits.

Too objective—lack of nexus of faith.

Counter theory to Anselm's in Abelard.

Efficacy of Christ's death lies in its *moral* power—satisfaction rejected.

Enkindles love in us and reconciles us to God.'

Bernard opposes Abelard : his doctrine—" The Head satisfied for the members."

Exaltation of the *will* of God in Aquinas.

God *might* have dispensed with satisfaction—transition to *acceptilation* view of Duns Scotus.

Aquinas recognises penal endurance in Christ's sufferings (so the Lombard, Innocent III., etc.).

III. The Reformation interest in Justification reacted on doctrine of Atonement.

Justification not merely forgiveness, but forgiveness *on a righteous basis*.

The atonement as foundation of the sinner's peace.

Atonement not grounded in God's *will*, but in His *nature*.

Lifted from the sphere of private rights (Anselm) and placed on ground of public law.

Necessity of satisfaction to the law in its *penal* as well as its *preceptive* aspect.

Breadth of Reformation idea in Luther and other Reformers.

Atonement grounded in God's love.

Yet a " forensic " aspect is not to be denied.

LECTURE VIII

The essential fact here is what Ritschl calls "the religious self-estimate" of godly men in the Church.

This "self-estimate" has always one mark—the consciousness of having received everything from grace, and of continued dependence on grace.

Illustrations from Bernard, etc.

The Reformation doctrine in continuity with the Church-consciousness in this vital respect.

The development of the doctrine of atonement called for a readjustment of the doctrine of justification.

II. The Reformation doctrine a response to practical needs.

Meaning of justification by faith.

Inseparableness of justifying faith from good works; but this not the *ground* of acceptance.

Harmony of Reformation with Pauline doctrine.

The Tridentine antithesis to the Protestant doctrine. The two contrasted :—

    (1) In the place assigned to *faith* in justification.

    (2) In the Romish doctrine of *preparation* for justification.

       Merit of congruity and merit of condignity.

    (3) In the view taken of *justification itself.*

    (4) In the Romish view of *good works* as *completing* justification and *truly meriting* eternal life.

    (5) In the treatment of *post-baptismal sin.*

The Romish doctrine of Penance, its *working system* of justification.

Penance as the "second plank"—its development in confession, absolution, satisfaction, etc.

Purgatory, indulgences, and masses.

The whole theory a practical denial of the grace of the Gospel.

III. Abiding elements in the Reformation doctrine.

Post-Reformation controversies; advantages of the Reformed Church in these :—

    (1) Constructive genius of Calvin.

    (2) Less hampered by sacramentarian compromise.

Anabaptist and *Mystical* opposition; reversion to justification by *imparted* righteousness.

The doctrine of Osiander.

The Reformers' vindication of their view.

The *Lutheran* controversies; relations of believers to the law, to good works, etc.

LECTURE IX

(2) Held to corporeal presence of Christ in the Supper,
and doctrine of ubiquity of Christ's humanity connected therewith.

The Lutheran Christology largely conditioned by doctrine
of Supper.

Controversies of Brenz and Chemnitz, etc.

Corporeal presence comes in the end to a presence
virtualiter.

Century of undisturbed Lutheran orthodoxy—age of *Lutheran
Scholasticism*.

More vital tendencies in hymnology, etc.

Reaction against arid dogmatism in *Pietism*.

Influence of Spener and Francke.

Subjectivity and decadence of Pietistic movement.

Its failure to satisfy intellect.

The *Calvinistic* development.

Calvin's genius and influence—general nature of his system.

Calvinistic doctrine of *predestination*.

God with Calvin is not *exlex*.

Defect of his conception—Love is subordinated to sovereignty, instead of sovereignty to love.

Need of supplement through the organic conception of the
divine purpose in history referred to under Augustine.

The *Arminian* protest against Calvinism in Holland.

Two schools of Calvinists—*supra*lapsarians (Beza, Gomar)
and *infra*lapsarians.

Arminius affirms conditionality of predestination and
universality of grace.

The "Remonstrants" under Episcopius—points of the
Remonstrance.

Synod of Dort (1618-19) condemns Arminianism, and reaffirms Calvinistic positions (in milder form).

Christ died *sufficienter* for all, *efficienter* for the elect
only.

Real antinomies of Calvinistic system unresolved—mediating
attempt in "Amyraldism."

Flattening down of doctrine in later Arminianism—Curcellæus,
Limborch.

The "governmental" theory of atonement of Grotius.

Christ a *penal example* to deter from sin—a "rectoral
expedient."

It lacks a ground in essential justice.

Parties in Germany since Schleiermacher—" mediating,"
" confessional," " liberal."

The later Ritschlian School.

(3) Growth of the *scientific* spirit—Changes in human thought,
and effects in theology.

Outcome in demand for a restatement of the problems of
theology, and recasting of the whole system.

The result not to be feared.

II. Review of particular departments.

  (1) Call for a new *apologetic*.

     Change from older point of view—more comprehensive
character.

     Place of Christianity in general system of the world.

     Faith and reason ("religious" and "theoretic") cannot
be sundered.

     Apologetic cannot be separated from positive exhibition of
the Christian system.

  (2) The doctrine of *God*. Two main tendencies in thought of
century :—

    1. Deistic tendencies corrected by more living grasp of the
divine *immanence*.

     Bearings on ideas of revelation, miracles, etc.

    2. More central place given to the divine *love*.

     Bearing on idea of the divine purpose—the "Kingdom
of God."

    Modern treatment of the *Fatherhood* of God—truth and
error in representations.

     The divine Fatherhood in relation to (1) Christ ; (2)
members of His Kingdom ; (3) the world in
general.

  (3) The doctrine of *man* and *sin*. These also profoundly
influenced.

    1. The higher philosophy aids us in apprehending the *God-
related* side of human nature.

    2. The evolution theory, in its naturalistic form, tends to
lower man in obliterating the marks of his distinctive
dignity.

     Bearings of theories of the origin of man on the
doctrines of sin and redemption

     Limitations of evolution theory, and compatibility with
higher spiritual origin of man.

     False antithesis of "evolution" and "creation."

I

IDEA OF COURSE—RELATION OF DOGMA TO ITS HISTORY—
PARALLELISM OF LOGICAL AND HISTORICAL
DEVELOPMENT

"Theology is peculiarly the science of revealed religion. Theologians exist only among people who believe in a revelation, whether exceptional and national, or common and universal. Paganism and natural religion produce philosophers only, not theologians."—REUSS.

"When once we depart from that method of treating Church history, which proceeds upon the theory that in the changes and in the advances of theological science the logically necessary development of thought must be traced, we have no longer any other point of view left to us than that which makes the religious and scientific experiences of the theological subject to form the sufficient basis for his particular theological views. For second or third class men this standard may suffice."—RITSCHL.

"The teleology of Revelation supplements that of Nature, and so, to the spiritually-minded man, they logically and mutually corroborate each other."
—J. G. ROMANES.

LECTURE I

Idea of Course—Relation of Dogma to its History—Parallelism
of Logical and Historical Development.

PERMIT me, in introducing this course, to express the
pleasure I feel in being permitted, as a voice from
across the Atlantic, to speak to this audience on some
of the highest themes that can engage human thought.
Increasingly is it borne in upon us that in the great
brotherhood of nations, the bonds of which we rejoice
to see drawn closer every day, the supremely unifying
influence is the faith of men in Jesus Christ. Sundered
by geographical situation, with different histories and
vocations, held apart by the engrossing and often
rival interests proper to the life of independent peoples,
we are again knit together by this faith we cherish in
the One Living Lord, by our share in the world-wide
fellowship of His Church, and by our labours in
common for the ends of His Kingdom. It is a saying
of one of the most beautiful of the early Christian
writings—the *Epistle to Diognetus*—that "what the
soul is in the body, that Christians are in the world."[1]
That soul throbs in Scotland ; it throbs in America ;
and the heart that feeds its pulses is the same in both
lands—the Christ that liveth, and was dead, and
behold, is alive for evermore.[2] If I seek to be a

[1] Ch. vi.   [2] Rev. i. 18.

helper of your faith and knowledge in regard to that great heritage of truth which has come down to us from the past, which has received its existing shape through long conflict with opposing forces, and is embodied as the expression of our faith in the historical creeds on which our Churches rest, I am confident I can rely on your sympathy, and on your desire to gain as clear an insight as possible into this important department of Christian study.

For, expressed in brief, this is the subject on which I am to have the honour of addressing you—How dogma has shaped itself in history, what law has guided its development, and what abiding value belongs to its products. I do not propose to discuss the history of dogma for its own sake, or as a matter of mere antiquarian interest. I am to ask whether there is a recognisable law in the progress of dogma, and, if there is, what help it affords us in determining our attitude to theological system now, and in guiding our steps for the future. This is a question, surely, as practical as it is pressing.

But can we rightly speak of a system of dogmatic truth? Systems, of course, there are—venerable, the products of age-long development, but are they truth? As you are well aware, dogmatics—theological system —is in these days in somewhat evil case. It is like a ship among the breakers, caught by adverse currents, battered and washed by heavy seas on every side. Will it survive the strain? Or will its timbers yield, its masts go by the board, its time-honoured structure collapse in melancholy ruin? This is what many hope ; what others fear ; and you, who are to be the teachers of the future, no doubt feel deeply the gravity of the crisis. Let us, for encouragement, glance as impartially

as we can at the situation, and observe the quarters
from which dangers principally threaten.

There are those, then, first, who would *exclude* dogma
from Christianity altogether, as having no rightful place
there.   The bond of union in Christ's religion, they
tell us, does not lie in intellectual conceptions, but in
participation in Christ's spirit.   To make Christianity
depend in any degree on "doctrines" or "dogmas" is
to falsify Christ's Gospel in its essence.   Disputes
about doctrine — dividing, distracting, rending the
Church — have not tended to the advancement of
Christianity, but have been the prolific cause of wrath,
uncharitableness, bitterness, and persecution.   On this
view, the development of dogma we are to study,
instead of leading to any stable results in the better
apprehension of Christian truth, is a gigantic monument
of human folly, a monstrous aberration of the human
spirit, an incubus on the intellectual and moral
progress of the race.   This type of objection to dogma
will probably be felt to put itself out of court by its
manifest exaggeration.   There are few who reflect
earnestly on Christianity but will concede that it
contains *some* elements of doctrine, however nebulous
these may be supposed to be ; or who will not admit
that it is inevitable that the human spirit should seek
some clothing of conception for its faith, suited to its
degree of knowledge and culture.[1]   The question of
"doctrine" or "dogma" resolves itself very much into

---

[1] Even so pronounced an evolutionist in dogma as Sabatier admits
that "a religion without doctrine, a piety without thought, a sentiment
without   expression,   are   things   essentially   contradictory" ;   that
"Christianity in its pure essence implies the absoluteness of God, that is,
His perfect spirituality and His perfect independence" ; and that the
"variability of dogma is not unlimited," but is "necessarily confined
within limits which, while not easy to define theoretically, are none the
less precise and fixed" (*Esquisse d'une Philosophie de la Religion*, pp.
405, 211, 400 ; E.T., pp. 336, 172, 334).

how rich we suppose the content of Christianity
to be.

A second class, accordingly, do not go so far.
They grant that these ultra-radicals overshoot the
mark, but they still regard the *actual* course of dogma
as, if not exactly a mistake—seeing that it followed a
path of historical necessity—yet a wide departure from
the original idea of Christianity; to that extent a
"pathological" rather than a normal and healthy
process.[1] Dogma, as we know it, is, it is contended,
the result of an initial misunderstanding of Christianity,
which has vitiated its development all through; an
amalgamation of primitive Christian ideas with conceptions borrowed from the Greek schools; "a work
of the Greek spirit," as Professor Harnack describes it,
"on the soil of the Gospel," the general outcome of
which was "the Hellenising of Christianity."[2] In this
process the Gospel contributes, indeed, its part; but the
Greek spirit, working with its own intellectual instru-
ments, and importing at every point its philosophical
notions, is the really controlling factor, and the
Christian element—a drop, shall we say, in a vessel of
foreign liquid—is so wrought upon, diluted, changed,
as to be often hardly recognisable. The requirement
of those who take this view, accordingly, is, that,
breaking with the past, we begin *de novo*, get back
behind even the apostles, and, starting from the
immediate impression of the historical Christ, set
ourselves to construct "a new theology" which shall
be free from all metaphysical pre-suppositions. The

[1] Harnack objects to this term, but it seems correctly enough to
describe the idea.

[2] *Hist. of Dogma*, i. p. 21 (E.T.); cf. pp. 46, 47. Dr. Allen, in his
Continuity of Christian Thought, has a similar view; only he regards
this union with the Greek spirit as a great good, and puts *Latin* theology
under the ban. This last is far from Harnack's judgment.

air is full of this cry for "a new theology"; only the new theology which the age demands seems still to seek. As an American representative[1] says of it, it is "not a theology, but a tendency." The attempts—Continental and transatlantic—which have been made to give it shape show chiefly how far its adherents are from agreement among themselves. Not a few of the new theologies seem ready enough to blend with science and philosophy, if only the watchwords are sufficiently modern; the best are by no means criticism-proof.[2] The fundamental assumption of this school, that the history of dogma has been a persistent straying into the paths of error, will be considered in the course of the lectures.

Lastly—to allude only to one other phase of the attack—assault is made, not only on the completed edifice, but on the certainty of the very *foundations* of dogma; for criticism, in the view of many, has been brought into play with such deadly effect on the records of the Old and New Testaments—the old conceptions of revelation and inspiration have received such damage—the progress of scientific knowledge has made it so difficult to entertain even the *possibility* of supernatural occurrences—that a structure of dogma built on so insecure a basis cannot have, it is thought, any claim to rational acceptance—not to say to rank among the sciences, and even vaunt itself as queen of them! We come here, I grant, to a real dividing line; for if it be really the case that the foundations of

---

[1] President Bascom.

[2] As a type of transatlantic opinion, I might instance an article on "Reconstruction in Theology" in the *Bibliotheca Sacra* for Jan. 1897. Its leading ideas are evolution, immanence of God, Christ the acme of development, rejection of the old dogmas, and replacement of them by evolutionary conceptions in which, for the most part, the Christianity of the New Testament would not know itself.

historical religion are subverted ; if God, in truth, has not entered by word and deed into history, and given to man sure and reliable knowledge regarding Himself, and His character and purpose ; if the Son has not truly come as the Saviour of the world, and the promise of the Spirit to guide into all truth has not actually been fulfilled ; then, beyond doubt, the legitimacy, and even the possibility of dogma—above all, the legitimacy of such a development of dogma as history presents to us—fall to the ground.   But with this also falls the entire Christian faith.[1]   My appeal at present, however, is not to those who have not this faith, but to those who have it ; those who, knowing something of the results of criticism in the past, retain a reasonable confidence that nothing will emerge finally from the critical movements of the present that can materially affect our conceptions of the great outlines of God's historical revelation, or obliterate those evidences of an organism of truth in Scripture which force themselves, almost without seeking, on every observant mind.

Must theology, then, whose daughter " dogma " is, in face of these hostile forces, vacate her throne, and resign her pretensions to have any sure and verifiable results to lay before men ?   So it is often argued, but I am far from thinking that this is the case.   While conscious, I hope, of the limits of thought on such a subject, I believe, as I have always done, that there is a place and need for doctrinal theology ; that there is a truth, or sum of truths, involved in the Biblical revelation, for which it is the duty of the Church to bear witness ; that Christianity is not something utterly formless and vague, but has an ascertainable, statable content, which it is the business of the Church to find

[1] Cf. Appendix.

out, to declare, to defend, and ever more perfectly to
seek to unfold in the connection of its parts, and in
relation to advancing knowledge ; that this content of
truth is not something that can be manipulated into
any shape men's fancies please, but something in regard
to which we should not despair of being able to arrive
at a large measure of agreement, if, indeed, the Protestant
Churches have not already so arrived.[1]   I believe also,
with more direct relation to our present subject, that, so
far from the history of dogma being the fatuous, illusory
thing that many people suppose, there is a true law and
logic underlying its progress, a true divine purpose and
leading in its developments, a deeper and more complete
understanding of Christianity in its many-sided relations
being wrought out by its labours ; and that, while its
advance has not been without much conflict, much
error, much implication with human sin and infirmity,
and is yet far from complete, that advance has in the
main been onward, and has yielded results which further
progress will not subvert, any more than the future
developments of science will subvert, say, such discoveries as the circulation of the blood, or the law of
gravitation.

The fact remains, however, that dogma, as we have
it, is a development in time—a work of the human
spirit operating on the matter furnished to faith in
divine revelation.   Is this to its prejudice ?   Or rather

[1] Assuming that there is, as above contended, an ascertainable doctrinal content in Christianity, it cannot but be to the advantage both of
the individual and of the Church to think out that content in as clear and
coherent a way as possible, and to give it as accurate statement as is
attainable.   In every other department of truth the advantage of clear
notions and of carefully thought out and methodised knowledge is
recognised.   I venture to say that what the Church suffers from to-day
is not, as so many think, too much theology, but too little theology, of
an earnest kind.

is it not a singular testimony to the depth and fulness of the Christian revelation that it has this age-long significance—a content which even yet the course of the centuries has not sufficed to exhaust?[1] I shall endeavour, in the remainder of this lecture, to illustrate a few of the relations of dogma to its history, which may help us to answer this question, and will bring out in a preparatory way what I mean by a law of progress in dogma, and show how this admits of being applied in corroboration or correction of the theological system.

I. I am well aware that the claims I have put forth in the above paragraphs for dogma—especially the assertion of the stability of many of its products—will sound to many utterly extravagant. Yet, even at this preliminary stage, I may be permitted to observe that, as already hinted, I affirm no more than is already involved in any assertion that theology is a *science*. For science universally proceeds on the assumption that something on the subject dealt with can be known, and that, if right methods are employed, sure results may be expected. It would renounce its claim to be science, if its course were a perpetual discovery that all previous steps had been wrong—that nothing could ever be made out and set down as certain. The scientific man, *e.g.*, does not go on the assumption that probably the law of gravitation will yet turn out to be a baseless specula- tion ; that chemistry may prove to be as illusory as alchemy, or astronomy as astrology. It will be said, naturally, that, while this is true of the experimental sciences, theology stands on a very different footing.

---

[1] Sabatier remarks that, "strictly speaking, there is no Church, except in Christianity, and no dogmas save Christian dogmas" (*Esquisse*, p. 271 ; E.T., p. 237). Does not this of itself point to a difference in the *nature* of the religion, to a fulness of doctrinal meaning in Christianity which other religions do not possess?

In many ways it does, but its scientific character nevertheless depends, as much as in the other case, on the
possibility of the attainment of definite and reliable
results, from which further advance can be made.
Physical science also recognises the law of progress.
It proceeds by small increments of knowledge ; there
may be, constantly are, mistakes, rash theorisings,
temptations to go off on false scents, to overstate
conclusions ; but these errors get corrected by experience, and the assumption in the midst of all is that
there is possible, and is being attained, a solid advance,
the building up of a stable fabric, through the slow
adding of truth to truth. My contention is, that this
must be the case also with theology, if it is to make good
its claim to be a science.[1] If I am right in thinking
that it is so, and that the history of dogma presents us
with an analogous advance, it is assuredly a truth which
needs very specially to be spoken at the present time,
when everything, theologically, is being flung into the
melting-pot, and doctrines, torn from their context in
history, and in the system of faith, are treated often in
the most arbitrary, dilettante fashion ; or, it may be,
have their character altogether changed through the
influence of some quasi-scientific, quasi-philosophical
theory, at the same time, perhaps, that a protest is
being raised against the importation of metaphysics
into Christianity !

But, first, what precisely *is* ¡ dogma ? I have
used the term hitherto without definition, but it is
desirable before going further to arrive at a somewhat

---

[1] This brings us back to the position that the real ground of the denial
of the possibility of theology, or of a science of dogma, is always at bottom
the denial that any source of sure knowledge exists, in revelation or
otherwise, of God and His will and relations to men.

nearer determination. In current usage the word is obviously employed in a wider and a narrower sense. When Professor Harnack, for instance, rebutting a contention of Sabatier, says that " Christianity without dogma, without a clear expression of its content, is inconceivable," since Christianity " not only awakens feeling, but has a quite definite content which determines, and should determine, the feeling," [1] he clearly does not use " dogma " in the stricter sense usual with him, but employs it as practically synonymous with " doctrine." Ordinarily " dogma " stands, in distinction from this, for those formulations of Christian doctrine which have obtained authoritative recognition in wide sections of the Church, and are embodied in historical creeds.[2] There are, indeed, three terms—" doctrine," " dogma," and " theology "—nearly related, but between which careful distinction ought to be drawn ; the more, that a prejudice is often connected with " dogma " which is not associated in the same degree with the two others. " Doctrine," as Harnack rightly declares in the above passage, is of the essence of Christianity ; it is the direct, often naïve, expression by Christian faith of the knowledge it possesses, or the convictions it holds, regarding God and divine things. It furnishes its basis and material to " theology," which also is, in its way, doctrine—doctrine in elaborated form. " Theology " may be described as the reflective exercise of mind

---

[1] *Hist. of Dogma*, i. p. 22 (E.T.).

[2] Originally " dogma " was " opinion," what seems good to one ; then the term was applied to the opinions, decrees, or doctrines of the philosophers ; in the Church it was equivalent to doctrines ; finally, it assumed the signification of doctrines ecclesiastically sanctioned. "Dogma," says Sabatier, " in the stricter sense, is one or more doctrinal propositions which, in a religious society, and as a result of the decisions of the competent authority, have become the object of faith, and the rule of belief and practice (*Esquisse,* p. 263 ; cf. p. 230 ; E.T., pp. 274, 239). Cf. Harnack, i. p. 14, ii. p. 202 (E.T.).

upon the doctrines of faith. It aims at taking accurate account of Christian doctrine, at giving it scientific shape and grounding, at reducing it to system in the light of a central principle, at exploring the problems which it suggests, and exhibiting, as far as may be, its reasonableness, and relations with other departments of truth. Theology, like doctrine, therefore, antecedes and has a broader range than "dogma," by which, as remarked above, is properly understood those formulations of Christian doctrine which have obtained ecclesiastical sanction, and are embodied in the creeds. Thus regarded, the labours of theology are seen to be the presupposition of dogma; the latter, in turn, becomes the basis of new theological endeavours. But there is much theologising that never attains to the rank of accredited dogma. Quite unwarrantably, it seems to me, does Professor Harnack restrict what he calls the "genesis" of dogma to the first three centuries, and view it as peculiarly a work of the Greek spirit. The theology of Augustine, *e.g.*, is as truly epoch-making as that of the Nicene Fathers, and is in no way characteristically Greek—the very opposite.[1] Equally inadmissible is his attempted restriction of dogma to the Catholic Church. Protestantism also has had its invaluable share in this work. Even the labours of theology from the time of the Reformation—especially the rich and fruitful developments of the past century—cannot be excluded from this survey; for, if no creed has emanated from these labours, they have yet profoundly altered, deepened, and enlarged the interpretation of the older creeds, and have effectually been preparing the way for that "reconstruction" of dogma

[1] In a note to the third edition of *Hist. of Dogma* (i. p. 2, E.T.), Harnack practically concedes the justice of a criticism of Weizsäcker's on this point.

in the light of modern needs which will come in its
own good time.

A main advantage which the study of the relations
of dogma to its history may be expected to yield is
the test which the history of dogma enables us to apply
to dogma itself. What our age chiefly feels the need
of, I dare say, in the midst of the confusions that beset
it, is some way of bringing theological doctrines to a
higher test than the individual judgment. Many
theories are afloat; new speculations; new constructions of doctrine; each man claiming the right to set
aside the past, and put his fresh-coined fancy in its
place. Is there any way of bringing these conflicting
opinions to an objective decision, or must it be in
theology as in no other branch of science, *quot homines,
tot sententiæ*? The days are past when we can appeal,
with the early Church, to fresh apostolic tradition; we
refuse to bow, with the Middle Ages, to decisions of
councils and canonists; we repudiate the Romanist
assumption of an infallible head of the Church; we
decline, with the rationalist, to submit everything to the
rule of natural reason. Yet in the evolution of dogma
the need is imperative for some criteria by which sound
and healthy developments may be discriminated from
such as are the reverse. Do such criteria exist?

Naturally, our minds turn here first to Scripture,
which must always be the *ultimate* test. There is one
use at least to which Scripture may always be put—
negative, and yet immensely important as clearing
away much that does *not* belong to the system of
truth for which the Church is called to contend. There
may be disputes about the authority of Scripture, but
there ought to be no dispute about this, that whatever
has no place in Scripture, or cannot be legitimately

deduced from it, is no part of the truth of revelation for which the Church is set as "the ground and pillar."[1] This, I take it, is the distinction between Protestantism and Roman Catholicism, and it warrants us in rejecting straight off a vast mass of what passes as Catholic dogma, and cuts no less at the roots of many of the theories of modern Protestantism.[2] On the positive side, equally, Holy Scripture is the ultimate source of our knowledge of the facts and laws of Divine revelation. But apart from the difficulties formerly referred to, there remains the fact that all systems equally appeal to Scripture, and there would still seem to be the need of a tribunal to decide on this appeal. It is easy to speak of appeal to Scripture, but it is to be remembered that this very application to Scripture cannot be divorced from that growing insight into its plan and purpose— into the organic unity and fundamental harmony of its doctrinal content—which is the result, partly, indeed, of our improved method of using it, but partly also of that very history of dogma which we propose to test by it. We are more dependent on the past than we think even in our interpretation of Scripture ; and it would be as futile for any man to attempt to draw his system of doctrine at first hand from Scripture, as it would be for a man of science to draw his scientific knowledge direct from nature, unaided by text-books, or the laborious researches of the myriad workers in the same field.

There are secondary criteria of the soundness of a doctrinal system which I should be the last to depreciate—which are, in fact, of the highest value. There is, *e.g.*, the inner coherence and correlation of

---

[1] I Tim. iii. 15.

[2] What, *e.g.*, will always keep the Church from making a dogma of Universalism is the fact that this doctrine is at least not plainly taught in Scripture—some will go further, and say, is expressly contradicted by it.

parts in the system itself—its *organic unity*—which
is a check against any member of the system being
wantonly tampered with, or dissevered from the rest.
There is, again, the correlation of the doctrines of the
system with *vital Christian experience*, by which I mean
not simply the casual experience of the individual, but
the experience of the Church as a whole—of its greater
as well as its humbler souls—its Augustines and Anselms
and Bernards and Luthers, as well as its obscurer saints
—and of these in their loftiest as in their deeper moods.
That only can be truth which is fitted to sustain such
experience, to plumb its depths, and to supply the full
provision for its need.   A species of value-judging this
to which none will take exception!   There is once
more the appeal to *the practical effects*—verification by
results.   One simple form in which this test can be
applied—apart from moral fruits—is that of workable-
ness.   There are denials, we know, of nearly all the
great doctrines of the evangelical creeds—of the deity
of the Saviour, of His atoning work, of regeneration by
the Spirit, of justification by faith—but it is singular
that those responsible for such denials seldom attempt
to establish a Church upon them.   Where they do, it
does not thrive.   The very Churches in which the
impugners of the doctrines promulgate their denials
rest on the public profession of the doctrines which
they seek to subvert, and would lose their vitality and
power, if cut away from faith in them.

These tests are all valuable, and I do not say
they are insufficient.   Still it may be felt that, in the
divergent state of opinion around us, they do not, after
all, sufficiently eliminate the subjective element: that
there is still need for a more objective criterion—one
which will lift us above the uncertainties and fallibilities

of individual judgment, and place our feet on more stable ground. Is there such a criterion? Absolutely, of course, there is not; but the nearest approach to it is probably the method I propose to follow in the present lectures—that of appeal to the rigorous, impartial, one might almost say, if sufficient time is given, the practically unerring verdict of *history*. Here is a tribunal before which the personal equation in the individual judgment is cancelled; the accidental elements in the thought of an age drop away, and only its abiding contribution to truth is retained. We are familiar with Schiller's saying that the history of the world is the judgment of the world. It is at least true that the history of dogma is the judgment of dogma. One thing I am absolutely persuaded of, that, whatever imperfections inhere in our existing creeds, no phase of doctrine which the Church has with full deliberation rejected—which, on each occasion of its reappearance, it has persisted in rejecting—need raise its head now with any hope of permanent acceptance. And this principle alone, as we shall see, carries us a long way. The history of dogma criticises dogma; corrects mistakes, eliminates temporary elements, supplements defects; incorporates the gains of the past, at the same time that it opens up wider horizons for the future. But its clock never goes back. It never returns upon itself to take up as part of its creed what it has formally, and with full consciousness, rejected at some bygone stage.

I often feel that, in our revolt against traditional "dogma," too little weight is given to this fact that the system of doctrine embodied in our creeds is the product of centuries of development, and long testing in the fires of controversy. I hope that before this course of lectures is finished it will be apparent that I am no opponent of real progress in theology. I plant

myself here, in truth, on the most modern of all
doctrines — the doctrine of evolution, supposed by
many to be fatal to the permanence of dogma.   There
has been evolution of doctrine in the past, and there
will be evolution in the future.   But evolution means
that there has been something evolving ; and *pro tanto*,
if the evolution has not been utterly fatuous, there
must be, as remarked about science, results of that
process put on record.   What I complain of in many
of the apostles of the " new theology " is that, in their
eagerness for the new, they really ignore this primary
article of their own creed.   For we do not, after all,
begin *de novo* in our search for a theological system,
any more than science, in its study of nature, begins
with an unpeopled world.   The thing which confronts
us when we look into the matter is, that in all the great
Protestant Churches there is a *system of doctrine in
possession*—a system professedly based on Scripture,
and embodied, in its essentials, in the acknowledged
Reformation Creeds.   I do not, of course, argue that,
because a doctrine is found in any or all of these
creeds, it is necessarily true ; but what I do say is, that
when we are in search of a criterion to determine
what does, and what does not, belong to the genuine
doctrinal content of Christianity, this practically consentient body of doctrine in the great Church Creeds is
not a fact to be ignored—is, indeed, a weighty fact to
start from—one which gives that body of doctrine a
strong *prima facie* claim on our consideration.   The
fact that these creeds are, as we are so often reminded
to their disadvantage, the products of historical development, is precisely the fact which gives them, to my
mind, their peculiar value as witnesses.   They are not
the creations of individual minds.   They have centuries
of development, of conflict, of witness-bearing, behind

them.   Their success in history is the counterpart of
the failure of the opposite views to commend themselves
—to hold their ground in battle.   They represent the
" survival of the fittest " in doctrine under the severest
possible strain.   Not one of these doctrines but has
been hacked and hewed at till, if it had not been
founded on God's word, and felt to be true to Christian
experience, the breath would have gone out of it long
ago.   Yet men fling it aside as if this simple fact that
it is old—has survived all this brunt of battle—were
sufficient without further ado to condemn it !   It is not
explained why, in every other sphere, the surviving
product in an evolutionary process should be the fittest,
and dogma alone should be an exception.

One answer, I know, that will be made to this line
of argument is that, seeing the evolutionary process is
not yet complete, we cannot tell what the future may
bring forth—what changes, what transformations ; nay,
by adhering to the old and obsolete, we place an arrest
on further progress, and deny the fact of evolution
itself.   A double fallacy, it seems to me, underlies this
objection.   First, there is a fallacy in the initial
assumption that an evolutionary process is one of
unlimited flux and change, and yields no stable
products in its course — an assumption contrary to
every principle of science ; and second, there is an
overlooking of the fact that a true evolution is *organic*,
i.e., is a continuation of the developments of the past,
not a reversal of them.   Genuine evolution illustrates a
law of continuity.   It is not a violent breaking with
preceding forms, but proves its legitimacy by its
capability of fitting into a development already, perhaps,
in large measure accomplished.   In like manner, the
test of a sound theological development is not its
independence of what has gone before, but the degree

of its respect for it, the depth of its insight into it, and its capacity of uniting itself with it, and of carrying it a stage further towards completion.

II. When, however, I speak in these lectures of the history of doctrine as a test of theological system, and of a law or logic in that history, I desire now to say that I have in view something much more specific than these general principles involved in *all* development. The late Dr. J. H. Newman, *e.g.*, in his famous essay on the *Development of Christian Doctrine*, laid down what we must recognise as sound general principles—the very soundest—however much we may differ from him in the application of them. The first note of a genuine development, he tells us, is Preservation of Type ; the second is Continuity of Principle ; the third, Power of of Assimilation ; the fourth, Logical Sequence ; the fifth, Anticipation of the Future ; the sixth, Conservative Action in the Past ; the seventh, Chronic Vigour.[1] The principles are excellent : by their help we might, I think, refute very successfully much that is advanced by Dr. Newman himself. Yet, just because of their generality, it is certain that, had we nothing more, we should be left at the end of our inquiry very much where we were at the beginning. The idea I wish to illustrate in these lectures is different. It is not in its nature recondite, yet it has not, so far as I have observed, been made much use of in discussions on the history of dogma. It is not general principles of evolution we are in search of, but the immanent law of the actual history ; and when we seize the nature of that law, it will not only, I conceive, prevent us ever after from regarding the development of dogma as a maze of irrationality, but will be seen to furnish us

[1] Chapter v.

with a corroboration, and in some measure a *rationale*, of our Protestant Evangelical Creeds ; will yield us a clue to their right understanding, and, what is not less important, an aid to their further perfecting.

Has it ever struck you, then,—you will not find it noticed in the ordinary books, but I am sure your attention cannot be drawn to it without your perceiving that there must be more underlying it than meets the eye—what a singular *parallel* there is between the historical course of dogma, on the one hand, and the scientific order of the text-books on systematic theology on the other ?   The history of dogma, as you speedily discover, is simply the system of theology spread out through the centuries—theology, as Plato would say, " writ large "—and this not only as regards its general subject-matter, but even as respects the definite succession of its parts.   The temporal and the logical order correspond.   The articulation of the system in your text-books is the very articulation of the system in its development in history.   Take, for example, any accredited theological text-book, and observe the order of its treatment.   What we ordinarily find is something like this.[1]   Its opening sections are probably occupied with matters of Theological Prolegomena — with apologetics, the general idea of religion, revelation, the relation of faith to reason, Holy Scripture, and the like. Then follow the great divisions of the theological system — Theology proper, or the doctrine of God ; Anthropology, or the doctrine of man, including sin (sometimes a separate division) ; Christology, or the doctrine of the Person of Christ ; Soteriology (Objective), or the doctrine of the work of Christ, especially the

[1] The order is generally practically followed even where the designations vary.

Atonement ; Subjective Soteriology, or the doctrine of
the application of redemption (Justification, Regeneration, etc.) ; finally, Eschatology, or the doctrine of the
last things.   If now, planting yourself at the close of
the Apostolic Age, you cast your eye down the course of
the succeeding centuries, you find, taking as an easy
guide the great historical controversies of the Church,
that what you have is simply the projection of this
logical system on a vast temporal screen.   A glance at
the subjects of my lectures, with the details that are
immediately to follow, should convince anyone of this.
Meanwhile, assuming for the moment that it is as I
say, let me ask you to reflect on what so remarkable a
coincidence implies.   One thing, I think, it shows
unmistakably, viz., that neither arrangement is arbitrary
—that there is a law and reason underlying it ; and
another thing which forces itself upon us is, that the
law of these two developments—the logical and the
historical—is the same.   One is apt, I know, to look
with suspicion on all attempts to force history into
systematic categories.   Hegel tried this with history
generally, and Baur applied the same method with no
small ingenuity to this very field of Church history and
doctrine.   It is not, however, in this metaphysical sense
I ask you to consider the presence of law in history.
The facts to which I point need no manipulation of
mine to make them suit the exigencies of a particular
theory.   They lie upon the surface, and claim an explanation from anyone who attentively observes them.[1]
Let us try, in the first place, to understand the law which
discovers itself in the *logical* arrangement, then consider
the closeness of the *historic* parallel.

[1] Harnack, whose own method is so different, is often struck with this
upcropping of "logic" in history.   Cf. his *History of Dogma* (E.T.), iii.
p. 170 ; iv. p. 254, etc.

In the sketch just given of the arrangement of the theological system, not only is the order followed the usual one, but it will be perceived that there is a reason for this order—a logical principle which determines it.   The method, briefly stated, is simply to take the doctrines in the order of their logical dependence ; in which one forms the presupposition of the other. The doctrine of redemption, *e.g.*, presupposes that of the Person of the Redeemer, and, prior to that, the doctrine of sin ; the doctrine of sin, again, throws us back on the general doctrine of man, and also on the character, law, and moral administration of God ; the doctrine of God, on the other hand, underlies everything—the doctrine of man, of sin, of Christ, of salvation, of the purpose of the world, of human destiny. It is possible, no doubt, to alter or invert this order— to begin, *e.g.*, as Dr. Chalmers did, with sin as the disease for which a remedy is provided ; or with some recent theologians, with the Kingdom of God as the goal of the divine purpose.   It is also true that it is only in the light of the later doctrines that the wealth and range of the earlier are fully discovered.   Yet in the logical order of dependence the sequence is as I have stated it.   Just as in nature it would be found impossible to expound chemistry adequately without some antecedent knowledge of physics, or biology without some knowledge of both chemistry and physics ; so in theology the derivative doctrine cannot be exhaustively expounded till those which it presupposes have, at least in some measure, been explained. This, indeed, is the principle adopted in the classification of the natural sciences—the simpler preceding the more complex—and the attempt to proceed otherwise in theology, to work, *e.g.*, with the doctrine of sin, or of atonement, without a previous investigation of the

Scriptural doctrines of God, of man, and of the relations of both, can only end in superficiality and
error.

Such, then, is the logical system, and the principle
on which it is constructed.   Looking next to the
development of doctrine as it lies before us on the
broad page of history, what do we find ?   As stated
before, simply this logical system projected on a vast
temporal screen.   The whole course of lectures will be
an illustration of this thesis, so that it is only a quite
general indication that is needed here.   Using, then, the
controversies which impelled the Church in the formation of its creed as a guiding clue, mark, in a rapid
survey, the exactitude of the parallel.   The second
century in the history of the Church—what was that ?
The age of *Apologetics* and of the vindication of *the
fundamental ideas of all religion*—of the *Christian*
especially—in conflict with Paganism and with the
Gnostics.   This was the twofold battle of the Church
in that age.   On the one hand, it had to vindicate in
its apologies its right to exist, and to be tolerated in
the Empire ; on the other, it had to defend its essential
conceptions against the lawless speculations, and disin-
tegrating tendencies, of a fantastic religious philosophy. [1]   It was not so much as yet the special
doctrines of the Christian faith that were in discussion—though these also were partly drawn in—as
rather the broad truths that underlie all religion : the
unity, spirituality, and moral government of God,
man's freedom and responsibility, the certainty of
judgment, the need of repentance, the idea of revelation, the canon of Scripture, the vindication of the
primary facts of the Gospel as against those who
allegorised them into transactions of the spirit-world, etc.

[1] Cf. Lecture II.

Professor Harnack and his school make it a reproach against the second century apologists that they converted Christianity into a natural theology. There is thus much truth in the charge, that what we call natural theology had, from the necessity of the case, a large place in treatises addressed to pagans. But what I have to point out now is, how in all this we are still in the forecourt of theology ; just as, in the same place in the logical scheme, or discipline preparatory to it, we find ourselves dealing with natural theology, apologetics, canonics, the ideas of religion and revelation, and the historicity of the Christian facts. The most fundamental questions, in short, are those which challenged first the judgment of the Church.

We pass to the next stage in the development, and what do we find there ? Just what comes next in the theological system— *Theology Proper*—the Christian doctrine of God, and specially the doctrine of the Trinity. This period is covered by the *Monarchian, Arian*, and *Macedonian* controversies of the third and fourth centuries, in which the Church was called to conflict with these various forms of error :—first, in opposition to Unitarian, Patripassian, and Sabellian perversions, vindicating the general doctrine of the personal Trinity ; second, as against the denials of Arianism, upholding the true and essential divinity of the Son ; and third, as against Macedonianism, asserting the true deity and personality of the Holy Spirit. [1] These classical controversies follow, it will be observed, the logical order of Father, Son, and Spirit, and represent positions won from the enemy, frontier fortresses captured, lines laid down, from which the Christian Church has never since been, probably

[1] Cf. Lectures III. and IV.

never will be, dislodged. Their results have entered into all the great creeds, and form, we may believe, an inalienable possession of theology.

What comes next? As in the logical system theology is succeeded by *Anthropology*, so in the history of dogma the controversies I have named are followed in the beginning of the fifth century by the *Augustinian* and *Pelagian* controversies, in which, corresponding with the change of theological activity from East to West, the centre of interest shifts from God to man—from transcendental discussions on the Trinity to the intensely real and practical questions of sin and grace, which the speculative East, with its stronger sense of freedom, was tempted to pass over all too superficially. [1] In the Latin Church, on the other hand, ever since the days of Tertullian—through Cyprian, Hilary, and Ambrose—the way had been preparing for the serious study of these questions. But it was the great mind of Augustine, initiated into their depths by dearly-bought experience, and led to more precise formulation of the issues through conflict with Pelagianism, that first brought them to an issue. No grander figure, despite his undeniable limitations, has ever risen in the Christian Church than Augustine—a man as peculiarly raised up and providentially fitted for the work he had to do as the Apostle Paul himself. [2] He, too, has won for the Church positions of which the Protestant doctrines of grace are the consistent development ; while Catholicism, after acknowledging his supremacy

[1] Cf. Lecture V.

[2] It is one of the outstanding merits of Harnack's work on Dogma that he is able to do so much justice to Augustine. Only Augustinian theology, with which sympathy is shown, needs to sustain it a stronger foundation than Harnack's picture of original Christianity yields.

through practically the whole Middle Age, has sunk back into·a species of Semi-Pelagianism.[1]

Augustinianism, however, in conflict with Pelagianism, is not the only great development of the Post-Nicene age.   As in the theological system *Christology* follows Anthropology, and forms the transition from the latter to Soteriology, so is it here.   From the time of Augustine's death we see the Church entering on that long and distracting series of controversies known as Christological—*Nestorian, Eutychian, Monophysite, Monothelite*[2] —which kept it in continual ferment, and rent it with the most unchristlike passions during the fifth and sixth, on even till near the end of the seventh, centuries. This is perhaps, hardly even excepting some in the Lutheran Church, the most unlovely series of disputes in the whole history of Christianity, and it is grievous to reflect that, of all things, it was the Saviour's Person that was the occasion of them.[3]   Yet even here, as impartial inspection will convince us, there was a logic in the process ; the best men knew the importance of the issues they were contending for, and the Chalcedonian decisions have been accepted by most Churches as, if not a final formulation—for what formula on such a subject can be regarded as final ?—at least marking off the bounds within which a true doctrine of our Lord's Person must move.

This concludes the development of doctrine in the ancient Church.   Meanwhile, growing up beside it, and threatening to check further advance in a healthy direction, was a vast sacerdotal system, with theological conceptions of its own, the baleful influence of which remained unbroken till the great revolt of the Reforma-

[1] Cf. Lecture V.
[2] Cf. Lecture VI.   Apollinarianism in the fourth century was an important prelude.   [3] *Ibid.*

tion. Yet the progress of doctrine was not at a standstill in the interval. Theology, Anthropology, Christology had each had its day——in the order of the theological system, which the history still carefully follows, it was now the turn of *Soteriology*. Hitherto the doctrine of atonement, while always, as I shall seek to show, held fast and central in the faith of the Church, had never been theologically investigated as the other doctrines had been, and many crude and tentative conceptions had maintained themselves side by side with profounder apprehensions.[1]   Now, with Anselm, in his *Cur Deus Homo;* the problem entered definitely into the mind of the Church for examination and solution, and Christological questions were brought formally into relation with Soteriological.   Anselm's theology, while embodying elements of deep truth, had the necessary defects of first great attempts, and it required the explicit antithesis of Abelard, who represents the principle of the *moral* as against the *satisfaction* theories of the atonement, to bring out into clearness the nature of the issues involved.[2]   The problem, however, was now definitely seized.   Bernard and Aquinas laboured at it, not without result; till, at the Reformation, when Christ's death was grasped in its full significance in relation to divine law, as the ground of the sinner's justification, the doctrine may be said to have reached in essentials the form in which it has entered into the greater Protestant Creeds.

Soteriology, then, holds the place we should expect on the theory of the parallelism of the logical and historical development; but, if our hypothesis holds good thus far, it is assuredly not refuted by the next step, that taken by the Reformers in the development of the doctrine of the *Application of Redemption*.[3]   This, as we saw, is the next great division in the theological

1 Cf. Lecture VII.   2 *Ibid.*   3 Cf. Lecture VIII.

system—*Subjective Soteriology*, as some term it—which includes the doctrines of Justification, Regeneration, Sanctification, and the New Life.   The parallel here is so obvious that I need not stay to enlarge upon it.   The Reformers, as is sometimes, not quite fairly, pointed out to their reproach, took over practically unchanged the results of previous developments in doctrine—the Theology, the Anthropology, the Christology, the doctrine of Atonement, of the older Church ;[1] but they concentrated all their own energy on the bearings of redemption on the relation of God to the individual sinner—on Justification, on Regeneration, on Sanctification, and Good Works.   These, as is well known, were the great living issues in the Reformation period—its special contribution to the history of doctrine.   And its results also abide.

What now shall I say of the remaining branch of the theological system, the *Eschatological ?*   An Eschatology, indeed, there was in the early Church, but it was not theologically conceived ; and a Mythical Eschatology there was in the Mediæval Church—an Eschatology of Heaven, Hell, and Purgatory—to which I shall refer hereafter.[2]   But the Reformation swept this away, and, with its sharply contrasted states of bliss and woe, can hardly be said to have put anything in its place, or even to have faced very distinctly the difficulties of the problem, as these force themselves upon the modern mind, with its larger outlook on the ways of God and providence.[3]   Probably I am not mistaken in thinking that, besides the necessary revision of the theological system as a whole, which could not properly be undertaken till the historical development I have sketched had run its course, the modern mind has given itself with special earnestness to eschatological questions, moved thereto, perhaps, by the solemn im-

[1] Cf. Lecture VIII.   [2] Cf. Lectures IX. and X.   [3] Cf. Lecture X.

pression that on it the ends of the world have come, and that some great crisis in the history of human affairs is approaching.[1]   Even here I do not anticipate that the great landmarks of Christian doctrine will undergo any serious change.   The chief result may be to teach us caution in speaking on a subject, so many of the elements of which are yet beyond our grasp.

III. I trust I have succeeded in showing in outline what I mean when I speak of a parallel between the theological system and the historical development of dogma, and of a logical law underlying both.   The law is, indeed, in both cases the same.   The development is not arbitrary, but is shaped by the inner reason and necessity of the case.   The simpler precedes the more complex ; fundamental doctrines those which need the former as their basis ; problems in the order in which they naturally and inevitably arise in the evolution of thought.   The result is, that instead of inextricable confusion in history, we see the creation of an organism ; instead of fatuity and error, the gradual evolution and vindication of a system of truth.   Thus there is created a test of the value not simply of the existing doctrinal system, but of any theory claiming to be an enlargement of, or substitute for, the older forms of faith.   I am very far from disputing that there is still room for fresh developments in theology. Existing systems are not final ; as works of human understanding they are necessarily imperfect ; there is none which is not in some degree affected by the nature of the intellectual environment, and the factors the mind had, at the time of its formation, to work with.   I do not question, therefore, that there are still sides and aspects of divine truth to which full justice has not yet

[1] Cf. Lecture X.

been accorded ; improvements that can be made in our conception and formulation of all the doctrines, and in their correlation with each other. All I am contending for is, that such a development shall be a development *within* Christianity and not *away* from it ; that it shall recognise its connection with the past, and unite itself organically with it ; and that it shall not spurn the past development, as if nothing of permanent value had been accomplished by it. As I have already tried to show, so far from this contemptuous attitude to the past being in harmony with the spirit of true evolutionary science, it is a flagrant departure from it. Every discovery of new law in science fits in with previous developments, and carries these a stage further forward ; avails itself of past generalisations as an aid to further progress ; verifies them through the new and wider truths to which they lead. So far as a theory is true, it at once explains previous facts, and is verified by them.

Yet here again, perhaps, there is need for a word of caution.   I am not sure that we do not err in speaking, as we sometimes do, of the room for advance in theology as if it were absolutely indefinite ; as if the chief part of the task of theology lay still before it ; as if as much remained to be done as though our fathers had never entered the field ; as if, in short, the work of theology were still only beginning.   It is not always remembered that in every department of knowledge, theology not excepted, we have, as in agriculture, to accept a law of diminishing returns.   In art and science this law manifestly holds.   In architecture, we cannot plan and build as if Greeks and Romans, Normans and Teutons, had not built before us ; in music, we do not expect to outrival the creations of Handel and Haydn, and Mozart and Beethoven ; in science, it is not certain that the discoverers and inventors of the twentieth century will have as large and clear a field for their operations as their predecessors. The great lines of the sciences, at all events, are mapped out, their foundations are laid, much of the structure is built, and this is work that can never be done over again. So in theology, I think, we have to recognise the fact that our fathers have laboured, and we have entered into their labours; that history has been in travail with these subjects for the past nineteen centuries, and has brought forth more than wind; that we are not dealing with human speculations, but with a divine revelation, the records of which have been in men's hands from the beginning, and on which men's minds have been directed with the intense desire and prayer for light; that Christ promised His Spirit to His disciples to guide them into truth, and not first to scholars of the nineteenth century; and that the pre-sumption—practically the certainty—is, that the great decisive landmarks in theology are already fixed, and that we are not called upon, nor will be able, to remove them. It is, of course, always open, even in science, to a man to frame a theory which goes on the assump-tion that all the developments of the past have been wrong—that, *e.g.*, the earth is not a sphere, and that the Copernican theory of the heavens is a mistake—but we generally regard him as not wise ! Within limits, it should not be otherwise in theology. The men behind us have laid the foundations, and we must be content, I take it, to build on the foundations they have laid. This leaves us still vast work to do, but it is not their work. We shall not make less progress by realising that there is firm footing for us in the past to start from. We may take encouragement from those who have gone before us that our labour need not be in vain.

II

Early Apologetic and Fundamental Religious
Ideas—Controversy with Paganism and
Gnosticism (Second Century)

"The Gospel has a demonstration of its own, more divine than any established by Grecian dialectics."—ORIGEN.

"Within certain limits, then, and on certain subjects, metaphysics are but another name for *thought*; and if we are to have such an understanding of Bible truths, and the fundamental ideas as I have described,—and persons who profess to be theologians ought not perhaps to have much less,—we cannot avoid the obligation of going through some kind of metaphysical thought."—MOZLEY.

"The historical vocation of Christianity will not be satisfactorily fulfilled where men rest contented with being firm in the faith, with the deliverance of souls from the world, but only there, where Christian knowledge or science is also held to be the vocation of the Church."—DORNER.

LECTURE II

Early Apologetic and Fundamental Religious Ideas—Controversy
with Paganism and Gnosticism (Second Century).

IT has been contended in the previous lecture that the
history of dogma, rightly understood, is but the working
out of the solution of the problem of what belongs to
the essential content of Christianity. The elaborate
doctrinal articles embodied in our creeds seem, indeed,
to stand far apart from the simplicity of the original
gospel, and in one sense do stand apart from it.
Still they are to be judged by their claim to unfold and
exhibit in a form which has borne the test of time the
content of that original revelation—to give developed
or *ex*plicit statement to what is *im*plicit, or only frag-
mentarily and unsystematically expressed, in its Scriptural records. Dealing, however, as I propose to do,
only with main epochs, I am warranted in passing over
preliminary stages, and in coming at once to the second
century, which I have already described as the age of
Apologetic, and of the *polemic against Gnosticism.* It will
be found that there is a deeper identity between these
forms of conflict than at first sight meets the eye. In
both Christianity is fighting for its very existence. In
both also it is driven back in its defence on the vindication of the ideas that lie at the basis alike of natural
and of revealed religion. I propose to show in this
lecture how that conflict was waged, and to illustrate

its typical character, and the abiding value of its results for theology.

I. The rise of a *written apology* in the second century is intimately connected with the characteristics of the age in which it had its birth. It was an age of preaching, teaching, lecturing, declaiming beyond all precedent. The foundations of the new order were laid in the previous century by the Emperor Vespasian, who, though himself anything but literary, conceived the idea of bringing about an alliance between the philosophers and the State, and instituted a salaried hierarchy of teachers in Rome and the provincial cities.[1] The seed thus sown came to its fruitage in the age of the Antonines. Renan happily hits off the reign of Marcus Aurelius in calling it "The Reign of the Philosophers."[2]   In this reign, once in the world's history, Plato's dream was well-nigh realised ; the State had a philosopher for its ruler, and philosophers monopolised nearly all the places of power. It was inevitable that, appearing in such an age, apology should run into literary and philosophic form—should wear, what it has in Justin, and most of the other apologists, the garb of a "new philosophy."[3]   The significant thing is that it should appear at all.   " It shows," as I have said elsewhere, " not only that the spirit of the age had affected Christianity, but also that Christianity had pushed its way into literary circles, and was attracting their attention.   It makes clear that the Christians were beginning to have confidence in themselves, were no longer content to be 'a dumb folk muttering in corners,' as their enemies scornfully de-

---

[1] Merivale, *Romans Under the Empire*, chaps. lx., lxvi.
[2] *Marc Aurèle*, chap. iii.
[3] Justin, *Dial. with Trypho*, 8.

scribed them, but were emboldened to present their case in the open court of public opinion, and to challenge a verdict in their favour on the ground of its inherent reasonableness." [1]

The bulk and range of the apologetic literature which comes down to us from this period awaken our admiration and surprise.   Most of the writers are men of learning and culture ; not a few are philosophers and rhetoricians by profession.   The earliest are Quadratus and Aristides[2] in the reign of Hadrian.   Justin Martyr is the centre of a distinguished group in the age of the Antonines.   Among them are included Tatian,[3] Justin's own disciple, Athenagoras, Theophilus of Antioch, Melito of Sardis, with Minucius Felix, founder of Latin Apology, whose dialogue *Octavius* Renan styles "the pearl of the apologetic literature of the reign of Marcus Aurelius." [4]   Tertullian, in the close of the century, brings up the rear.   Origen might legitimately be included in our list, for, though he belongs to the next century, his great classic is a reply to Celsus in this. The works of these writers represent a wide area. There are two or three from Athens ; several are from Rome ; two are from Asia Minor ; one is from Syria ; one is from Pella, in Macedonia.   No fewer than seven of the apologies are addressed to emperors ; some, as those of Theophilus and Minucius Felix, are directed to individuals ; others are general, as Tatian *To the Greeks.*   It is, moreover, a noble and elevated

---

[1] *Neglected Factors in the Study of the Early Progress of Christianity,* pp. 184-194.

[2] The apology of Aristides has recently been recovered.   On the strength of a Syriac title some place it in the next reign.

[3] Better known as the author of the *Diatessaron,* or Harmony of the Gospels, likewise recently discovered.

[4] *Marc Aurèle,* chap. xxii.

spirit which breathes in most of them : the tone of men in whom already stirs the consciousness of coming victory. What fine dignity, for example, marks the exordium of Justin's first apology : " To the Emperor Antoninus Pius, and to his son Verissimus (Marcus Aurelius), the philosopher, and to Lucius, the philosopher, the adopted son of Pius, and to the sacred Senate, with the whole people of the Romans, I, Justin, the son of Priscus and grandson of Bacchius, native of Flavia Neapolis, in Palestine, present this address and petition on behalf of those of all nations who are unjustly hated and wantonly abused, myself being one of the number." " For," he goes on, " we have come, not to flatter you by this writing, nor please you by our address, but to beg that you pass judgment after an accurate and searching examination, not flattered by prejudice, or by a desire of pleasing superstitious men, nor induced by irrational impulse or evil rumours which have long been prevalent, to give a decision which will be against yourselves. For us, we reckon that no evil can be done us, unless we be convicted as evil-doers, or be proved to be wicked men ; and you, you can kill, but not hurt us." This was a new way of addressing emperors. No sycophancy or subserviency here ; but noble, fearless, yet dignified utterance ; the language of a man who pleads for truth rather than for safety : the tone which befitted a true freeman of Christ !

It is a truism to say that every age calls for an apologetic suited to itself. By a not unnatural illusion, we are apt to think that the demands on the apologist in the nineteenth century are more severe and testing than in any previous time. I am far from sure that this opinion is correct. The character of the assault has altered ; the conditions of the defence are different ; but I should greatly question whether the Christian Church has a heavier task imposed on it to-day than had the Church of the second century. A little reflection will show us that it was a very complex apologetic indeed which the Church of that time had to undertake ; and, if we fairly consider it, our feeling, I think, will be one of admiration that, with all its draw-backs, it accomplished its task so well. It is easy, no doubt, to sit in judgment on the work of the men by the help of whose shoulders we have mounted to the height we now occupy ; who were the pioneers in their several departments. Justin's work, *e.g.*, is, we may admit, defective in many ways. It is unsystematic, desultory, uncritical. His exegesis is often fanciful ; his use of allegory is excessive. He founds arguments on the Greek text which the Hebrew will not sustain. But even such criticisms may be carried too far. Justin's apology would not do for us ; but I venture to think that, with all their faults, his books contain a mass of reasoning, parts of which are even yet not antiquated. Those who depreciate his originality should remember how little had yet been done in the way of either apologetic or theology. Many of his arguments are trite only because they are now familiar. It seems to me that Justin blocks out his argument, taking it as a whole, with considerable skill ; and that many of his thoughts—that, *e.g.*, of the spermatic Word—are both original and profound. We shall do greater justice to the complexity and difficulty of this second century apologetic if we reflect on the double conflict the Church of that age had to sustain. It had to defend itself as a proscribed body against the *outward* attacks made on it in the name of the laws, and this at a time when its numbers were small, its prestige was *nil*, and the cloud of odium and calumny that enveloped it seemed well-nigh impenetrable ; and it had to defend itself against the keen and unscrupulous *literary* attacks of opponents like Fronto, Celsus, and Lucian, who fought it with intellectual weapons. In what follows it will be convenient to glance at the literary attack first ; then to look at the apology by which this and other assaults were met, as it shaped itself under the actual conditions of its environment.

We find, then, what the literary conditions of the age might lead us to expect, that the rise of apology had for its counterpart *written attacks* on the Christian religion. We shall err exceedingly if we underrate either the keenness or the intellectual ability of these attacks. Celsus (*c.* 160 A.D.) is here the classical representative.[1] Baur does not speak too strongly when he says : " In acuteness, in dialectical aptitude, in many-sided culture, at once philosophical and general, Celsus stands behind no opponent of Christianity."[2] With him begins what may be called the formal literary assault on Christianity, that assault prolonged through so many centuries, and revived with new vigour in our own day. His *True Word* (λόγος ἀληθής), in which he assails the Christian faith, is known to us only through the extracts from it in Origen, but these are so copious, and are so often given in Celsus's own words, that it is possible to reconstruct the greater part of the work, as has been done, in fact, by Keim. The plan, in particular, is easily made out. With considerable ingenuity Celsus brings forward first a Jew, whose task it is to advance against Christianity all the objections and calumnies that can be raked together from

---

[1] Cf. *Neglected Factors*, etc., pp. 192-94.
[2] *Church History of First Three Centuries*, ii. p. 141 (E.T.).

the point of view of the synagogue.   This done, the
Jew is dismissed, and Celsus conducts the argument in
his own person.   We now have the subject looked at
from the standpoint of the true philosophy.   Jew and
Christian are good enough to play off against each
other, but in the eyes of the wise man of heathenism
their positions are equally absurd.   The view of the
world on which Celsus proceeds is in some respects
different from the modern one ; in others, it has a
surprisingly modern look.   It is one which excludes
beforehand all revelation, incarnation, and miracle.
The world is bound in an iron band of necessity, and
its course cannot be altered.   In such a system, as
Origen says, " free will is annihilated." [1]   Matter is the
source of evil, and the quantity of evil is fixed and
unalterable.[2]   With this conception Celsus turns on
Christianity, and everything in it is necessarily an
offence to him.   Scarcely anything in the way of cavil
has escaped him.   The objections of later critics of
the Gospels—of the Deists, of Voltaire, of Strauss—
are with marvellous completeness anticipated here.   But
it is on the doctrine of Redemption that he pours the
vials of his fullest scorn.   Redemption was to Celsus
an incredibility, because he regarded it as an impossibility.   If the sum of evils is a fixed quantity, it is
clearly beyond any one's power to do aught to diminish
it.   A change from bad to good in human nature he
thought barely conceivable.[3]   Pardon of sin could
have no place in his system.   That the world was
created, or is governed, for man's benefit is to him the
most ridiculous of ideas.   To strike at the Gospel he
does not hesitate to degrade man in the scale of
creation below the rank of the brutes.[4]   It is peculiarly

---

[1] Origen, *Against Celsus*, iv. 67.   [2] iv. 62.   [3] iii. 67-69.
[4] iv. 23-25, 78, 79.

an offence to him that Christianity is a religion for sinners. The proclamation in the *Mysteries* is to those who are of pure heart and upright life ; but the Gospel invites the wicked, the worthless, and the vile.[1] I need not pursue his attack into greater detail ; but, relatively to his own age, it may be safely said that it was as formidable and effective a piece of criticism as any that comes from the heavy artillery of unbelief to-day.

Yet the singular thing is that, so far as is known to us, this work of Celsus fell utterly flat in his own day. We do not even hear of its existence till eighty or ninety years later, when Origen, at the instance of a friend, undertakes a refutation of it. It had in any case no effect in stopping the triumphant march of Christianity to victory in the empire. Why was this ? Why did so clever a book, written by so clever a man —a book which already exhausted the main objections to Christianity as these have always been presented— fail ? I cannot here even attempt to sketch the line of Origen's magnificent reply, but there are a few reasons that lie on the surface which bring out, I think, at least the main causes of its failure, and for that very reason are instructive. *One* reason, it may be confidently affirmed, was the obvious *unfairness* of the book. Celsus did not even attempt to be fair. He set himself studiously to twist, ridicule, misrepresent, to put the worst possible construction upon everything. This might amuse pagans, but could produce no effect on Christians, or on those who saw how Christians lived. These needed no argument to refute Celsus. Believers knew from their own experience that he did not speak the truth ; did not do justice to their books, their religion, their morality, their lives. Akin to this,

---

[1] Origen, *Against Celsus*, iii. 59.

as a *second* reason, was the strange blindness in the book to the moral and spiritual grandeur of Christianity. Celsus saw nothing of this, or, if he did, would not acknowledge it. But every one else was not so blind, and when the truth in Jesus was set before men, they beheld its spiritual glory, and felt its saving power. In presence of that vision the objections of Celsus vanished like spectres before the dawn. A *third* reason of failure was the inadequacy of the explanations Celsus had to offer of Christianity. This is the test which all systems of unbelief have to encounter. It is not enough that Christianity be refuted : it must be explained, and Celsus had no satisfactory explanation to offer. Driven to an issue, he has no better hypothesis to suggest than imposture on the part of Jesus and His disciples. But the human conscience will never reconcile itself to this as an adequate explanation of a system like Christianity. It recoils from it, and till unbelief can get rid of this idea, and in coarser or subtler forms it has never succeeded in doing so, it will not carry general assent. A *fourth* reason of the failure of the book was the strange perversity with which Celsus turned the things which are the glory of Christianity into an argument against it. This applies to its invitations to the poor, the ignorant, and the sinful, which to Celsus were such a "rock of offence." A *last* reason that may be given was that Celsus, in rejecting Christianity, had no substitute to offer. His view of the world was not one which would stand in the light either of reason, or of the heart's needs, before the Christian one. Men felt that in the doctrine of a Father-God who loved them, and had sent His Son to save them, and called them to be His children, they had something which the cold rationalism and cheerless fatalism of Celsus could not give them. *His* spirit would not attract them where Christianity failed. Thus his argument broke down, and the Gospel went on its way unharmed. The case is a typical one. The same causes that explain the defeat of Celsus give the reason why the story of the Cross finds its weekly entrance into myriads of hearts, while the learned tomes which were to grind the Christian religion into powder lie on the shelves unread.

This brings me now to speak of the task of the *Christian Apology* itself. I have said that if we fairly consider the magnitude and difficulty of this task, the feeling in our minds will be one of admiration at the ability with which it was accomplished. We shall best understand the shape it assumed if we look at it in the light of its threefold aim, as *Defensive, Aggressive,* and *Positive.*

In the first place, Christianity had to vindicate its right to *exist,* to clear itself from the calumnies and aspersions that were ignorantly or maliciously heaped upon it. This was its *Defensive* task. It had to undertake this task in relation to both Jews and Gentiles. It had to encounter and refute the slanders and misrepresentations of the ancient people, their perversions of Gospel facts, and denial of the Messiahship of Jesus. It had a yet more difficult task in relation to the Gentiles. Here Christianity stood outside the protection of the laws, and, as a religion proscribed and persecuted, had to plead for bare toleration, for the mere right to be. It had to show cause why the enactments against it should be removed, and it should be admitted to full legal recognition. In doing this, it had to encounter, as I before hinted, a mass of superstition, odium, prejudice, ignorance, of the density of which we can now form little conception. It raised its voice for justice with the whole might of the Roman State against it. This first part of its apologetic work it will be admitted that the early Church accomplished nobly and successfully. The vindication of the Christian faith from the calumnious charges brought against its adherents occupies a large space in all the *Apologies* (Justin, Tertullian, etc.). The accusations are met by pointing to the absence of evidence in support of the charges ; by showing the inconsistency of the conduct alleged with the spirit and precepts of the Gospel ; above all, by appeal to the public testimony of the characters and lives of Christians, which presented so marked a contrast to the heathen debasement around them.

The second part of the Christian Apology was *Aggressive*, and here its relation to Judaism necessarily differed from its relation to heathenism. The Christians acknowledged the reality of the Old Testament revelation. They had therefore, to a certain extent, common ground with the Jews, and it was on this common ground that the argument proceeded. What they had to show *the Jew* was that the Mosaic Law, the divine origin of which was admitted, was in its nature temporary ; that there had been an earlier dispensation when the Fathers did not observe the law ; and that their own Scriptures predicted a time when God would make a new covenant with His people, and bring in a more spiritual system. This laid on the apologist the task of distinguishing between the temporary and eternal elements in the law ; of demonstrating its typical and shadowy character ; of proving the Messiahship of Jesus—all points requiring delicate and careful handling, and in dealing with which we need not wonder if the defenders of Christianity occasionally stumbled. In relation to *Paganism*, the first attitude

of the apologist was necessarily polemical. He must
clear the ground of existing errors to gain a hearing for
his own side.   All the apologists, accordingly, devote
a good deal of attention to the exposure of the folly
and absurdity of idolatry, and of the puerile and
immoral character of the pagan mythology.   In this
they got abundant help from the heathen poets and
philosophers themselves.   No true apology, however,
can ever be entirely negative.   The Christian writers,
therefore, did not content themselves with simply
assailing the popular religions, but put forward in their
stead the great truths of natural religion.   They
proclaimed with a clearness and assurance in striking
contrast with the vacillation of the schools the great
doctrines of the unity of God, of His universal providence, of His moral government, of the future life, of
a judgment to come.   For many of these doctrines
they could again adduce the testimony of heathen
writers ; but here a marked difference appears in the
ranks of the apologists themselves.   One school
—of which Tatian, Theophilus, Tertullian,[1] may be
regarded as types—took up a strongly hostile attitude
to heathen philosophy and learning.   Their work was
done when they had shown the errors, contradictions,
absurdities, into which heathen writers had fallen.
Another and nobler school—best represented by Justin
and Origen—took a more liberal view of their relation
to philosophy, and gladly availed themselves of any
rays of truth in the heathen wisdom.   They recognised
as clearly as the others how inadequate was the
guidance of reason, and did not fail to show the conflicting and confused nature of the opinions of the

---

[1] But Tertullian knew how to avail himself of the philosophers when it
suited him.   What was true in their teaching this school supposed to be
borrowed from Moses and the prophets.

ancient pagans. But their relation to heathen learning did not exhaust itself in this negative attitude. With Paul they did not spurn the argument, "As certain of your own poets have said."[1] Here comes in the doctrine of Justin, already adverted to, of the spermatic Word. All men, he holds, have in them a portion of the divine Word. "Whatever things," therefore, he boldly claims, "were rightly said among all men are the property of us Christians."[2] Sages and law-givers had a *portion* of this Word; in Christ we possess the *whole* Word. Christ, therefore, furnishes the canon by which to distinguish the true from the false in the teaching of antiquity.

But, finally, the task of this apologetic was also a *Positive* one—in relation, I mean, to Christianity itself. It was not enough that the rival systems of idolatry should be overthrown, or even that the truths of natural religion should be established in their place. The positive character of Christianity as a revelation from God must also be made good. The apologists asserted the Divinity, the Messiahship, the supernatural birth, the resurrection, the heavenly reign of Jesus, and maintained that through Him a new and final revelation had been given by God to men. An indispensable part of their apologetic work, therefore, was to establish the reality of this alleged revelation, and here the lines of evidence chiefly relied on were the following. A main place was always given to the argument from *prophecy*, and it may be claimed for the apologists that their handling of this argument, if frequently uncritical, was yet in substance sound. The passages principally insisted on were those which the Church has always

[1] Acts xviii. 28.
[2] *Second Apol.* 13; the doctrine of the spermatic Word is chiefly found in *First Apol.* 46; *Second Apol.* 8-13.

regarded as Messianic (*e.g.*, Is. liii.), and which will
probably retain that character despite the light thrown
by criticism on their historical relations.   The same
stress was not laid on *miracles* as in later times, chiefly
because miracles were not so often challenged as
ascribed to sorcery.   But Quadratus, the earliest
apologist, is said to have dwelt on the Saviour's
miracles;[1] and Origen, in his reply to Celsus, well
shows that it is not the miracle as a mere work of
power, but the miracle in its moral character, and its
relation to the agent, which affords the proof of the
divine.[2]   Appeal, again, is repeatedly made, as by
Justin and Origen, to the remarkable *spread of
Christianity* as an evidence of its inherent spiritual
energy.   This argument had peculiar force at a time
when every violent means that paganism could employ
was being used to check its victorious progress, yet it
came forth triumphant over all.[3]   But the crowning
argument was the appeal to the *changed characters and
lives* of the followers of Christ—the *moral* miracles
wrought by the Gospel in the souls of men.   With a
changed life came changed relationships—a new ideal
of marriage, purified family life, a new conception of
social duty, new works of love, etc.   The argument
was irresistible that a religion which produced such
fruits could not be other than divine.[4]

At this point, however, we come on a question
of considerable importance for the right understanding
of the apologists and their work.   It is the question
raised by Professor Harnack and those who think with

---

[1] Eusebius, iv. 3.   [2] i. 68; ii. 49-51.

[3] Cf. Justin, *Dialogue*, 177; Tertullian, *Apology*, i. 37; Origen,
Against Celsus, i. 27; ii. 13; iii. 24; viii. 26, etc.

[4] This appeal runs through all the apologies. Cf. especially Justin,
Tertullian, Origen (i. 9, 26).

him, as to how far the apologists we are studying had
any proper grasp of the distinctive nature of Christianity at all. According to this scholar,[1] the apologists
have all but completely fallen away from a right
apprehension of a Christian Gospel. The substance
of Christianity for them lay solely, he thinks, in its
rational content—in its doctrines of God, of virtue, of
a future life—and the only value of the objective facts
of Christianity (the incarnation, resurrection, etc.) is
to give certification and assurance of these truths.
Christianity is a system of natural religion with supernatural sanctions. The doctrines which I have called
those of natural religion—God, immortality, virtue—
are the essence of the matter, all else is the machinery
of revelation and attestation. As I cannot acquiesce
in this verdict, at least without very considerable modi-
fication, it is proper that I should give one or two
reasons for my dissent.

It is an obvious preliminary consideration that the
works we are dealing with are *apologies*, and not
doctrinal treatises. They are, that is, books written
with a perfectly definite end, viz., to refute the
calumnies brought against the Christians, and to
vindicate for them the right to be allowed to live
quietly and peaceably under the laws in obedience to
their own consciences. Addressed to pagans and
idolaters, they naturally adopted the lines of argument
most suitable for such an audience. They do not
enter into the specialties of the Christian religion, about
which the pagans knew nothing and cared less, but
keep to the broad truths in which the contrast between

---

[1] Cf. *Hist. of Dogma*, ii. 7, 8, 169-230 (E.T.). Harnack here follows
von Engelhardt. Neither can carry through his view consistently, and
the qualifications both are compelled to make go far to neutralise the
original thesis.

their own faith and that of the established idolatry was most palpable. As well might Paul be blamed for confining his preaching before Felix to righteousness, temperance, and judgment to come,[1] or for starting from the basis of natural religion in his address to the Athenians,[2] as these apologists for not discussing the interior doctrines of Christianity before persons not yet persuaded of the elementary truths of Theism. Writers in our own day are not usually found debating the mysteries of justification or regeneration in treatises intended to refute the agnosticism of Mr. Huxley or Mr. Spencer.

With this reservation, it may be freely granted that the apologists do give prominence to what I have called *the fundamental articles of religion*, and with united voice endeavour to convince their opponents of the truth and reasonableness of these. The truths they thus declared included the being, unity, and spirituality of God ; His free creation of the world, and its dependence on Him for continued existence ; His providence and moral administration ; the reality and immutability of moral law ; the certainty of a day of judgment, and of a future state of rewards and punishments. It is evident that these were truths which it was necessary to bring forward and strongly to emphasise in the face of prevailing idolatry, of Epicurean atheism, of Stoical pantheism and fatalism, of the denial by all classes of creation, and often of providence as well.[3] It would be a very unsafe inference from this, however, that the apologists knew nothing of the more specific Christian doctrines, or did not discuss these doctrines among their fellow-Christians. Harnack himself admits this,[4]

---

[1] Acts xxiv. 25.   [2] Acts xvii. 22 ff. ; cf. xiv. 15-17.
[3] Prof. Harnack allows that "this was the very thing required" (*Hist. of Dogma*, ii. 171 (E.T.)).
[4] "It is," he says, "intrinsically probable that their works, directly

though it seems to blunt the edge of much of his own argument. It was not against the specific doctrines of the Christians that objections ordinarily were directed, but against their non - compliance with established worship, their disuse of images, temples, etc. When objections *were* made against the special doctrines, as by Celsus, they were taken up and answered. But even the eight books of Origen's reply to Celsus would give us a very poor idea of the content of Origen's theology.

A further fact which it is necessary to insist on is that the doctrines mentioned as put in the foreground by the apologists are *very real parts of the Christian system.* A truth does not cease to be Christian because it is also in accordance with reason, though this would seem to be the presupposition of much of the criticism of the apologists. The doctrines of the unity of God, of His moral government, of judgment to come, and of a future state of rewards and punishments, *are* fundamental parts of the Bible system, and as such need to be expounded, defended, and enforced. It is true also that these doctrines were not clearly and firmly grasped by the heathen world, and that Christianity gave new distinctness and certitude to them. Why then should the apologists not give them prominence? These are, in truth, the foundation doctrines of all, and until they are acknowledged no progress can be made.

addressed to the Christian Church, gave a more full exposition of their Christianity than we find in the apologists. This can, moreover, be proved with certainty from the fragments of Justin's, Tatian's, and Melito's esoteric writings. . . . . If we compare Tertullian's *Apology* we easily see how impossible it is to determine from that work the extent of his Christian faith and knowledge. The same is probably the case, though to a less extent, with Justin's apologetic writings" (*Hist. of Dogma*, ii. pp. 169, 220). One must take into account also the doctrine of "reserve" —the so-called *disciplina arcani*—in the early Church (Origen, *Against Celsus*, i. 7; cf. Newman's *Arians*, i. sect. 3; Hatch's *Influence of Greek Ideas*, etc., pp. 293-98).

I have gone thus far on the assumption that the apologists do, as alleged, contain essentially nothing more than a rational theology and cosmology—the Logos doctrine, on this view, being part of the cosmology. I would now, however, go a step farther, and *contest the justice of this assumption.* Professor Harnack has afterwards to qualify his sweeping judgment, and acknowledge that in the case of Justin, at least,[1] if not of others,[2] a good many elements of a more distinctive character are present. But the admission is again retracted, and Justin's doctrine reduced to " moralism," by explaining that in Justin Christ appears solely as a teacher who reveals the above-named truths, by the knowledge of which man is able in his own power to attain to repentance and virtue, and so make himself worthy of eternal life. Christ has given to men the perfect law. They are saved by obedience to it, and need no help beyond right instruction.[3] One would require very powerful reasons before crediting the author of the *Apologies* and of the *Dialogue with Trypho* with this frigid legalism—this doctrine of salvation by one's independent efforts—which is an utter subversion of grace,[4] and would mean a relapse into the worst error of Judaism. But I cannot agree that Justin is fairly chargeable with this doctrine. Justin's theology has many defects, but it is simply not the case that he regards Christ's incarnation, life, death, and resurrection, as intended only to give confirmation to a rational scheme of truth, or that he ignores an objective redemption. His teaching has many positive Christian elements. With the other apologists he did much to lay the foundations of the doctrine of the Trinity. He

---

[1] ii. pp. 203, 220.   [2] P. 169.

[3] ii. pp. 221, 227 ; cf. pp. 216-20.

[4] " If, as all seems to show, the thought of a specific grace of God in Christ seems virtually neutralised," etc. (ii. p. 227).

is explicit on the incarnation. He recognises, if inadequately, the weakening of the powers of human nature through sin, and speaks of man in his fallen state as the child of necessity and ignorance.[1] His writings abound in statements which show that he attributed a redeeming efficacy to the death of Christ, and that not simply through its moral effect, but objectively, and in itself.[2] He knows of the call to repentance and faith, and of the remission of sins of God's free grace, as the result of obedience to that call. Baptism is to him "regeneration" or "new birth"; and in his eucharistic teaching he affirms a mystical incorporation with Christ.[3] Even the doctrines formerly alluded to, while their rational character is insisted on, are not set forth by Justin and his fellow-apologists as bare truths of natural religion, but are exhibited as truths of revelation, and are bound up with definite Christian elements. The creation of the world, *e.g.*, is connected with the Logos who historically became incarnate in Jesus Christ; the doctrine of immortality is associated with the resurrection, and with Christian hopes; there is a judgment, but it is Christ who is judge, etc. What may legitimately be said in criticism of the apologists, I think, is :—1. That the philosophical training of some of them, blending with the habit of thought of the age, gave a predominatingly philosophical cast to their writings, and led them to view Christianity rather as a "new philosophy" than

[1] *First Apol.* 10, 61. Man is affirmed to be held in bondage by the wicked demons, "taking as their ally the lust of wickedness which is in every man, and which draws variously to all manner of vice."
[2] *E.g., Dial.* xiii. 94-96. Von Engelhardt can only get over these passages by putting a forced and arbitrary construction on expressions which would naturally be understood otherwise.
[3] *First Apol.* 61, 65, 66. It is granted that "the apologists strove to get beyond moralism" (Harnack, ii. 227). There is no sign of such "striving," and why should they strive if their view was as represented?

as a method of salvation ; and, 2. That then, as still, the peculiar business of the apologist tended to draw his eyes away from the more distinctive doctrines of Christianity to those which could be rationally defended, and in this way did injury to the proportions of truth. But it is only in a relative sense this can be affirmed of them ; and against it is to be set the service they rendered in uniting Christianity with the best and truest thinking of the ancient world on God, the soul, virtue, and the life to come.

From a review of the whole, I think it will be evident that, as I said at the beginning, we have no reason to be ashamed of this second century apologetic. It had a difficult task to perform, and it did it well. It was not a shallow and meagre, but a large and complex apologetic—dealing with many antagonists, and with a great variety of sides of truth. It was an apologetic, too, that had all the force of reality about it. Men felt they were engaged in an earnest and deadly struggle, and had no time for mere sword-play. They wrote with a purpose, and their purpose gave power and decision to their pens. The Church was grateful to them then, and we may remember them with gratitude to-day.

II. I now proceed to observe that, while the battle I have described was being fought by the apologists against the assaults of paganism *without*, the Church was exposed to a subtler and far more deadly peril, and had to brace itself for a more onerous struggle *within*, in its controversy with what is known as *Gnosticism*. If the former—the apologetic—contest represents the conflict of truth with error on its *rational* and *ethical*, the struggle with Gnosticism may be said to represent this conflict on its directly *religious* side ; for the questions in the Gnostic contest unquestionably go deeper, and touch Christianity in its central and most vital parts.   Here we come to closer quarters than we have yet done with the theory of the Greek origin of dogma.   In the view of Prof. Harnack, the Gnostics are not heretics at all ; they are raised to thrones of honour as "the first Christian theologians."[1]   They only, this authority thinks, sought to bring about in an acute way that Hellenising of Christianity which the Church afterwards accomplished by a more gradual process.[2]   I confess I feel it difficult to know what to make of the theory of Christianity involved in such a dictum.   Prof. Harnack overlooks that there is theology and theology.   There is a theology which keeps true to the basis of Christian facts, and seeks to interpret them to knowledge ; and there is a theology, the centre of gravity of which lies outside of Christianity altogether, which would subvert these facts, and dissipate Christianity into a cloudland of human imaginations.   That the triumph of Gnosticism, notwithstanding the germs of truth in some of the higher systems, would have meant the dissolution of historical Christianity and certain ruin of the Church, is granted by writers of nearly every school.   "The crisis," says the late Dr. Hatch, "was one the gravity of which it would be difficult to over-estimate.   There have been crises since in the history of Christianity, but there is none which equals in its importance this, upon the issue of which it depended for all time, whether Christianity should be regarded as a body of revealed doctrine, or as the *caput mortuum* of a hundred philosophies— whether the basis of Christianity should be a definite and definitely interpreted creed, or a chaos of specula-

[1] i. pp. 227, 255 (E.T.).   [2] i. pp. 226, 227.

tions."[1] How that which would have been the destruction
of Christianity, and subversion of the possibility of dogma,
can be claimed as a legitimate stage in the development
of dogma within Christianity I fail to apprehend.

Gnosticism is one of the most singular phenomena
of the second century, or of any age. We have seen
something of the literary character of that century in
its earlier part. But, beyond this, the age was one of
syncretism—of the clash and conflict of systems, of the
meeting and commingling of streams from East and
West, of restless, feverish excitement in thought and
religion, an age marked by a great welter of opinion on
all subjects human and divine. The air was sultry
with superstition, yet in the midst of the confusion
were deep, unsatisfied religious cravings, and a strong
desire on the part of the bolder minds to grasp the
secret of existence, which, despite Greek philosophy
and Oriental mysteries, seemed still to elude them.
Into this mass of conflicting opinion Christianity
entered as a powerful ferment, and the intensity of
the ferment can best be measured by the magnitude of
the effects which it produced.[2] The elements of the
prevailing systems began to adjust themselves in new
relations under the action of the Christian ideas :
systems of the strangest and most bizarre character
grew up, and multiplied themselves with fungus-like
rapidity ;[3] finally, vast and complicated theories were

---

[1] *Organisation of the Early Christian Churches*, p. 96. The fluid
character of Prof. Harnack's thinking is strikingly shown in his easy
grouping of Irenæus with " Paul, Valentinus, and Marcion " ; his ranking
of Marcion and the Valentinians as " scriptural theologians," and his statement that "Irenæus and Hippolytus merely followed them," etc. Cf.
Hist. of Dogma, ii. pp. 237, 250.

[2] Cf. *Neglected Factors*, etc., pp. 194-99.

[3] Irenæus compares them to "mushrooms growing out of the
ground " (i. 29).

formed, which aimed at being at once a philosophy of God and of the universe, a divine theodicy, a philosophy of Jewish and Christian revelation, and a basis of religious practice. Baur has truly said : " Gnosticism gives the clearest proof that Christianity had now become one of the most important factors in the history of the time ; and it shows especially what a mighty power of attraction the new Christian principles possessed for the highest intellectual life then to be found either in the pagan or in the Jewish world." [1]

We shall, nevertheless, utterly miss the significance of this remarkable phenomenon if we regard it as mere perversity—inexplicable craze and hallucination. Gnosticism was, in its own way, an attempt at the explanation of things, and the questions it dealt with were such as, for the most part, spring out of the nature of our intelligence, and cannot but impress themselves on the thoughtful mind. Such questions were—the relation of infinite and finite, the explanation of the evil and imperfection of the world, the meaning of this groaning and sighing for deliverance which is through all things, the nature of the Christian revelation, its relation to past stages of revelation and to the general philosophy of history, the manner and nature of redemption. On all these questions the Gnostics would not be put off with commonplace answers. They had the true aristocratic contempt for the answers which passed current in the Church. They were not content to be told that God created the world. How could the infinite produce the finite ? Whence came matter, the very antithesis, as they conceived it, of spirit ? It was not enough to tell them a tale of the serpent tempting the woman in Eden. They must get behind that.

[1] *Hist. of Church*, ii. p. 1 (E.T.).

Whence this evil and imperfection which seem inherent in the very nature of things ?   It was not enough to say, Christ has come to redeem the world.   What is it in man which makes him capable of redemption ?   How came man to be what he is, and what is the explanation of the differences that prevail among men in respect of gifts, fortune, position, and spiritual capacity ?   Whence this yearning of the soul, which seems to be shared by so much else in nature, for truth and blessedness and freedom ?   Admit the reality of revelation, how explain the contrasts between the old revelation and the new ?   And how is the whole related to the general theory of the universe ?   Such are the problems—deep and important enough, and legitimate enough too, if only we are content with such answers as are possible, and put our questions with proper humility.   The fault of the Gnostic did not lie in his questions, but in his answers—in the unsoundness of his methods, and the vain conceits of his own fancy which he put in place of knowledge.

Gnosticism, then, as the name denotes, professes to give " knowledge," an absolute knowledge, which only the higher class of minds could appropriate.   The infinitely varied shapes assumed by the systems render it almost impossible to classify them, or even to give an account of their leading ideas which shall not be open to objection.   We might as well attempt to classify the products of a tropical jungle, or the shapes and hues of the sunset clouds, which change under our view as we look at them.   There are the *early* and *incipient* forms of Gnosticism, with their roots in the apostolic age, of which Cerinthus may be named as a representative ; there are the *inchoate* or *semi-developed* systems, of which the Ophite (so-called from the *rôle* of the serpent in the mythology) is the principal group ; finally, there are the *fully-developed* systems, those of Basilides, Valentinus, and Marcion, with their respective schools. These last—at least the systems of Basilides and Valentinus, for Marcion stands apart—were really, as already hinted, great religious philosophies, the pro- totypes of those absolutist systems which have sprung up in Germany in our own century, and profess to explain everything. Basilides, with his powerful specula- tive grasp and all-embracing evolutionary process, might be termed the Hegel of the movement ; Valentinus, with his robe of phantasy and triple fall and redemption, was its Schelling ; Marcion, with his severe practical bent, his doctrine of faith, and his antithesis of the just God and the good, might, without straining, be named its Ritschl.[1] The thing which chiefly strikes us in these systems is the mythological dress in which con- ceptions at bottom metaphysical are clothed. It is not easy to say how far this belongs to the essence of the thought, or is a poetic or allegorical veil consciously thrown over their conceptions by the inventors of the systems. It is difficult to believe, *e.g.*, that the adventures of the mystic Sophia in Valentinus are meant to be taken as literal history, and not rather as part of a great divine poem—the symbolising of truths or ideas which could not otherwise be so well expressed. It is as if the categories, say of the Hegelian logic, were translated into the language of emanation, and represented as æons evolved one from the other in series.[2]

[1] The chief authority on Basilides is Hippolytus, on Valentinus is Irenæus, and on Marcion is Tertullian.

[2] Harnack speaks of " mythological powers translated into an aggregate of ideas " (i. p. 249). We are disposed to regard it rather as a system of ideas translated into the language of mythology. It is possible to over- rate, but Harnack, I think, underrates the importance of the vesture, and regards the Gnostics as attaching less meaning to it than they did (i. pp. 233-235).

Absolutely common features of the Gnostic systems there are none ; we can but present outstanding or typical features. In general, God is conceived of as an Unfathomable Abyss (βυθός), between whom and the finite creation is interposed a long chain of æons or powers,[1] emanations of the divine, constituting in their totality the Pleroma or Fulness of the divine essence. The world is not a creation of divine power, but is the result of a rupture or fall in the Pleroma. In some systems matter stood alongside of God as an independent evil power ; in others it is explained as a result of the development, or is derived from a spiritual fall. In all the systems a distinction is made between the Demiurge, framer of this visible creation and God of the Old Testament, and the Supreme God revealed in the fulness of time in Christ. The God of the Old Testament is an inferior and imperfect Being—limited, passionate, vengeful—while the God of Christ is identified with the primal source of virtue, goodness, and truth. Christ Himself is either a celestial Being, an Æon, who appears in a phantasmal body among men for their redemption (Docetism), or is the earthly Jesus, with whom the higher power temporarily associates itself. Men are distinguished into two classes—spiritual and psychical ; sometimes into three—spiritual and hylic (material), with the psychical (soulish) as an intermediate class. The spiritual alone are capable of the higher knowledge, in which consists salvation. The practical influence of the system was twofold, according as, on the one hand, the doctrine of the evil of matter was made the ground of ascetic practice ; or as, on the other hand, the spirit sought to show its superiority to the flesh by unrestrained indulgence in licentiousness. The system of Marcion avoided the transcendentalism

---

[1] The Basilidean theory had originally no æons.

of æons, but opposed the God of the Old to the God of the New Testament, and was docetic in its view of Christ.

Here, then, was a crisis threatening the very life of the Church, which called for the most strenuous efforts of the ablest minds to resist it. The Gnostic sects— some of them rising to the dignity of influential schools —must have embraced no inconsiderable portion of the total membership of the Church of the time. They honeycombed the Church in every direction, and with their alluring speculations drew off the "elite" who wished to combine philosophy and culture with their Christianity. We can best see how largely Gnosticism bulked in the Church consciousness of the period by observing the space which it occupies in the literature of the period. With slight exception, heresy to the Fathers of the close of the second and beginning of the third centuries is simply Gnosticism. "The whole of Irenæus, a great part of Tertullian, the whole of Hippolytus nearly, and not a little of Clement of Alexandria, are devoted to its refutation. This does not take account of lost treatises." [1] But the work which these Fathers undertook was effectually done. The main body of the Church also consistently and resolutely withstood these Gnostic theorists. [2] Next to the fact of its rapid rise, accordingly, the most remarkable thing about Gnosticism is its short-lived character. It had a brilliant, meteoric course, but the acute crisis, at any

[1] *Neglected Factors*, etc., p. 195. The other heresies combated are principally Ebionitism and the nascent Monarchianism of the end of the second century. The latter belongs properly to the next period.

[2] "For Justin," says Harnack, "about the year 150, the Marcionites, Valentinians, Basilideans, and Saturnians are groups outside the communities, and undeserving of the name 'Christians'" (i. p. 250 E.T.). In *Dialogue* 80, Justin describes, but does not name, these parties.

rate, in connection with it soon passed away. It sprang up towards the end of the first century; had reached its height about the middle of the second century; was already in its decadence, though still a force to be reckoned with, by the end of that century; then it vanished, leaving only obscure traces of itself in scattered sects.[1]   It had only one important revival, that of Manichæism in the third century, if that appearance on Persian soil can be so described.   Gnosticism was, in fact, the product of a peculiar age, and of a peculiar set of conditions in that age, and when these changed it passed away like an unwholesome dream.   We can compare it to nothing so much as to an exhalation from a marsh, kindling up into strange and variegated, but illusive lights, will-o'-the-wisps that vanished when the morning broke.

A movement of this kind, however, could not come and go without powerful reactive effects on the Church itself, and lasting gains to the theological development. Inevitably, in the course of this conflict, the Church was driven back on the deepest grounds of its religious convictions, and compelled to formulate and defend the ideas which lay at the foundation of revealed, nay, of all religion.   This is what Professor Harnack calls the "Hellenising" of Christianity, and regards as on the same plane with the efforts of the Gnostics themselves.[2] In his view the Fathers simply fell into the error of their opponents in availing themselves of the weapons of the Greek philosophy, and, especially through their Logos doctrine, gave Christianity an intellectual character which differed not in kind, but in degree, from the

---

[1] A church of the Marcionites lingered on for a considerable time.
[2] Cf. *Hist. of Dogma*, ii. pp. 247, 305, 321, etc. (E.T.).   Thus also Kaftan in his *Truth of the Christian Religion.*

Gnosticism they were combating. It would again require strong evidence to make good a theory intrinsically so improbable ; and that evidence, I am persuaded, an unbiassed study of the facts will not yield us. If it were true, the Fathers themselves must have been strangely deceived, for, by Professor Harnack's own admission, to them Greek philosophy was the parent of all heresy.[1] The chief end these Fathers of the old Catholic period had in view was *conservation*—the preservation of the faith as they had received it—and the last thing they thought of was to give over Christianity to philosophy, or construct a new Gnosticism in room of that which they combated.[2] If in fulfilment of their task they could not but feel impelled to set over against the Gnostic systems — which, as we saw, were simply gorgeously illuminated philosophies of God, man, and the universe—their own conception of what may be called the Christian philosophy of the world, this was in the line of sound development, and does not imply a departure from the Christian basis, unless in so far as it can be shown that Christianity is *wrongly* interpreted. And this is not done by simply alleging against it the Logos doctrine !

It was an unfortunate necessity of its position in this controversy, that the Church had to enter into conflict with its formidable adversaries destitute of most of the *defences* it afterwards possessed against error— without a fixed canon of Scripture, without a generally

---

[1] *Hist. of Dogma*, ii. p. 247.

[2] Dorner's estimate of the period is very different from Harnack's. " A glorious period," he says, " when Christian faith and Christian science flourished, began about the middle of the second century, and so rich a harvest was reaped, for the latter especially, that at the end of the century hardly any one could wish that the Church might have escaped the Gnostic s orms " (*Person of Christ*, i. p. 254, E.T.).

recognised creed, without even a court of ecclesiastical
appeal, such as the council afterwards became.   Everything was yet to make—at least to define ; and it was
precisely one of the gains of the Gnostic controversy
that it compelled the Church to provide itself with
these means of defence, and erect bulwarks against the
inroads of unauthorised speculation, which not only
served the immediate end of safety, but were of abiding
value.   In this region, I know, many things are still in
dispute, but competent scholars are tolerably agreed as
to the general outcome.[1]   Dr. Hatch is justified in
attributing to Irenæus and Tertullian the special
credit of striking out the conception of the "Apostolic"
as that which was to guide the Church at this crisis ;[2]
but it is not less important to observe that, in laying
stress on this conception, these Fathers do not claim to
be introducing anything new, but only to be expressing
what the Church had always recognised, but had not
before the same occasion explicitly to state.

The first important gain to the Church from the controversy in which it had been plunged, was the collection of a body of *New Testament Scriptures*, or the
formation of a New Testament canon.   It is not
that the Church did not know itself before this time
possessed of inspired and authoritative writings.[3]   The

[1] Cf. Ritschl, *Enstehung d. alt.-Kath. Kirche* (1857), pp. 336 ff. ;
Dorner, *Person of Christ*, i. pp. 257-58 (E.T.) ; Harnack, *Hist. of Dogma*,
ii. pp. 18-93 (E.T.) ; Hatch, *Organisation*, pp. 93-97.   In conjunction
with the resistance to Gnosticism, resistance to the powerful, enthusiastic,
and schismatic movement of the middle and latter part of the second
century known as Montanism gave a strong impulse to the changes I
describe. See below, pp. 90, 125.

[2] *Organisation*, pp. 96, 123.

[3] This against Harnack.   The use of the N. T. writings as Scripture by
Irenæus and Tertullian shows quite clearly that it was not they who
created that idea, but that the writings they appeal to had long attained
an established and authoritative position.   Of the twenty-four columns or
so of references to Scripture in the index to the translation of Tertullian's

Gospels in particular had long been in use in the churches, and collections had early been made of Paul's Epistles.[1] Such collections, however, grew up naturally, informally, with a view to purposes of edification, and with no idea consciously present of forming what we mean by a Canon of Scripture. We have only to recall how near the Church of the second century stood to the Apostolic Age, and what stress was still laid on living Apostolic tradition, to see how far it would lie from men's minds to erect these writings of Apostles and Apostolic men into a permanent rule of faith and practice for the whole Church. Now, under pressure of the Gnostic controversy, when the Church was faced by the mutilated Canon of Marcion,[2] and saw its borders overrun by pseudonymous and apocryphal productions, it was inevitable that it should be impelled to set about in right earnest making a collection of the books which it *did* regard as Apostolic — which it knew from their history and long-established use to be so—and that these should be definitely separated from the floating mass and raised to a position of exclusive authority. With this went the other motive of finding in these Scriptures— thus collected and unified—a basis from which to assail the theories of its opponents, and to defend the Church doctrine against their attacks. To this end it was necessary to lay stress on that in the writings which gave them their authority — viz., their Apostolic character, or origin either directly from Apostles or

work against Marcion, fully half are to the New Testament. On the controversy between Zahn and Harnack on this point, see *Studien und Kritiken* for 1891.

[1] Besides 2 Pet. iii. 17, see the free quotations from these epistles by Polycarp and others.

[2] Marcion accepted only one Gospel, viz., Luke's, and that in a mutilated form, and ten Epistles of Paul. The word "Canon" is used here anticipatively.

from men belonging to the first Apostolic circles, and
having Apostolic sanction for their work. Thus grew
up towards the end of the second century the definite
conception of a collection of New Testament Scriptures
—of a *New Testament*, as it now begins to be called—
which henceforth takes its place beside the Old Testament as of equal validity and authority with it. Lists
are drawn up of the sacred books, and the Church
Fathers of the period show the clearest consciousness
of dealing with a code of writings of Apostolic origin,
inspired character, and normative authority.

It was soon apparent, however, that the mere fixing
of the Canon of Scripture was not enough. There
arose next the question of the *interpretation* of
Scripture when men had it. The Gnostics were not
to be silenced by simple appeal to a book. They
did not always admit the authority of Scripture ;
but even when they did, they had their own ways
of eliciting from it the sense which they desired.
The writings of the Fathers are full of specimens
of the extraordinary exegesis by which their opponents
managed to educe their far-fetched mythological conceptions from the simplest Scripture words. The
Fathers themselves are far from free from the vice
of allegorical interpretation ; but, as any one will see
on comparison, their use of Scripture was sobriety itself
compared with that of the Gnostics whom they combated.[1] The question, in brief, was no longer as to
the Canon of Scripture, but as to the sense to be drawn
from Scripture. It was here that the Fathers fell back
on a *second* line of defence, sought by them not in
Greek philosophy, but in what they named *The Rule of
Faith*—the constant and steadfast tradition of the truth
which had been maintained in the Churches from Apos-

---

[1] Cf. Irenæus, i. 9, 4, and *passim*.

tolic days. They said—There is something prior to
the Scriptures. The Church was founded by the oral
word of the Apostles and their followers. Their testimony has been handed down in all the great Churches ;
has taken definite shape in the practically consentient
forms of their baptismal confessions. Consult it there,
and you will find it uniform and single—one definite,
Catholic tradition, which all the Churches possess, and
which they unitedly carry back to an Apostolic
source.[1] It aided this appeal that by the middle
of the second century the baptismal formula of the
Churches had already crystallised into tolerably
settled shape—into a form substantially identical
with our Apostle's Creed.[2] In other words, to the
wanton speculation of those who sought to impose
on Scripture a sense it would not bear, they opposed
the consentient testimony of all the great branches
of the Church from the days of the Apostles downwards. This, no doubt, was the introduction of the
principle of tradition, which in its later development
wrought so much harm. But it was a legitimate use of
that principle at a time when tradition was still living.
It was used not to supersede or set aside Scripture, but
to corroborate it ; not to set up a rival authority, but
to act as a check on the wantonness and extravagance
of an interpretation which otherwise would have no
limit.

Of more doubtful utility was the *third* line of defence
set up, in the attempt to secure, in turn, a guarantee for

[1] Cf. Irenæus, i. 10 ; Tertullian, *Prescript. of Heretics*, 13, 18, 20, 21,
28. On the connection with baptismal confession, cf. Irenæus, i. 9, 4 ;
Tertullian, *Against Marcion*, i. 21, etc.

[2] I need only refer to the controversy which has been waged on the
Continent on the history of this oldest symbol. The English reader may
consult Dr. Zahn's small book (translated), or Dr. Swete's work on the
same subject. For comparative tables, cf. Schaff, *History* (ante-Nicene),
ii. pp. 528-38.

the purity of the tradition, in *a continuous historical episcopate*, conceived of as, by divine ordinance, the depository and guardian of the truth.   Pre-eminently, of course, the truth was to be sought for in those great Churches, *e.g.*, Rome, Antioch, Corinth, believed to have been founded by Apostles ; and lists of the succession of bishops in some of these Churches are carefully given in proof of the possibility and reality of this transmission of Apostolic doctrine.[1]   That an important truth lies in this conception of a chain of faithful witnesses to Apostolic tradition is not to be denied ;[2] but the precise form given to it of an Apostolical succession of bishops must be contested.[3] It is not necessary to accept Apostolic episcopal succession to see in the victory over Gnosticism a triumph of the *fides catholica et apostolica*.

The gains to *doctrinal* theology as the result of this second-century conflict with Gnosticism are not less striking.   The first part of the work of the great Anti-Gnostic Fathers—Irenæus, Tertullian, Clement, Hippolytus, etc.—was, like that of the Apologists, polemical. They had to carry war into the enemy's camp—to show the baselessness, the unchristian character, the immoral tendencies, of the Gnostic imaginings.   No one who studies the great work of Irenæus *Against Heresies*, or Tertullian's powerful treatise *Against Marcion*, will deny the ability with which this work was performed.   But the principal task forced on the Church was positive ; and here the very searchingness of the Gnostic attack—the fundamental character of

---

[1] Cf. Irenæus, iii. 1-4 ; iv. 26 ; Tertullian, *ut supra*, 32 ; Eusebius, *History*, iv. 4, 5, 11, 19, 20, 22, etc.

[2] Cf. 2 Tim. ii. 2.

[3] Canon Gore admits that the first links in some of these chains of bishops are somewhat "idealised" (*Church and Ministry*, p. 306).

the questions it raised, some of which, as that of the
relation of the Old to the New Testament, the
Church had been tempted to overlook or too easily to
glide over—compelled its representatives to grapple
with the profoundest theological problems.   They had
to rescue the Christian idea of God from the mythological speculations that defaced it ; to secure the idea
of creation against that of involuntary emanation ; to
vindicate, as Paul had to do earlier, the glory of the
Son against the tendency to merge Him in a crowd of
Æons ;[1] to defend, with John, Christ's true humanity
against a variety of docetic denials ; to uphold the unity
of revelation and the identity of the God of the Old
Testament with the God of the Gospel ; to do battle
for the historicity of the great facts of Christ's
life—His Virgin-birth, His miracles, His death, His
resurrection—against theories that resolved them into
allegories ; to vindicate the universal receptivity of
men for the Gospel as against Gnostic exclusiveness
and pride.   Will any one say that the work here also
was not well done, or that the results bear any real
resemblance to ideas of Greek philosophy ?[2]   I am
not concerned to deny that in the speculations of
some of the Fathers—in the Alexandrian school especially—there is a sensible influence of Platonic and
Stoical philosophy on the Christian construction.   Even
this need not be condemned as altogether evil, for
Christianity has its kinship with, and its right to
assimilate, the highest thoughts of all philosophies.
But it will be found that it is precisely the element
which was most baneful in Platonism—its conception
of God as abstract Being ($\tau\grave{o}$ $\breve{o}\nu$), exalted above all

[1] Cf. Lightfoot's *Colossians*, p. 102.
[2] Cf. Harnack's own list of the results in *Hist. of Dogma*, ii. p. 317
(E.T.).   It is not easy to see where in that list " Hellenism " comes in.

definite predicates—which later theology wrought to
overcome.   If, on the other hand, we take the theology
of such as Irenæus as a type of the *constructive* work
of the period, we find, despite the fact that his ideas
are nowhere systematically presented, a wealth of
profound thoughts, some of which modern theology is
only beginning fully to appreciate.   We shall have to
return to this system further on.[1]   Meanwhile I only
observe that a theology which takes the incarnation
for its centre ; which uses this as the key to the
doctrines of God, of creation, of man, of redemption,
of the final issue of things ; which unites creation in
the closest way with redemption ; which sees in Christ
the " recapitulation " of humanity—its central Personage
and New Head ; which represents Him as gathering
up all created things into one in Himself ;[2] which
explains the redemption of sinners on the same
principle of One representing all in the obedience He
rendered to God, His victory over Satan, and His
endurance of what was due to the righteous ordinance
of God connecting death with sin—a theology of this
kind, I say, is one regarding which it is not presumptuous
to hold that the Church has yet a long way to travel
before it leaves it behind.

[1] Cf. Lect. VII.   [2] Eph. i. 10.

III

The Doctrine of God; Trinity and Deity of Son and Spirit—Monarchian, Arian, and Macedonian Controversies (Third and Fourth Centuries)

" Heresies of different kinds have never originated from any matter in which the principle involved was not important and beneficial to human life." —ORIGEN.

" The natural heresies in Christianity are the Docetic and Nazaritic, the Manichæan and Pelagian."—SCHLEIERMACHER.

" Truth of any kind breeds ever new and better truth ; thus hard granite rock will crumble down into soil, under the blessed skyey influences ; and cover itself with verdure, with fruitage and umbrage. But as for Falsehood, which in like contrary manner, grows ever falser—what can it, or what should it do but decrease, being ripe ; decompose itself, gently or even violently, and return to the Father of it—too probably in flames of fire."—CARLYLE.

LECTURE III

The Doctrine of God; Trinity and Deity of Son and Spirit—
Monarchian, Arian, and Macedonian Controversies (Third
and Fourth Centuries).

THE work of the Anti - Gnostic Fathers had to be
accomplished before the Church was fully prepared to
enter on the construction of its peculiar doctrines.
Once, however, the foundations had been laid, and the
issues cleared, in the conflict with pagan polytheism and
Gnostic emanationism, new questionings arose, and the
Church, with a sure instinct, went boldly to the heart
of the matter in the determination of the Christian
concept of God as Triune, and the vindication of the
supreme Deity of Son and Spirit. These doctrines
were early drawn into the field of controversy by
heretical denial. The controversies which deal with
them are those known as the Monarchian, Arian, and
Macedonian, in the third and fourth centuries. There
were, however, preparatory developments to which it
will be necessary to give attention. I shall give first
an account of the earlier stages in the history of the
doctrines; then proceed to speak of the controversies
by which these earlier conclusions were tested.

I. The doctrine of the Trinity is that which, above
all, it has become customary to trace to the influence
of Greek metaphysics. It is well, therefore, to remember that it was the uniform contention of those

who fought this battle against the various forms of
heretical denial, that the doctrine they contended for,
while not theologically formulated, lay in the faith of
the Church from the first, as involved in its confession
of Father, Son, and Spirit.   The last charge the
Fathers of that age would have pleaded guilty to was
that they were bringing in new doctrines, or importing
speculations from philosophy which had no scriptural
basis.   Their aim here, as in the Gnostic controversies,
was conservation—the defence of vital interests of the
faith against theories which they believed compromised
or negated them.   Their appeal, accordingly, was, as
before, always to Scripture and to continuous Christian
tradition.   When, for example, Hippolytus, or whoever
wrote the book entitled *The Little Labyrinth*, in the
commencement of the third century, was refuting the
Unitarians of his day (the Artemonites), he appealed
confidently to Scripture, to the teaching of earlier
writers, and to Christian psalms and hymns.   "Per-
chance," he says, "what they allege might be credible
were it not that the divine Scriptures contradict them.
. . . For who knows not the works of Irenæus and
Melito, and the rest, in which Christ is announced as
God and Man?   Whatever psalms and hymns were
written by faithful brethren from the beginning celebrate
Christ as the Word of God, asserting His divinity."[1]
On both sides of the controversy it was always felt
that the estimate put on the Person of Christ was
the decisive thing for faith and for theology.   But
the confession of the true Deity of Son and Spirit
necessarily carried thought back to Triune distinction
in the Godhead itself; and baptism in the Threefold
Name[2] was a continuous acknowledgment that this

[1] Euseb. v. 28.
[2] Matt. xxviii. 19 ; cf. 2 Cor. xiii. 14 ; 1 Pet. i. 1 ; Rev. i. 4, 5,

distinction belonged essentially to the Christian idea.

The earliest impugners of the divinity of Christ known to us were the Jewish-Christian *Ebionites*, who certainly do not represent the living, progressive element in early Christianity, but stood from the first on a low level, and from their failure to grasp the essential nature of the Gospel, grew only the more reactionary and impoverished in their views as time went on. To them Jesus was simply a man on whom for His piety the Spirit of God descended at the Baptism, qualifying Him for His Messiahship. Even the better-minded section of this party—the Nazarenes —cut off from the great developing body of Gentile Christianity, and cramped by their environment, tended, as in every such case of arrested development, to become more and more a mere sect—an historical anachronism. Ebionitism disappeared about the fifth century.

We cannot look generally to the *Apostolic Fathers*, as they are called—Clement of Rome, Barnabas, Hermas, Ignatius, Polycarp, and the rest[1]—for much aid in the development of doctrine. Of the more consequence is it to notice that the Christology of these Fathers is, as a rule, remarkably strong and clear. The key-note of all is struck, as Harnack correctly says,

etc. ; *Didache*, ch. 7. Dorner truly says of the baptismal formula that it " requires us to regard the Father as the Father of the Son, and the Son as the Son of the Father, and therefore does not signify a paternal relation to the world in general, but to the Son, who, standing between the Father and the Spirit, must be somehow thought of as pertaining to the sphere of the divine, and therefore denotes a distinction in the divine itself."—*Syst. of Doct.* i. p. 351 (E.T.).

[1] The designation covers generally the writers and literary remains of the immediately sub-apostolic age.

in the opening words of Second Clement,[1] "Brethren, we ought so to think of Jesus Christ as of God, as of the Judge of quick and dead." Ignatius, whose chief theological interest lies in his opposition to docetic denials of the reality of Christ's humanity, is no less decided in his assertion of Christ's true divinity, calling Him "Our God, Jesus Christ."[2] Even the recently-discovered *Didache*, doctrinally so meagre, is pronounced enough here. Baptism is to be administered in the name of Father, Son, and Spirit, and Christ is addressed in the eucharistic prayers as "the God of David."[3] I mention these Fathers, however, chiefly to refer to a theory of Professor Harnack's, which stands in connection with his general view of early Church doctrine, but to which I am unable to assent. In Professor Harnack's judgment we must distinguish in the writings of this period not one but two Christological types, named by him respectively the *Adoptionist* and the *Pneumatic*. In the former Jesus is regarded as a man in whom God, or the Spirit of God, dwells, and who, after His probation on earth, is adopted by God and raised to heavenly glory; in the latter He is regarded as a heavenly Spiritual Being, the highest after God, who has assumed flesh, and after His work on earth returns to heaven. In the one we have a man who has become God, in the other a quasi-divine Being who has become man.[4] On this theory I would submit the following remarks. In the first place, I would point out that the only writing Professor

---

[1] Really an ancient homily.   [2] *Ephesians*, xviii.

[3] Chap. x. The expression is so strong that some editors have taken the liberty of expunging it. But Harnack, Lightfoot, Schaff, etc., defend it.

[4] Cf. *Hist. of Dogma*, i. 188-99 (E.T.). Harnack's own mind would appear to incline to some form of what he calls the Adoptionist Christology. This colours his treatment in more places than one.

Harnack can adduce for his " Adoptionist " Christology is the allegorical *Shepherd* of Hermas.[1]   It is conceded that the Christology of the rest of the group (Clement, Barnabas, Ignatius, Polycarp, etc.) is what he calls " Pneumatic."   In the next place, I would question the justice of his description of even the " Pneumatic " Christology.   He finds the prototype of this in the Epistle to the Hebrews, the Epistle to the Ephesians, and the Johannine writings, in the New Testament. But it is at least misleading to represent these Scriptures as teaching only the incarnation of a heavenly, spiritual Being, without recognising that this Being is expressly held to be in the fullest sense divine.   If the Apostolic Fathers teach a doctrine of the Son's divinity as high as that of John, or Paul, or the Epistle to the Hebrews, I do not think we can reasonably ask more.   But, finally, does even Hermas teach only an " Adoptionist " Christology?   I cannot admit that he does.   There are, indeed, ambiguous elements in Hermas's Christ- ology, but they turn rather on another point—the relation of the Son to the Spirit of God.   With regard to Christ Himself there seems little doubt that he meant to assert a true incarnation of the pre-existent Son.   In one place,[2] for instance, Hermas is shown a rock and a gate, and is told that they denote the Son of God.   How, he asks, can this be, seeing that the rock is old and the gate new?   It is replied—the Son of God is more ancient than all creation, and became the Father's counsellor in His creation.   For this reason He is old.   But the gate is new, because He was made manifest in the last days, that they who are to be saved may enter through it into the Kingdom

[1] A popular early allegory in three parts—Visions, Commands, and Similitudes.
[2] Similitude ix. 12.

of God.   This surely is not " Adoptionist " Christology ! [1]   What Harnack describes under this title is
really the view of Paul of Samosata towards the close
of the third century.[2]

In the *Apologists*, whose general position and work
I discussed in last lecture, we find, as was to be anticipated, a considerable theological advance.   It is
granted—and it is something to have it admitted—
that these writers held firmly by the Trinitarian formula,
and, further, unanimously believed that it was the
Second Person of the Trinity, the " Logos," one in
essence with the Father,[3] who became incarnate in
Christ.   A serious charge is nevertheless brought
against the apologists by the newer school.   It is
alleged, first, that they shifted the centre of gravity in
Christian theology, and led it into a wrong track, in
introducing this Logos speculation at all ; [4] and second,
that the Logos with these Fathers is a cosmological,
and not primarily a Christological, conception — is,
therefore, a part of that " natural theology " into which
they are reproached for converting Christianity.   It is
the cosmological interest, it is held, and not the
Christian, which drew them to the doctrine of the
Logos.   Is this charge just ?   Only, I think, in a very
partial degree.   First, as to the origin of the notion,
while Philo of Alexandria has a doctrine of the Logos,
it is an unwarrantable assumption that the apologists

[1] Pfleiderer, Dorner, Salmon, Donaldson, etc., do not take Harnack's
view of the Christology of Hermas.   Harnack seems to attach generally
a quite disproportionate importance to this writing, which is of the
slightest theological merit.

[2] See end of Lecture.

[3] Cf. Harnack, ii. p. 211 (E.T.)—"The inner essence of the Logos
is identical with the essence of God Himself."

[4] Thus Kaftan in his *Truth of the Christian Religion.*

got their idea from Philo, and not from a much nearer source—the Apostle John. John's Gospel we know to have been in their hands, and Theophilus expressly founds on it,[1] but Philo is never once mentioned in their pages.[2] It is different with the Alexandrians, who do use Philo.[3] Besides, the argument for the divinity of Christ, and for distinctions in the Godhead, is not founded on this term alone, but is based broadly on the Gospel testimony, and on Old Testament Scripture.[4] Next, as to the cosmology, while it is true that, as befitted their apologetic aim, they gave special prominence to the rational side of this doctrine, and, as theologians and Christian philosophers, used it, as the apostles also did,[5] to connect the Christology with the cosmology — thus lifting Christianity clear away from and above all Judaic limitations[6]—I cannot hold it as established that the cosmological was the primary interest to their faith. The first thing with these writers was incontestably the fact of the Logos *incarnate ;*[7] from this they moved back, with the New Testament, to the connection of the Logos or Son with creation. The result was their conviction that the principle of revelation was likewise the principle of creation, and *vice versa*—a very important basis for

[1] Chap. xxii.

[2] Siegfried seeks to trace resemblances, but can adduce no allusions or quotations, *Philo von Alex.*, pp. 332 ff. This is the more remarkable that Plato and other philosophers are constantly noticed. As Siegfried finds Philo everywhere in the New Testament—in the Synoptics, Pauline Epistles, James, as well as in the Fourth Gospel and Hebrews—his resemblances must be taken with caution.

[3] *E.g.*, Clement, *Stromata*, i. 6, 21, 23, etc.

[4] Cf. Justin's *Dialogue, passim.*

[5] John i. 2; 1 Cor. viii. 6; Eph. iii. 9; Col. i. 15-17; Heb. i. 2; Rev. iii. 14.

[6] Cf. Ritschl, *Entstehung* (1857), p. 307.

[7] Cf. Dorner on Justin, *Person of Christ*, ii. p. 265 (E.T.)—"The doctrine of the Logos is thought out by him not *a priori*, but from history," etc.

the refutation of Gnosticism, and for a sound philosophy of religion.

Still, it is to be conceded that the Logos doctrine of the apologists is not yet that of the later Nicene theology, and that, judged by this standard, it has serious defects. It would be too much to expect that an attempt of this kind would be successful all at once, and neither was it. The task these writers had before them was admittedly a difficult one. They were practically agreed in their doctrine of the Logos, and aimed at conserving Christ's entire and perfect divinity. But in carrying back the distinction of Father and Son into the Godhead, they could not decline the obligation of showing how this was reconcilable with monotheism. The task was laid on them of reconstructing their doctrine of God so as to include the distinction of Father and Son—also of Spirit. They had to attempt not only a theology of the Person of Christ, but a theology of the Trinity. And the theory they constructed, while the precursor of the Nicene, shows logical gaps which subsequent controversy was bound to bring to light. The chief difference was, that, while attributing to the Logos a real and eternal mode of subsistence in God, they did not, apparently, regard this mode of subsistence as personal, but held that the " coming forth " or " begetting " ($\gamma\acute{\epsilon}\nu\nu\eta\sigma\iota\varsigma$) of the Son as a distinct hypostasis was immediately prior to creation, and with a view to it. That is to say, the *Logos* was eternal, but His personal subsistence as *Son* was not. Further, as against the Gnostic view of involuntary emanation, this generation of the Son for the work of creation was represented as an act of the Father's *will*. This is the view of Justin probably, of other leading apologists certainly ;[1] and it continued

[1] Justin, *Second Apol.* 6; Athenagoras, 10; Tatian, 5; Theophilus,

long to be the view in the Latin Church. Tertullian, *e.g.*, expressly says : " There was a time when the Father had no Son." [1] It will be evident that this Logos doctrine of the apologists gave a certain point of support to the later Sabellian and Arian constructions : to the Sabellian, in the idea of the Logos as a modal, not personal, distinction in the Godhead ; and to the Arian, in the admission that there was a time when the Son was not, and that He was produced by an act of the Father's will. Yet nothing could be further from the minds of the apologists than to give support to either of these views. Their doctrine differs dia-metrically from that of the Arians in that they held the Son to be truly of the Father's essence ; and it differs from the Sabellian, in that they affirmed the existence of three distinct *hypostases*, or persons, in the Godhead, antecedent to and since the Creation.

This brings me to the consideration of the *Anti-Gnostic, especially the Greek, Fathers*, by whom the real foundations of this doctrine of the Trinity were laid. In Irenæus, the earliest of these Fathers, the enuncia-tion of this doctrine is full and clear. He frees its statement from those ambiguities we have seen adhering to it in the apologists, and firmly asserts the eternal subsistence, the full divinity, and the personal distinct-ness of the Logos who afterwards became incarnate in Christ. " The Logos," as Harnack expounds him, " is the revelation-hypostasis of the Father, 'the self-revela-tion of the self-conscious God,' and, indeed, the eternal self-revelation. For according to him the Son *always*

ii. 10. Bishop Bull labours hard to bring these writers into line with Nicene orthodoxy, but, as Dr. Newman admits, in vain. Cf. Bull's *Defence of Nicene Creed*, bk. iii. chaps. ii. v. ; Newman's *Arians*, App. note 2. See Harnaek's *Hist. of Dogma*, ii. pp. 210-12 (E.T.).

[1] *Against Hermogenes*, 3.

existed with God, *always* revealed the Father, and it
was always the *full* Godhead that He revealed in
Himself.   In other words, He is God in His specific
nature, *truly* God, and there is no distinction of essence
between Him and God." [1]   Tertullian, as we have
seen, followed in the steps of the apologists in his
doctrine of the Son ; yet in controversy he struck out
many important thoughts, and had a decisive influence
on the nomenclature of theology.   It is to him, *e.g.*,
we owe such expressions as " generation," " one substance," " three persons." [2]   He conceives of the Trinity
as a *dispositio* or *economia* in God which anteceded the
Creation, and defends the unity by the thought that
the unity is not abrogated when it derives the Trinity
from itself. [3]   But he is as emphatic as the Nicene
Fathers in affirming that Son and Spirit are of "one
substance " with the Father. [4]

It is, however, the Alexandrian theologians who
had most effect on the development of our doctrine,
and this is the place, perhaps, at which a few words
ought to be said on the general character of this
important school.   Alexandria was the most wonderful city of the ancient world, in an intellectual respect,
after Athens.   It is difficult to give an adequate idea
of it, with its motley population, its seething life, its

---

[1] *Hist. of Dogma*, ii. p. 264 (E.T.).   He grants that Irenæus " does
not utilise the distinction in the interest of cosmology."

[2] Some confusion arose from the fact that the Latin writers used
"hypostasis " as the equivalent of " substance," while the Greeks took it
in the sense of " person."   This ambiguity was subsequently cleared up
(Council of Alexandria, 362 A.D.).

[3] *Against Praxeas*, 3, 5.

[4] *Ibid.* 2.   It is unfair when Harnack says (ii. p. 258), " Here then
the Gnostic doctrine of æons is adopted in its complete form, only with
limitation to three."   Tertullian (sect. 8) repels this very objection, and
cogently shows the difference of his view from that of the Valentinians.

clashing of a hundred rival philosophies and religions, its fusion of Greek, Jewish, and Oriental modes of thought—the city of Philo, where Basilides taught, where Neo-Platonism had its birth, where Athanasius was afterwards to rule. It is easy to forecast the character of the theology which would grow up under such conditions. As earlier, in Philo, we have the blending of Jewish ideas with Greek philosophy, so now it was to be anticipated that the attempt would be made to wed Christianity to the thought and culture which were the predominant influences in this busy intellectual centre. This is, in fact, what happened. The new spirit found its embodiment in the famous Catechetical School of the city, commenced by Pantænus, then presided over with such distinction by Clement (till 202 A.D.), and subsequently by Origen (till 231 A.D.). It is the characteristic of this school that it takes a genial view of heathen culture, does not cut itself away from it, but rather seeks to assimilate what is good in it to itself. It believes that the God of the Gospel is also the God of the first Creation, and that all learning and science —all development of the God-given faculties of man— are sacred, or are capable of becoming so. It thus seeks to connect Christianity, as the principle of a new humanity, with the whole circle of man's intellectual and moral interests. It does this, at the same time, on Christian ground, not seeking, as is sometimes charged against it, to exalt knowledge above faith, but holding rather that the true knowledge must always be based on faith, love, and obedience.[1] In tendency the school was speculative, idealising, spiritualising. But it is not an Antichristian Gnosis, but a Christian one, which it seeks to develop. The great teachers take their stand

[1] In Clement the Word first exhorts, then trains, then teaches.— *Pædagogue*, i. 1, 2.

explicitly on the Christian " Rule of Faith "—the *canon ecclesiasticus*—and on the Scriptures, to which appeal is made as a final authority.[1]   Origen, in his *First Principles*—the earliest extant attempt at a systematic theology — very properly distinguishes between the things certainly believed by the Church, and his own speculations on points not included in the Church's teaching, to which he does not attach the same authority.[2]   With all its faults, I venture to think that the Alexandrian School had an ideal we do well to cherish, and bore witness to a truth of no slight importance, viz., that Christianity is the principle of transformation for *all* our humanity.[3]

In this school, accordingly, though not in an unchristian sense, we get the nearest approach to Professor Harnack's theory of a fusion of Christian with Greek modes of thought.   On our present subject of the doctrine of God, we find in the Alexandrian Fathers both advance and defect.   Clement's mind is superlatively idealistic ; but on the Trinity he holds that the Logos or Son is eternally pre-existent with the Father.[4] Thus, like Irenæus, he frees himself from the view of the apologists that the personal subsistence of the Son began with the Creation.   Still, the personality of the

[1] Cf. Clement, *Stromata*, vi. 15 ; vii. 16, " Scripture the criterion by which truth and heresy are distinguished " ; Origen, *First Principles*, Preface.

[2] i. 6.

[3] As against the charges of Platonising, etc., brought against these Fathers, we should note Harnack's admissions that Clement's superiority is shown " in his contriving to preserve at all points his connection with the faith of the main body of Christendom," and in " the rejection of all conceptions that could not be verified from Holy Scripture, or at least easily reconciled with it " ; that " Origen was an exegete who believed in the Holy Scriptures, and, indeed, he viewed all theology as a methodical exegesis of Holy Writ " ; and that, despite trammels, there are passages in both Clement and Origen " which reproduce and set forth the preaching of the Gospel in a surprisingly appropriate way " (ii. pp. 327, 335, 376).

[4] Cf. *Stromata*, v. 1 ; vii. 1-3, etc.

Son seems always with this Father in danger of again merging into the simple attribute of the divine Reason. Origen, on the other hand, emphasises the personal distinction, and gives the doctrine a development which marks real progress. Both he and Clement treat God in His exaltedness too Platonically ; but Origen's distinction from the Gnostics is seen in the fact that, as his critic admits, he "attributes self-consciousness and will to this superessential essence, in opposition to Valentinus, Basilides, and the later Neo-Platonists. . . . He conceives of God in a more living, and, so to speak, in a more personal way, than the Greek philosophers." [1] That is to say, his doctrine is not that of the Gnostics or philosophers at all, and Professor Harnack is at fault in continually seeking to suggest a fundamental identity.

Origen's peculiarity on the doctrine of the Trinity was twofold. First, to him is due the introduction into theology of the notion of the "eternal generation" of the Son — meaning by this an ineffable timeless origination from the Father's essence which is to be distinguished from Creation. Origen's view on this point may fitly be regarded, as Dorner suggests, as the higher unity of the views of preceding theologians. The apologists and Tertullian held a γέννησις of the Son,—a generation, or coming forth into hypostatic existence, —but it was not eternal. Clement recognised the eternal distinction ; but his was a Trinity, so to speak, *in statu,*—a stationary Trinity,—in which the personality of the Son was only precariously secured. Origen overcomes this by introducing into the doctrine the conception of living movement or process,—of an ever-circling life in the Godhead,—in virtue of which the Son is eternally begotten of the Father, and the Spirit

[1] Cf. *Stromata*, ii. pp. 349-50.

eternally proceeds from both. That is, he retains the notion of the γέννησις, but carries it back to eternity.[1] Dorner justly remarks in proof of the value of this conception that, whereas other conceptions of Origen —his doctrine of eternal creation, of the pre-existence of souls, of final restitution, etc.—have never obtained ecclesiastical recognition, "his doctrine of the eternal generation of the Son, on the contrary, attained, through its own weight, the position of a corner-stone in the doctrinal edifice of the Church."[2]

Origen had thus secured the hypostasis of the Son : was there not a danger now of imperilling the divine unity? This is the second peculiarity in his view— the way in which he seeks to safeguard the divine unity in the midst of these distinctions. This he endeavoured to do through his doctrine of subordination. The Father, in His absolute, underived existence, is held to be the primal source (ἀρχή) of the Godhead ; the Son, though the perfect image of the Father, has *derived* existence. The Spirit is derived in a degree yet further removed. The Father, therefore, is alone the Most High God : Christ, though divine, is related to the Father as a derivative and subordinate Being. Origen stayed himself on the words in John, "My Father is greater than I."[3] He speaks even of the Son as a "second God" (δεύτερος θεός).[4] It is easy to see that this view gave a ready point of contact to later Arianism. For if full Godhead is made to consist in the attributes of self-existence, ingenerateness, etc., and these are reserved for the Father, and declared to be incommunicable, how can the Son, who is denied

[1] *First Principles*, i. 2, 3 ; iv. 28, etc. Cf. Dorner, *Person of Christ*, ii. pp. 108-16.
[2] ii. p. 114.　　　　　　　　[3] John xiv. 28.
[4] *Against Celsus*, v. 39. Similarly, the apologists and Tertullian. Cf. Tertullian, *Against Praxeas*, 3.

these attributes, be said to have perfect divinity ?
Here is a weakness in the theory of Origen which the
later Athanasian doctrine had to overcome ; and it is
not difficult to trace whence this weakness arises.   It
arises precisely from that undue influence of the
Platonic conception of God as the incomprehensible
τὸ ὄν,—Being raised above finite determinations, almost
above existence itself,—to which Origen's own doctrine
of eternal, living movement in the nature of God
furnished the antidote,[1] but which it was left for future
theology more perfectly to purge out.   I do not deny,
therefore, a relative Greek influence in the formation of
Alexandrian doctrine : I hold only that it is not, as
Harnack and others would make it, the moving spring
in the development, which here, as elsewhere, follows its
own logic, despite partial deflections.

II. The way is now open for the consideration of
the series of controversies by which the conclusions
which we have found shaping themselves in the
preceding development were put to the proof.   It will
be seen as we go on that they follow the logical order
of the subjects—the *Monarchian* relating (mainly) to
the Father, the *Arian* to the Son, and the *Macedonian*
to the Holy Spirit.

As the second century was the period of the Gnostic
heresies, so the third century was pre-eminently the
period of the *Monarchian* heresies.   And as out of the
conflict with the Gnostic opposition the Church
emerged with a clearer grasp of the great fundamental
truths of religion, so out of the conflict with

---

[1] I have observed above that Origen never quite surrenders himself to
this conception, indeed, has positive elements in his idea of God (self-
consciousness, will, etc.) wholly incompatible with it.   Cf. Dorner, ii.
pp. 130-44.

Monarchianism it emerged with a firmer grasp of the Christian concept of God—of that view of God, namely, which is involved in its own assertion of a real incarnation, and a real work of the Spirit. In light of what has been said in the previous pages, it is not difficult to understand how the forms of heresy I am to describe should have originated. As soon as an explicit doctrine of the Trinity began to be formulated, it was inevitable that it should be opposed, if on no other ground than that of its alleged novelty. The question was bound to arise, How is the doctrine of a Trinity to be reconciled with the fundamental article of the unity of God?[1] The divine " Monarchia "—the sole government of God, as against Polytheism—seemed imperilled. But not only the theological interest ; even the Christological interest seemed put in danger by the process of the development. The strong subordination-ism of certain of the Fathers,—*e.g.*, of the apologists and Origen,—the way in which they sought to secure the distinct hypostasis of the Son by speaking of Him as a " second God,"—the precarious way in which they connected the Logos with the Father's will,—evoked the feeling that not the unity of God alone, but the true divinity of Christ Himself was compromised. It was not, after all, very God who was manifested in Christ. It was these two interests in combination— the theological and the Christological, the interest in the divine unity and the interest in the Son's divinity— which wrought to produce the type of heresy we call Monarchian : which led, *e.g.*, in the Patripassians, to the rejection of the hypostatic Logos altogether, and to the assertion that the Father Himself had become incarnate

[1] Tertullian, in his treatise against Praxeas, gives a vivid account of the fears and prejudices entertained by many (sect. 3) ; so also Hippolytus, *Refut. of Her.* ix. I. Both Fathers retort the charge of novelty on their opponents.

in Christ. Only thus, they thought, could they make sure that in Him they had the true and absolute God. These profounder interests were crossed, of course, in many minds by shallower ones : by the simple recoil from mystery, the desire to have everything made plain, level, easy to the common understanding, the lack of appreciation for the deeper elements of Christian doctrine. Enough has been said to show, however, that the heresies I speak of are not to be set down to sheer love of error—few serious heresies are—but are clearly explicable from the nature of the case and the circumstances of the time. Neither are they to be set aside as of slight interest to ourselves. The third century will be found swarming with theories which bear the most singular resemblance to those of our own day—of which many modern theories, indeed, are little more than reproductions ; and in studying the grounds on which the Church rejected them, we are gaining no small assistance in the solving of our own problems.

Monarchianism, as a form of error, goes back to the last quarter of the second century. Tertullian is the first who gives it this name.[1] It denotes in general, as already explained, the tendency which emphasises the unity of God, and rejects the personal Trinity. This rejection, however, may take place in two widely different forms. Where, on the one hand, the theological interest is strong and the Christological interest is weak, we have naturally an exaltation of the divine unity at the expense of Christ's true divinity— an *Ebionitic* or *Unitarian* Monarchianism. Where, on the other hand, the Christological interest is predominant —where, *i.e.*, the motive is to safeguard Christ's true

---

[1] *Against Praxeas*, 3 ff.

divinity—we have an identification of Christ with the One Person of the Godhead, who is then viewed as assuming this particular mode of manifestation—a *modalistic* Monarchianism : in its earlier form Patripassianism, in its more developed form Sabellianism. We have therefore two classes of Monarchians : (1) the Ebionitic, Unitarian, or dynamical Monarchians ;[1] and (2) the modalistic Monarchians in their two divisions of Patripassians and Sabellians. I proceed to a brief review of both.

At the head of the Ebionitic type of Monarchianism, perhaps of both forms, is the obscure sect of the *Alogi* in Asia Minor (*cir.* 170-80 A.D.),—Synopticists, we might call them,—who, from an Antimontanistic motive,[2] held fast by what they regarded as the Christology of the Synoptic Gospels, and rejected the Logos doctrine of the Gospel of John. Hence their name, "deniers of the Logos." It is not clear whether they admitted the divinity of Christ in any form ; we know that at least they accepted the supernatural birth.[3] Thereafter, for several decades, the chief theatre of the movement was Rome. There, in the beginning of the third century, an aggressive, purely *Unitarian* form of Monarchianism had vogue—first under one Theodotus of Byzantium, a currier, who was excommunicated by the Bishop

---

[1] I reject Harnack's name "Adoptionist" for this group, both as in itself unsuitable, and as a name already specifically appropriated to a heresy of far later date (eighth century). See below, p. 206.

[2] Montanism, formerly referred to, was an enthusiastic prophetic movement which claimed to inaugurate the era of the Paraclete. It originated in Phrygia in the middle of the second century, and attained to large dimensions. Tertullian was its most noted and only great convert.

[3] Epiphanius, 51. They rejected also the Apocalypse. Harnack attaches to this obscure party a quite unmerited importance—speaks of them even as "the first to undertake within the Church a historical criticism worthy of the name of the Christian Scriptures and the Church tradition" (iii. p. 19).

Victor ;[1] then under a younger Theodotus, a banker ; finally, in the kindred party of the Artemonites, so-called from their founder Artemon. The older Theodotus was a man well versed in Greek culture. He is said to have taught that Christ was "mere man" (ψιλὸς ἄνθρωπος), but admitted His supernatural birth. The descent of the Spirit upon Him at the Baptism was the reward of His pre-eminent piety. Even so He was not God, though some of his party are said to have taught that Jesus *became* God after the resurrection—a view akin to that of Paul of Samosata.[2] The views of the Artemonites were not dissimilar. They were refuted in the work entitled *The Little Labyrinth*, by Hippolytus or a presbyter Caius, to which allusion has already been made. What interests us in these discussions is that the appeal of the Church writers is above all to Scripture, which they accuse their opponents of abandoning for Euclid, and Aristotle, and Theophrastus, and Galen.[3]

Of weightier significance is the other type of Monarchianism—that which I have named the modalistic. Its earlier *Patripassian* form had a brief but curious history. The essence of this view, as already

---

[1] Harnack says that "his is the first instance of which we are certain, where a Christian who took his stand on the rule of faith was yet treated as a heretic" (iii. p. 21). But it may be doubted how far it would be allowed that Theodotus stood on the rule of faith. The author of *The Little Labyrinth* says of his party, "They have set aside the rule of the ancient faith" (Eus. v. 28).

[2] See below. The authorities are Hippolytus (vii. 23), Eusebius (v. 28), Epiphanius (54).

[3] They accuse them further of falsifying and corrupting the Holy Scriptures. This again delights Harnack, who finds in it evidence that the party pursued grammatical exegesis and textual criticism in order to correct the MSS. of Holy Scripture. "Instead of simply accepting or capriciously trimming the traditional text, an attempt was made to discover the original. How unique and valuable is this information !" (iii. p. 25).

explained, is that the Father Himself had become incarnate in Christ, and suffered in and with Him.   It is
difficult for us at first to conceive how any one could
maintain this identification, seeing that Christ, as Son,
is definitely distinguished from the Father—could hold,
in short, that Father and Son were the same.   Yet the
theory was not only held, but, as Tertullian testifies,
met for a time with a wide measure of acceptance.[1]   It
established itself in Rome during several episcopates,
was favoured by the Roman bishops, and had an
influential following among the laity.[2]   The earliest
representative of the view known to us was Praxeas, a
confessor of Asia Minor, and strong opponent of the
Montanists.   He came to Rome, probably in the
episcopate of Eleutherus (170-90 A.D.), and not only
induced the latter to recall letters of peace he had sent
out on behalf of the Montanists, but persuaded him to
adopt his own views.   Thereby, Tertullian says, he did a
twofold service to the devil at Rome—" he drove away
prophecy, and he brought in heresy ; he put to flight
the Paraclete, and he *crucified* the Father." [3]   Afterwards
he went to Carthage, and disseminated his views there.
Tertullian claims to have converted him ; but the " tares "
he had sown sprang up, and gave occasion to the
African Father's treatise.   Praxeas represents the Patripassian view in its crudest form.   The One Almighty
God, the Father, he taught, has literally become incarnate
in Jesus Christ.   In proof he alleged the passages : " I
am God, and beside me there is none else " ;[4]   " I and
my Father are one " ;[5]   " He that hath seen me hath
seen the Father " [6]—treating these three passages,

---

[1] *Against Praxeas*, 1 ; Hippolytus, ix. 1.
[2] Novatian wrote against their tenets in the middle of the century.
[3] *Against Praxeas*, 1.   [4] Isaiah xlv. 5.
[5] John x. 30.   [6] John xiv. 9, 10.

Tertullian says, as if they were the whole Bible. Pressed with the difficulty of how the Father could be at the same time the Son, he took refuge in the distinction that the Spirit, or divine element in Jesus, was the Father, and the flesh which he assumed constituted Him the Son. The objection that the theory subjected the Father to passivity and suffering he avoided by saying that the Father suffered in *sympathy* with the suffering of the flesh. Tertullian had no difficulty in showing that, under pretext of Monarchianism, Praxeas really introduced a new duality. The flesh is the humanity, and the Father is but an indwelling Presence. Son and Father, while affirmed to be one, are again separated, and the theory veers round into a dynamical one. A much subtler form is given to the Patripassian doctrine by another representative, Noetus of Smyrna, probably under the bishop Victor (190-200 A.D.). His school was active under the two succeeding episcopates—those of Zephyrinus (200-18 A.D.) and Callistus (218-23 A.D.), both of whom gave countenance to the error.[1] The peculiarity of the doctrine of Noetus lies in his bold assertion that the Father, by a change in His mode of being, literally *became His own Son.* He is quoted as saying, " When, then, the Father had not been born, He was justly styled Father ; and when it pleased Him to undergo generation, He became His own Son, not another's. . . . On account of the birth that had taken place, He confessed Himself to those beholding Him a Son, no doubt ; yet He made no secret, to those who could comprehend Him, of His being a Father." [2] This view Noetus grounded in the speculative doctrine that it lies in the nature of God to combine in Himself contrary modes

[1] Cf. Hippolytus, bk. ix. This Father also wrote a special work against Noetus.
[2] ix. 5.

of being. When challenged for his views by the Church, he boldly defended himself by saying, "What evil am I doing, in glorifying one God?"[1]   He was, however, excommunicated, and formed a separate school.   Still another name may be mentioned as representative of this view—Beryllus of Bostra, in Arabia, whom Origen had the satisfaction of recovering from his errors.   Our information regarding Beryllus is very scanty,—one obscure passage in Eusebius,[2]—but he seems to have held in some form a doctrine of divine self-limitation, or, as he calls it, "circumscription" ($\pi\epsilon\rho\iota\gamma\rho\alpha\phi\acute{\eta}$)—analogous, perhaps, to the modern "kenosis."   The divine in Christ, he says, was not a divinity of His own ($\iota\delta\iota\alpha \ \theta\epsilon\acute{o}\tau\eta s$), but of the Father ; and this divinity, since the incarnation, exists in a circumscription of being which did not belong to it before.

In various ways, in these earlier attempts, we have seen the idea developing itself of *modes* in the divine existence.   We are now to see this idea wrought out in a more complete fashion by *Sabellius*.   Sabellianism has its advantage over previous theories in that it seeks to do justice to the Trinitarian distinction undeniably involved in the New Testament revelation, and aims at giving a rationale of that distinction in harmony with Monarchian principles.   Briefly stated, its solution is— the substitution of a Trinity of revelation for an immanent Trinity : of a Trinity of *modes* or *aspects* of the one divine Being for a Trinity of Persons. Sabellius, the author of the heresy, began his career in Rome, where he was excommunicated by Callistus— himself a Patripassian.[3]   Thereafter his doctrine had a powerful revival in North Africa about 260 A.D., and yet another in the fourth century, when Athanasius,

---

[1] *Against Noetus*, 1.   [2] vi. 33.   [3] Hippolytus, ix. 6, 7.

Basil, Hilary, etc., were drawn into the controversy. So far as its general principle is concerned, Sabellianism has had many modern defenders and representatives, —*e.g.*, Schleiermacher,—and it reappears in various popular forms without always being recognised for what it is.[1] Our sources of information regarding its ancient form are fragmentary and defective, but the general character of the system can fairly well be made out.[2]

Sabellius starts with God in His absolute, self-identical unity—in His silent, indrawn life—prior to all movement and revelation, and this he calls " Monas." But the Monas does not remain in this absolute, self-enclosed condition : it unfolds or expands itself—the silent God becomes the speaking God. In this transition to revelation or speech the Monas is termed " Logos." Logos, on this reading of the Sabellian theory, is not the Son, but the principle of *all* revelation—the Monas in the act of revealing or unfolding itself—God speaking.[3] A difficult point in the theory is the place left for creation. The Sabellian Trinity of Father, Son, and Spirit, has nothing to do with creation. It presupposes the world of time and space, and relates only to history. We must apparently assume some more general act of God's self-expansion, within which His special acts of revelation then take place.[4] The system properly

[1] Some of these are discussed in the author's *Christian View of God and the World*, Note A to Lecture VII.

[2] The most helpful are the notices in Athanasius in his *Orations* (iii. 4, 36 ; iv. 2, 3, 10-25). Elsewhere in Hippolytus, Epiphanius, Theodoret, Gregory Nazianzen, Basil, etc.

[3] Thus Schleiermacher, Baur, Dorner, etc. Neander differs, without, however, giving a clear view. The Logos was not the Son before the Incarnation (Athanasius, iv. 15, 21, 22). Basil (Ep. 210) quotes a statement that God, being one, was transformed as need arose, and dialectically revealed Himself (διαλέγεσθαι) now as Father, now as Son, now as Holy Spirit.

[4] Some such view is implied in Athanasius, iv. 10-13.

begins when we reach the stadia of Bible revelation. The modes of God's revelation Sabellius illustrates by various metaphors—especially by the Stoical figures of expansion (πλατυσμός, ἔκτασις) and contraction (συστολή), or by the arm outstretched and taken back again.   It is less a free act which such images suggest than a rhythmical movement of the divine nature—an alternate expansion and contraction of the Monas according to a law of internal necessity.   The Triune revelation belongs, as already said, altogether to the sphere of history, and, indeed, religious history.   God as Father is made known in the Old Covenant and the Law ;[1] God as Son in the Incarnation in Jesus Christ ; God as Spirit in His indwelling in the hearts of believers in the Church.   Under these aspects, it is pointed out, God enters into continually closer and more perfect relations with humanity.   God had still an outward relation to mankind in the Law ; in Christ He dwelt among them as an individual ; in the Holy Spirit He is the animating principle in the souls of believers.   On the nature of this Trinity, in contrast with the Church doctrine, it is to be remarked—first, that it is only a Trinity of revelation.   It is one and the same God— the original Monas—who reveals Himself in these three forms, or, as Sabellius calls them, using the word in his own sense, πρόσωπα—faces, aspects, manifestations. Second, the revelations are successive.   The Trinity is

---

[1] The relation of the Father to the Monas is another difficult point in the Sabellian system.   Strictly, the Father was only one of the three forms of manifestation (*prosopa*) of the Monas, yet it seems likely that in looser speech the Monas was also sometimes spoken of as the Father.   Cf. Athanasius, iv. 13, 14, etc.   Another name given to the Monas was Son-Father (υἱοπάτηρ).   Cf. Athanasius, *On Synods*, 16.   Athanasius no doubt gives the genuine Sabellian view when he says (*Orat.* iv. 13), " Then it is no longer proper to speak of the Father as expanding, but the Monas is productive of three, so that there is one Monas, then Father, Son, and Spirit."

a successive, not a simultaneous one. There are the successive outstretchings of the divine arm, and one has to be retracted before the other can take place. The πρόσωπον of the Father ends before that of the Son begins ; and that of the Son ends before that of the Spirit begins. The effect of this, thirdly, is, that the incarnation, like the other πρόσωπα, is only a transient phenomenon. As God had ceased to be Father before He became Son, so He must cease to be Son before He can become Spirit. The form of Son comes to an end with the resurrection and ascension. Sabellius is even reported to have taught that the humanity of Christ was then reabsorbed in the divine.[1] Thus the permanent significance of Christ's person is altogether lost. We know nothing of what views Sabellius held of redemption, but it may be inferred from the principles of his system that the goal of the whole development is that the finite creation shall be reabsorbed in Deity, who thus again becomes all in all.

Reviewing the Sabellian system as a whole, we cannot but see that it had considerable comprehensiveness and breadth, and was fitted to prove a formidable rival to the Church doctrine. It gave Monarchianism a developed character, and perhaps wrought out its principle in as plausible a form as any it has since assumed. It compelled the Church clearly to face the hypothesis of a modal Trinity as an alternative to its own doctrine. Yet it is evident also that the theory, in the shape it received from Sabellius, was anything but truly Christian. Its basis, to begin with, was Pantheistic—a Pantheism, as the Fathers saw, akin to that of the Stoics ; it failed, moreover, at every point to do justice to the facts of the Christian revelation. It is not in the Old Testament, or as Legislator, that

[1] Epiphanius, ii. 62, 1.

God is revealed peculiarly as Father.[1] But waiving
this, Father and Son in this theory have no relation to
each other.   The Father is not the Father of the Son ;
the Son is not the Son of the Father.   It is a contradiction of the Christian view to speak of the Father
as non-existent since the appearance of the Son ;[2] and
still more to represent the incarnation as only a
temporary appearance.   The whole Christian hope is
bound up with faith in the continued existence of the
Redeemer.   To speak of the union of the Godhead
with Him as coming to an end is to dissolve the
connection of believers with Christ, and destroy the
existence of the Church itself.   In comparison with
these, other objections are of minor account.   It is an undeniable weakness in the theory that it fails to subsume
all God's revelations under this form of Trinity, and
gives us only a chapter out of a much larger book—
leaves out of account, in particular, the initial manifestation of God in creation, and the whole providential
manifestation of God in history outside Israel.   God's
activity in creation and in the general government of
the world is plainly not suspended while He is mani-
festing Himself in the dispensational Trinitarian modes.
This touches the theory more nearly than we might
suppose, for it breaks up the idea which lies at the
foundation of the system, that God can exist only in
a single mode or πρόσωπον at a time.   It demonstrates,
on the contrary, that God can reveal Himself simultaneously in different modes, and does so.

I have now, as a final step, to ask you to look at

---

[1] This applies also to many modern theories, which identify the Father
with the Creator or Lawgiver.

[2] It was no doubt the perception of this difficulty which led to the
identification of Father and Monas already referred to.   But this breaks
up the consistency of the whole theory.

the culmination of this whole Monarchian movement in Paul of Samosata, Bishop of Antioch, 260-70 A.D., who represents the phase of *dynamical* Monarchianism. Reflection will readily suggest to us how near akin, without intending it, the Sabellian view of the person of Christ is to the Ebionitic, and how easily the one passes into the other. The point of difficulty in the Sabellian theory lies in knowing what to do with the humanity of Christ after the ascension. The supposition of its absorption when the πρόσωπον of the Son comes to an end is too violent to be long entertained ; the tendency, therefore, is to represent the divinity and humanity as separable, *i.e.*, to connect the two only dynamically. And this brings us back to Ebionitism. It is not, however, the logical issues only of the Monarchian movement which we see illustrated in Paul of Samosata : in his person also we have a conspicuous example of the essentially irreligious spirit which was a marked feature of the development. The Ebionitic Monarchianism of the early Church was a shallow product at the best, with hardly a trace of religious depth or earnestness in its course. In this respect Paul of Samosata is its classical representative —its born high priest. The chief source of our information regarding him is a circular letter sent out by the bishops and clergy who condemned him ;[1] and, after every allowance has been made for party prejudice, it is a most extraordinary picture which it presents to us. Discarding the grave and modest deportment which became a Christian bishop, Paul seems to have lived in a style of ostentatious splendour, combining with his ecclesiastical office a civil magistracy which

---

[1] Eusebius, vii. 30 ; cf. Gibbon, *Decline and Fall*, ch. xvi. The cautious Neander remarks that we cannot refuse the testimony in this case : Harnack lightly brushes it aside.

brought him a large salary. By this and by unblush-
ing ecclesiastical maladministration, he rose to a
position of inordinate wealth. His pride, luxury, and
oppression made him odious to his brethren. He was
as vainglorious as he was rich ; had erected for his use
a lofty tribunal and throne ; appeared in public with a
crowd of attendants making way before him ; strutted
through the Forum reading his letters and dictating
answers. But his behaviour in church was most
offensive of· all. He banished from the Church the
hymns sung in honour of Christ, and had hymns
composed in his own honour and sung by a choir of
women at the Easter festival. His preaching was of a
theatrical description, accompanied by extravagant
gesticulations and stampings ; and the people were
encouraged to applaud with the waving of handker-
chiefs, and were rebuked if they did not. His private
behaviour was equally scandalous. Yet his wealth and
power were such, owing to the favour of Queen Zenobia,
that few dared to touch him.

This was the man, then, in whom Monarchianism
now came to its head. His system is a development
of that of the earlier representatives of Unitarian
Monarchianism—the Theodotians and Artemonites—
but differed from theirs in that he held that Christ,
commencing as man, was raised by progressive de-
velopment ($\pi\rho o\kappa o\pi\acute{\eta}$) to the dignity of Son of God,
obtaining for His excellence divine rank.[1] The Logos
in God, he held, was simply what reason is in man.
Christ was mere man : He was, as Paul expressed it,
"from below" ($\kappa\acute{\alpha}\tau\omega\theta\epsilon\nu$). He does not, however, seem
to have denied the supernatural birth. The union of
the Logos with Christ did not differ, except in degree,

---

[1] Cf. Epiphanius (65), Eusebius, etc.

from his union with any other man.   In degree, nevertheless, it did differ, for the power of the divine
penetrated Christ's humanity as it did that of no other.
This indwelling of the Logos, or divine wisdom, or
power in Christ is one, not of person, but of quality
(κατὰ ποιότητα).   Through His interpenetration by
the divine power Christ advanced progressively till
He became God (τεθεοποιῆσθαι).   He is raised to
divine rank — from man became God (ἐξ ἀνθρώπων
γέγονε θεός).   Paul can therefore speak of an apotheosis
—a deification of Christ; but deity or Godhead here
only means that Christ, for His peculiar merit, was
deemed worthy by God of divine honours—not that
He became God by nature.   It was a Godhead of
rank, not of essence.   It was deification by grace.   But
this view the Church emphatically rejected.[1]   Two
influential Synods (264, 269 A.D.) were convened at
Antioch to deal with it.   At the first Paul succeeded
in imposing on the bishops by plausible subtleties; at
the second his sophistries were exposed, and his views
were definitively condemned.   It was, nevertheless,
three years afterwards before the orthodox party was
able to dispossess him.   A point of interest in connection with this Synod (269 A.D.) is that it rejected the
term *homoousios* (ὁμοούσιος), which later became the
watchword of Nicene orthodoxy, because of its abuse
by Paul.   This again is evidence that in these discussions it was not terms—Greek or other—the Church
was fighting for, but things.

I have been particular in stating this view of
Paul of Samosata mainly for the reason that it is in
principle not different from many theories at present

---

[1] This fact refutes the notion that it was familiarity with the apotheosis-
idea of heathenism which led to the ascription of divinity to Christ.

current among us—is, indeed, the type of dynamical
theories for all time. We have seen the essence of it
to be that, while in nature only man, Christ is raised to
Godhead—an honorary Godhead—through the working
of a divine power within Him. The relation of the
Godhead to the humanity is a dynamical one ; but it
ends in the exaltation of Christ to divine rank. This
accords with a tendency quite prevalent in recent
theology to assign to Christ the predicate " Godhead,"
while not really recognising in Him more than man.[1]
The dilemma in which this whole class of theories is
placed is obvious. If true Godhead is ascribed to
Christ He cannot be only, or merely, man ; if conversely Christ is held to be in nature and person man
only, however exalted by possession of the divine
Spirit, it is not in a real, but simply figurative sense,
that He can ever be spoken of as raised to Godhead.
Godhead is not a thing that can begin in time, or be
conferred as a degree of honour on a created being.
This view, therefore, under all its disguises, remains a
Unitarian one. If the supposition *could* be entertained
—though contrary to all right reason—that a Being
not originally divine could by development attain to
the rank of Godhead, this would land us in the equally
extraordinary result, from which even a theory like
Rothe's[2] is not free, that since the incarnation a new
person has literally been added to the Godhead. This
surely is reduction to absurdity.

[1] *E.g.*, Schultz, *Die Gottheit Christi.* Lipsius, Beyschlag, and many
Ritschlians, speak in the same way.
[2] Cf. *Christian View of God and the World*, Lecture VI.

IV

Same Subject Continued—Arian and Macedonian
Controversies (4th Century)

"God gives man nothing in a finished state. All His gifts are so bestowed that man shall have abundant work to do with them. This is specially true, not only of man himself, but also of the Bible."—ROTHE.

"For if he who speaks of two Hellenises, therefore he who speaks of one Sabellianises. But this is not so! God forbid. For as he who says 'Father and Son are two' confesses one God; so let him who says 'One God,' think of two, Father and Son, as being one in the Godhead."—ATHANASIUS.

"One need not be an orthodox trinitarian to see that if Arianism had had its way, the theology of Christianity would have become of a kind in which no philosopher, who had outgrown the demonism of ancient systems, could for a moment acquiesce."—T. H. GREEN.

LECTURE IV

Same Subject continued—Arian and Macedonian Controversies
(Fourth Century).

THE Monarchian controversies of the third century
on the Trinity and the supreme divinity of Christ were
but preludes to the great pitched battle of the Arian
controversy in the fourth. The fundamental question at
issue was how these peculiar assertions of the Christian
faith were to be reconciled with the unity of God ; above
all, how the relation of Christ to the Father was to be
conceived of, so as, on the one hand, not to compromise
His true divine dignity, and, on the other, not to
endanger the divine *Monarchia*. This question could
only be answered, as it was answered, through the
stating of all possible alternatives, the testing of each,
and the rejection of such as were found inadequate.
We are to see this process exemplified with regard to
the deity of the Son and Spirit in the controversy now
to be reviewed.

Ere the Arian controversy had broken out, a
decisive change had taken place in the external fortunes
of the Church. The struggle, prolonged through three
centuries with the forces of a persecuting paganism, had
issued in the decisive defeat of the latter. In 313 A.D.,
following on the last terrible persecution by Diocletian,
came the edict of Milan, giving universal toleration,

and in 323 A.D. Constantine, having overthrown his last rival Licinius, became sole ruler in the empire. The next year, 324 A.D., saw the so-called establishment of the Christian religion, an event which, outwardly favourable, introduced a new factor into the history of the development of dogma—one nearly always hurtful and disturbing — I mean the exercise of imperial authority. Ere, however, this fateful step was taken, the Church was involved in the controversy we are to study.

It was not, however, in external respects only that a change had taken place in the condition of the Church. The Church triumphed because it was already internally the strongest force in the empire. Even in the third century it was formidable—compactly organised, ably directed, influential not only in numbers, but in the rank of many of its members.[1] Its recognition by Constantine in the fourth was but the acknowledgment of a preponderance of influence already won. In an intellectual respect the advance was equally great. Theological tendencies were assuming distinct shape, and marked contrasts had begun to develop themselves in the schools. One such contrast must be referred to here for the sake of the profound influence it exercised on after theology, that, viz., between the schools of Alexandria and Antioch. The commencement of the Alexandrian school has already been described. Its chief representatives during the fourth century were, first, the renowned Athanasius, and after him the three great Cappadocian Fathers, Basil, Gregory of Nazianzus, and Basil's brother, Gregory of Nyssa. Throughout it retained the liberal, speculative, idealising character imparted to it by its master, Origen ; but in its newer

[1] See the evidence in my *Neglected Factors*, etc. (Lect. II.), on the extent to which Christianity had permeated the higher ranks of society.

form it kept clear of, and overcame Origen's subordinationism.[1]   The Antiochian school had opposite characteristics.   It was sober, literal, grammatical, rational ; in
Coleridge's phrase, was a school of the understanding
rather than of the reason.   We have seen the influence
exercised in Antioch by Paul of Samosata, and the
leaven of his teachings, no doubt, continued to operate
after his removal.   The true founder of the Antiochian
school, however, was Lucian, martyred in 311 A.D., who
stamped on it its predominant exegetical, and in part
rationalising, character.[2]   From this school came Arius
and most of the leaders of the party who supported
him.[3]   Professor Harnack goes further, and gives a
very definite and detailed account of the opinions of
Lucian, of which I will only say that it seems to me
largely hypothetical, and not borne out by the authorities.[4]   To Harnack Lucian is simply the Arius before
Arius.   He adopted the Christology of Paul of Samosata,
and combined with it the Logos doctrine.   His doctrine
is Paul's, with the difference that, instead of a man, it
is a created heavenly being who becomes God.   The
stress is laid on creation out of nothing, and on deification by progressive development.   There is, however,
no evidence that I know of that Lucian was a disciple
of Paul of Samosata,[5] or that he held that the Logos

---

[1] It kept free also from most of Origen's heretical peculiarities (eternal
creation, pre-existence of souls, etc.), though Gregory of Nyssa, nearest to
Origen in spirit, follows him in his restitutionism.

[2] A good characterisation of the school is by Neander, iii. p. 497 ff.
(Bohn's ed.).   Distinguished later representatives were Diodorus of
Tarsus, Theodore of Mopsuestia, Chrysostom, and Theodoret (see Lecture
VI.).

[3] Arius calls Eusebius of Nicomedia his "fellow-Lucianist" (Theod.
Ecc. Hist. i. 5).   Philostorgius, the Arian historian, gives a list of Lucian's
pupils in this party (ii. 14).

[4] iv. pp. 3-7 (E.T.).

[5] It goes against this connection that Eusebius, the historian, who
acted with Eusebius of Nicomedia and other friends of Arius, speaks in

was created out of nothing, or that Christ became God by progressive development.[1]   That his views tended in some way to Arianism we may indeed fairly conclude ; it is certain, further, that he stood with his school during three episcopates outside the communion of the Church, and was only reconciled to it shortly before his death.[2]   This, however, hardly warrants us in attributing to him so fixed a type of doctrine as that just indicated.

I. The Arian dispute took its origin about 318 A.D. in Alexandria, where Arius, a leading presbyter, had come into conflict with his bishop on the subject of the Trinity.[3]   Arius is described to us as a tall, spare man, ascetic in habits and dress, with long, tangled hair, and a curious practice of twisting about, but withal of fascinating manners and address, and not without a considerable mixture of craft and vanity.[4]   Of this last the introduction to his book called the *Thalia*—" I am that celebrated man who has suffered many things for God's glory, and being taught of God, has obtained wisdom and knowledge "[5]—is sufficient witness.   Notwithstanding his apparent smoothness, he was a man of strong and vehement passions.   He soon gathered round him a multitude of supporters, and was unwearied in the dissemination of his views.   The condemnation

the history in the highest terms of Lucian (viii. 13 ; ix. 6), but gives the most condemnatory accounts of Paul and his doctrines (vii. 27, 29, 30). Against this the vague expression of Alexander, Bishop of Alexandria, in an epistle against Arius — "Whom Lucian, having succeeded" (διαδεξάμενος), etc. (Theod. i. 4)—is hardly decisive.

[1] Nothing of this kind is suggested, but the opposite is shown by the the creed ascribed to Lucian at the Council of Antioch, 241 A.D.

[2] Theodoret, i. 4.

[3] The accounts in the histories vary as to the precise circumstances of origin of the quarrel, but admit of being readily harmonised.

[4] Cf. Stanley, *Eastern Church*, iii. 5.   [5] In Athan. *Orations*, i. 5.

of his opinions by a local council (321 A.D.) only fanned the flame of controversy. Feeling on both sides became intensely keen. Each party sought to strengthen itself by inviting the support of influential bishops ; the whole Church was soon in turmoil ; the very theatres resounded with ridicule of the disputes of the Christians.[1] Constantine, whose chief anxiety was for the peace of his empire, was deeply chagrined at this unexpected outbreak about matters, as he regarded them, of trifling importance, and wrote urgently to both Alexander and Arius, beseeching them to exercise mutual forbearance. When this failed, and his eyes, perhaps, had become more open to the gravity of the issues, he conceived the idea—by an inspiration of Heaven, as he thought—of summoning a council of the whole Christian world to decide the matter.

The controversy thus opened affords a favourite text for those who are disposed to make light of theological controversy generally. The whole contention, this class would have us believe, was a hopeless logomachy—a dispute about trifles, in which the essence of Christianity was in no way involved. Gibbon has made merry over the whole world convulsed about a diphthong.[2] So, for that matter, it is only a single letter which makes the difference between "theist" and "atheist!" Profounder minds judge the controversy very differently. Harnack, despite his theory of the Greek origin of dogma, makes it very clear that it was Christianity itself that was at stake. "Only," he says, "as cosmologists are the Arians monotheists, as theologians and in religion they are polytheists. Deep contradictions lie in the background : a Son who is no Son ; a Logos who is no Logos ; a monotheism which

[1] Cf. Socrates, i. 6. [2] *Decline and Fall*, xxi.

does not exclude polytheism ; two or three *ousias*, who are to be worshipped, while still only one is really distinguished from the creation ; an indefinable nature which first becomes God when it becomes man, and which still is neither God nor man. . . . The opponents were right ; this doctrine leads back to heathenism. The orthodox doctrine has, on the contrary, its abiding worth in the upholding of the faith that in Christ God Himself has redeemed man, and led them into His fellowship.   This conviction of faith was saved by Athanasius against a doctrine which did not understand the inner nature of religion generally, which sought in religion only teaching, and ultimately found its satisfaction in an empty dialectic." [1]

The historical significance of Arianism lay, as I have already hinted, in the fact that it brought to expression certain tendencies already working in theology, and compelled the Church to face them and give judgment upon them.   We saw how, in the preceding period, there were influences tending to exalt the divine " Monarchia " at the expense of the distinct hypostasis of the Son ; how, on the other hand, as the result of Origen's influence, there was a strong current of subordinationism on the part of those who held that hypostasis. This tendency, I remarked, was strengthened by—if it had not its main cause in—the Platonising way of regarding God as the self-caused, unspeakably

---

[1] *Grundriss,* i. p. 141 ; cf. *Hist. of Dogma,* iv. p. 41 (E.T.).   Mr. Froude tells us that in earlier years Mr. Carlyle had spoken contemptuously of the Athanasian controversy, of the Christian world torn to pieces over a diphthong, but later told him that he perceived Christianity itself to have been at stake.   If the Arians had won it would have dwindled away to a legend (*Life in London,* ii. p. 462).   I may add the judgment of Professor Schultz in his *Gottheit Christi.*   " The Arian Christology," he says, " is inwardly the most untenable and dogmatically worthless of all the Christologies that meet us in the history of dogma " (cf. ii. p. 65).

exalted, incomprehensible Being, who alone was God in the highest sense. This led, first, to God being put at an infinite distance from His creation ; next, to the necessity of interposing some middle being to effect the transition to the latter ; third, to the Son who was begotten for this purpose being put in the second rank, as not having those attributes which were supposed to constitute absolute Godhead. Subordinationist tendencies of this kind were active in the Church before Arius, *e.g.*, in Lactantius, in Eusebius of Cæsarea, probably in Lucian ; but it was only when definite expression was given to them, and their logical consequences were fairly drawn out by Arius, that their import was fully seen. In brief, Origen had spoken of the Son as occupying a secondary relation to the Father, while at the same time upholding His eternal generation and identity of essence with God. These two tendencies could not but come ultimately into collision. If the identity of nature with the Father was maintained, full and true Godhead must be granted to the Son, and the subordinationist elements, so far as in conflict with this conception, must be eliminated. If, on the other hand, the subordinationist standpoint was adhered to, in combination with the abstract, Platonising view of God, the Arian doctrine was the logical outcome.

It is not so much my object to enter into the details of the history of this controversy—which my limits do not permit—as rather to bring out the great issues involved, the principles at work, the logic, as I venture to call it, of the movement. It will help to this end if, before looking at the proceedings of the Nicene Council, we glance at the parties involved, and at the positions they severally occupy. This will show with tolerable clearness the course which the historical development was bound to follow.

By the time of the opening of the council three parties had shaped themselves with some definiteness.

First, the *Athanasian* party—to name Athanasius as its outstanding representative — was the only one of the three that had a perfectly unambiguous ground. The Son, in its view, was of the same essence (ὁμο-ούσιος) with the Father—very God of very God. In this view the genuine Christian interest was conserved which Athanasius constantly came back on, viz., that no creature, but only God, can unite us with God.[1] He was not less clear on the other point that a true incarnation is needed in order to redemption. Only the divine Son could atone for the sins of the world.[2] In thus bringing the deity of the Son into direct connection with man's salvation, he takes a step beyond the Fathers who connected it primarily with the creation, and in some of his positions well-nigh anticipates Anselm.[3] Yet he invariably contended that he introduced nothing new, but was defending what had always been the faith of the Church.[4]

At the opposite pole to the Athanasian was, second, the pure *Arian* party, led at first by Arius, and at a

[1] Cf. *Orations*, ii. 69, and *passim*. Harnack says, "Is the divine Being, who has appeared on earth, and has united man with God, identical with the highest divine Being who rules heaven and earth, or is He a half divine Being? That was the decisive question in the Arian controversy" (*Grundriss*, i. p. 136).

[2] Cf. specially his *Incarnation of the Word*, written before the Arian controversy. Harnack says, "The theology and Christology of Athanasius are rooted in the thought of redemption" (*Hist. of Dogma*, iv. p. 26).

[3] Cf. Harnack, iv. 29 ; Dorner, *Person of Christ*, ii. pp. 248-60.

[4] Cf. Harnack, p. 45. "Athanasius always appealed to the collective testimony of the Church in support of the doctrine which he defended," etc. So, on p. 22, of the Bishop Alexander : "Conscious that he is contending for nothing less than the divinity of Christ, the universal faith of the Church." The doctrine of Arius, on the other hand, is new (p. 41).

subsequent stage in the controversy by Aëtius and Eunomius (whence in the later Fathers the name *Euno-mians*). The general procedure of Arius is thus characterised by Dorner : " In the sphere of the relative, his movements are easy and skilful ; in the handling of the lower categories of logic he evinces dialectic address, but he applies them as a standard to every-thing, and is unable to rise to anything higher. He is entirely destitute of the strictly speculative faculty." [1] In his treatment the distinction of the Son from the Father was pushed to its extreme logical limit. His starting-point was from the term Son, which he held necessarily implied the priority of the Father. The Son, he taught, was a created being—created " out of nothing." He was the first and greatest of the creatures, and was brought into existence that through Him the world might be created. He was not eternal ; was not of divine substance ; was mutable, *i.e.*, could fall into sin ; was not able to comprehend the Father. It was on the ground of His foreseen merits as man that He received the names of Logos, Son, etc.[2] The Son, the Arians granted, is pre-temporal, before all ages ; but this was because they held that time began with the creation of the world. This idea they expressed by the formula, " There was when He was not " ($\mathring{\eta}\nu$ $\mathring{o}\tau\epsilon$ $o\mathring{v}\kappa$ $\mathring{\eta}\nu$).[3]

Intermediate between the two parties now described stood a third, the *Semi-Arian* or subordinationist party, distinguished from the Athanasian by their rejection of

[1] ii. p. 239.
[2] On the opinions of Arius, see Athanasius, *Orations*, i. 5, etc. ; Socrates, i. 6. Arius embodied his views in his *Thalia*, and in songs, set to popular airs, which were diffused among the people (*Philostorgius*, ii. 2).
[3] Harnack says, "With Arius the Son belongs to the world side, while, with Athanasius, He, as belonging to God, stands over against the world" (iv. p. 29).

the term ὁμοούσιος. They would go no farther than
the vague statement that the Son resembled the Father,
or was " of *like* substance " (ὁμοιούσιος)[1] with the Father.
But here two classes are specially to be distinguished.
There was, *first*, a disingenuous, time-serving section—
the *Eusebians*, as they are commonly called, from their
leader Eusebius of Nicomedia, one of the most active
supporters of Arius—whose real views were strongly
Arian, but who scrupled at no evasion which might
disguise their opinions, and employed the basest methods
of intrigue and violence against their opponents. They
have been called the Herodians of the Arian controversy.   Later on they fell back from the ὁμοιούσιον
formula, and took refuge in the bare declaration that
Christ was "*like*" (ὅμοιος) to the Father (whence their
name " Homœans "); or urged that Scriptural terms
only should be employed.   They are at this stage
known as *Acacians*, from their new leader Acacius.
But, *second*, there was another and larger section—the
sincere Semi-Arians, as we may call them—subordinationist in tendency, whose chief objection was to the
word ὁμοούσιος, which to their mind had evil associations,[2] rather than to the doctrine represented by it.
In the later stages of the controversy, this party,
repelled by the unabashed Arianism of some of their
allies, drew nearer to the orthodox, and ultimately
accepted their formula, though still without complete
unity of view.

Such, then, were the parties whose opinions came

---

[1] "Ὁμοιούσιος is in fact nothing, and when used of the real Son is
consequently either nonsense or false " (*ibid.* p. 33).

[2] It was, they held, novel, unauthorised, had Valentinian and Sabellian
associations, had been condemned by the Council at Antioch in the case
of Paul of Samosata, etc.

into collision in the famous Council of Nicæa. Let us follow out a little further the logical bearings of the Arian view as discussed then and after. Some of the evasions of the system—that, *e.g.*, about time—it was not difficult for Athanasius and others to strip off. The phrase, "There was when He was not," meant nothing unless a time relation was imported into it. It was only fitted to throw dust in the eyes of the simple, who felt as if Arius was asserting some quasi-eternity of the Son when he admitted that He was born before all ages. Again, it was easy to show that on the Arian theory "begetting" meant nothing else than "creating." The Son was a creature, neither more nor less : the relation of the Father and the Son was a purely causal one. And this, when brought to the point, Arius freely admitted. The Son, he said, was created "out of nothing." Further, the reason why the Son was created is, that God is so exalted that He cannot immediately create a world. An intermediate being is needed to fill up the gulf between God and His creation. But, since the Son is Himself a creature, it is plain that the same difficulty occurs in regard to Him. The difference between God and the creature must always be infinite. If, then, God is too exalted to create a world, He is likewise too exalted to create the Son ; a new being is needed to fill up the gulf between the Father and the Son ; another to fill up the gulf between God and this new being, and so *ad infinitum.*

These objections lay on the surface. But, in truth the creatureship of the Son being admitted, Arianism could run only one logical course ; and the logical stages are, as usual, virtually also the historical ones. Arius naturally *began* by trying to exalt the Son as high as he could—by bringing his view as near the

Church doctrine as possible. He was led to this also by his view that the Son was the intermediary of creation. For if God is too high to create the world, the Son must be represented as a very exalted being if God is to create *Him*. The Son in this way is brought so near to God that the incomparableness between Him and God is on the point of disappearing, and there seems no need for violent opposition to the Church doctrine.[1]   Arius, in one letter, even speaks of Christ as " perfect God " ($\pi\lambda\eta\rho\eta\varsigma$ $\theta\epsilon\delta\varsigma$) and " unchangeable " [2] —expressions quite contrary to the tenor of his ordinary doctrine. But, *next*, these high predicates bestowed on Christ could not conceal the fact that, in the view of Arius, the Son was only a creature—not truly of the essence of God ; that the Father's relation to Him was, as said, only a causal one.[3]   From this he quite logically developed his other propositions, that the Son was temporal, mutable, incapable of comprehending God, etc.   It is now the *distance* between God and the Son which is the ruling thought, and in this lies the real nerve of the Arian doctrine.   But now, if the Son is only a creature, foreign in essence to God, on what ground is He to be called either Logos or Son ?   He is no longer Son by nature ; why give Him this name? Arius answers that He receives the title on the ground of God's foreknowledge of His merits as *man*.   Sonship is taken from the divine side, and based on human merit.   The transition is made to a view not unlike that of Paul of Samosata.[4]   The pre-existent hypostasis becomes what Dorner calls a " cumbersome, confusing, cosmological appendage, which ought to

---

[1] Thus Dorner, ii. p. 237.   [2] Theodoret, i. 5.

[3] *Ibid.*   "This is really the cause of our persecution (that the Son had a beginning), and likewise because we say that He is from nothing ($\epsilon\xi$ $o\dot{v}\kappa$ $\check{o}\nu\tau\omega\nu$)."

[4] Cf. Athanasius, *Orat.* i. 5, and throughout.

have been cast aside with the occupation of this new point of view." [1] There was, besides, on this view, no work for Christ to accomplish which required this higher nature. Historically, therefore, the person of Christ became increasingly lowered in the hands of the Arians ; as, generally, it is the case that, wherever Arianism has appeared, it has tended to work round into Unitarianism. [2]

II. The first of the so-styled ecumenical Councils was summoned to meet at Nicæa, in Bithynia, in May or June 325 A.D. There, after some preliminary proceedings, it was formally opened with much splendour by the Emperor in person. A brief narrative of its doings will suffice. It consisted of about 300 (traditionally 318) bishops, [3] but a throng of presbyters, deacons, acolytes, etc., swelled the attendance to one or two thousand. The moving spirit in the debates on the orthodox side was the youthful Athanasius, deacon of Alexandria, who was present to assist his bishop. The avowed Arians were few in number. Even with the Eusebians they numbered barely a score. [4] A creed proposed by the partisans of Arius was rejected with horror : the creed itself was torn ignominiously in pieces. [5] The leadership of the middle party was assumed by Eusebius of Cæsarea, who now submitted a creed, which he said he had been taught as a catechumen at Cæsarea ; but this also, notwithstanding the great influence of its proposer, and the support of the Emperor, was rejected on

[1] ii. p. 242.
[2] See, as respects England, the valuable appendix by Dr. P. Fairbairn, in Dorner's *Person of Christ*, v. pp. 337-466.
[3] Cf. Athanasius, Socrates, Theodoret, etc.
[4] Philostorgius the Arian reckons 22.
[5] Theod. i. 8.

account of the ambiguity of its expressions.[1]   Something was needed which would mark accurately the distinction between the two parties, and this, it is said, was unintentionally supplied by Eusebius of Nicomedia himself in the term ὁμοούσιος.[2]   The majority of the Council saw that the formula that the Son was " of the same substance " with the Father expressed exactly what they were contending for, and precluded the ambiguities by which the Eusebian party sought to evade the force of other terms.   It met, accordingly, with their acceptance.   The Emperor also now saw that if unanimity was to be secured, it was only on the ground of this formula it was to be had. He therefore threw his influence into this scale, and the triumph of the *homoousion* was secured.   A new creed was drawn up on the basis of that of Eusebius, and its acceptance was enforced by imperial decree.[3] This seems to me a more probable representation of the course of events than that frequently given, which makes the majority of the Council belong to the Semi-Arian party, and supposes that it was the Emperor's will that forced on them the acceptance of the *homoousion* formula.   It seems clear that the Emperor's

---

[1] The creed is given, Socrates i. 8, Theod. i. 12.   Athanasius tells in an epistle (*Ad Afros*, 5, 6) that when the creed was read the Eusebians were seen exchanging nods and signs to intimate that they could accept its language in their own sense.

[2] Ambrose, *De Fide*, iii. 15.   Eusebius had written that " If we say the Son is true God and uncreate, then we are in the way to confess Him to be of one substance (ὁμοούσιος) with the Father."   " When," says Ambrose, " this letter had been read before the Council assembled at Nicæa, the Fathers put this word in their exposition of the faith, because they saw that it damped their adversaries ; in order that they might take the sword which their enemies had drawn, to smite off the head of those opponents' own blasphemous heresy."   This is probably the γράμμα of Eusebius referred to in Theod. i. 8.   But the accounts are confused.

[3] Two Arian bishops who declined to sign were, along with Arius, banished.   Eusebius of Nicomedia and another signed the Creed, but refused to sign the anathemas attached, and were banished later.

sympathies, so far as they were manifested, were all the other way. Eusebius of Cæsarea was his adviser, and he had given his approval to the Eusebian Creed. It was evidently only when he saw that the Athanasian formula alone had any chance of acceptance by the Council as a whole, that he gave it the weight of his support. This is not inconsistent with the view that the majority of the Council were originally more or less undecided ; and only as the discussion went on came clearly to perceive that it was the essence of the faith, as they had always held it, that Athanasius was doing battle for.

This famous Symbol, oldest of the ecclesiastical creeds —if we except the so-called Apostles' Creed, of which it is really an expansion—does not quite correspond in its original form with the shape in which we now have it. It runs thus—" We believe in one God, the Father Almighty, Maker of all things visible and invisible ; and in one Lord Jesus Christ, the Son of God, begotten of the Father, the only-begotten, that is, of the substance of the Father, God of God, Light of Light, very God of very God, begotten, not made, being of one substance ($\delta\mu oo\acute{v}\sigma\iota o\varsigma$) with the Father ; by whom all things were made both in heaven and on earth ; who for us men and for our salvation, came down, and was incarnate, and was made man ; He suffered, and the third day He rose again ; ascended into heaven, and will come to judge the quick and the dead. And in the Holy Ghost. But those who say, ' There was when He was not,' and ' Before He was begotten He was not,' and that ' He was made of nothing,' or who say that the Son of God is of another ' substance ' or ' essence,' or that the Son of God is ' created,' or ' changeable,' or ' alterable,' are anathematised by the Catholic and

Apostolic Church." It will be seen that the Creed consists of two parts—the Creed proper, or doctrinal part, declaring the Catholic faith, and the anathe-matising part, condemning the errors of Arius. Of the changes subsequently made may be noticed, first, the omission of two clauses, viz., " only-begotten, that is, of the substance of the Father, God of God," and " both in heaven and on earth," and later, of the whole anathematising part ; on the other hand, besides the insertion of various clauses, as " only-begotten " before the words " Son of God," the phrase " before all worlds " after " begotten of the Father," especially a con-siderable addition after the words " the Holy Ghost." [1] The changes will be readily seen if the shorter original form is compared with the Creed as given in the prayer-books.

The Council had spoken, but its decision, far from terminating the controversy, was in a sense only the beginning of it. The battle was transferred to the Church at large, and went on with varying fortunes for the next half-century—till the time of the Council of Constantinople in 381 A.D. The Church was now to reap the fruit of its ill-advised concession to the emperors of the power of interference in ecclesiastical affairs—a power which made the settlement of doctrine, the determination of the Christian faith, too often an affair of imperial caprice and court intrigue, and intro-duced the principle of persecution formerly employed against the Church *into* the Church, in the relation of parties with each other. In this long conflict of the Nicene faith with its adversaries, the man who stands out above all others is the noble Athanasius. The history of the Arian controversy after Nicæa is little

---

[1] See below, on Council of Constantinople, p. 123.

more than a history of the persecutions of Athanasius. Hooker does not exaggerate when he sums up the situation in his famous sentence—" So that this was the plain condition of these times : the whole world against Athanasius, and Athanasius against it."[1]   In the midst of these trials the character of Athanasius shines out in splendid greatness. He is, as Stanley says, of all the saints of the early Church, the only one who has actually kindled the cold and critical pages of Gibbon into a fire of enthusiasm.[2] To say that Athanasius was the greatest man of his age is to say very little. In comparison with the shifty, intriguing, unscrupulous men opposed to him—in comparison with the emperors who drove him into banishment— he towers as a giant in moral stature and strength of purpose. In good report and evil report he held to his faith without wavering. The means by which he fought his battles were conspicuously in contrast with those of his opponents. He sought to conquer by argument, by persuasion, not by violence. In the hour of victory he was generous and forbearing. The men against whom he was pitted, on the other hand, relied on nothing so little as on the justice of their cause. Their sole design, as the history of the period shows, was to ensnare, circumvent, and destroy him, and to this end no acts were too base, no measures too mean, to be employed. Five times he was driven into exile, and the men put in his place were a disgrace to humanity and religion.[3]   On this moral ground alone, apart from all question of truth and error, the Arian party of the fourth century stands condemned.

[1] *Ecc. Polity*, v. 42.
[2] *Eastern Church*, Lect. vii. 2.   "Athanasius masters Gibbon," the late Principal Cairns once remarked to the writer.
[3] Cf. Gibbon on George of Cappadocia and others.

Of the special phases of the conflict I can only speak in the most summary manner. It was not long till the policy of Constantine changed, and he brought back Arius and sought to force him on the Church—a step only frustrated by the sudden death of the heresiarch in the hour of his triumph (336 A.D.). But it was under Constantine's successor, Constantius—a man of narrow and despotic spirit, feeble and irresolute, the tool of wily plotters, without his father's genius, but with all his father's love of intermeddling in ecclesiastical affairs—that the crisis became really acute. The chief landmarks in the history are the (Semi-Arian) Council of Antioch in 341 A.D., remarkable for the number of its creeds; the (orthodox) Council of Sardica in 343 A.D., from which the Eusebian party withdrew, and set up a rival council at Philippopolis; the multiplied councils and creeds of Sirmium, 351, 357 A.D. (Arian), 358 (Semi-Arian), 359; finally the twin Councils of Ariminum and Seleucia, 359 A.D., in connection with which, after prolonged resistance, force prevailed to secure subscription to a court-formula, and, in Jerome's memorable phrase, "the whole world groaned, and was astonished to find itself Arian." Space fails to tell how after this the parties among the Semi-Arians gradually diverged; how the persecution of the sincere section under Valens drove them into the arms of the orthodox; how the vicissitudes of fortune brought Theodosius to the throne of the East, and gave a new turn to affairs in the capital, where the preaching of Gregory of Nazianzus had already wrought a change in the temper of the people; how at length, in 381 A.D., the Council was summoned at Constantinople with which the history of the Arian controversy closes. This Council, when it did come, was purely an Eastern one; and it is only the subsequent adoption of its decisions by the Church generally which gives it its title to the name "ecumenical." To it are traditionally ascribed those enlargements of the Nicene Creed formerly referred to. This is now known to be a mistake. The additions which the Nicene Creed received were not the work of this Council, but had their origin earlier. Most of the clauses, *e.g.*, are found in the Creed of Cyril of Jerusalem about 350 A.D., and in a Creed of Epiphanius of Salamis, about 374 A.D. The Creed thus enlarged was at most adopted and endorsed by the Council of Constantinople—the "Council of the 150"—and even of this there is not contemporary evidence. It is first attributed to this Council by the Council of Chalcedon in 451 A.D.

Such, then, was the doctrinal outcome of this long and weary controversy, and it can be judged how far it was a triumph of Greek philosophy, or how far a victory of Christian faith. The truth is, the whole strength of Athanasius was put forth to rescue the Christian idea of God from influences derived from Greek philosophy which threatened to subvert it. Sohm, in his spirited sketch of Church history, justly says that the struggle of the Nicene Council "was not a barren dispute about words, not a struggle to introduce one more speculative idea into theology. It was a struggle for the final expulsion of pagan philosophy from Christian territory, that the essence of Christianity might not be sought in a logical explanation of the universe, nor its result in the establishment of a philosophical theory. The Hellenisation of Christianity was successfully combated by Athanasius and the Nicene Council." [1]

---

[1] p. 56 (E.T.). This verdict, so opposite from Harnack's, yet receives support from many of Harnack's own admissions. "There was no philosophy in existence," we are told, "possessed of formulæ which could present in intelligible form the propositions of Athanasius" (iv. p. 48). With Athanasius "the religious and Biblical argument is the chief

The Nicene affirmations are "metaphysical" only in the sense that all affirmations that relate to being or essence—affirmations, *e.g.*, of the existence, personality, absoluteness, eternity of God, or, for that matter, of our own personal identity and freedom—are metaphysical. But such affirmations are none the less necessary. Ordinary speech is saturated with them, and could not get on without them. What can be truthfully affirmed is that, just because the Nicene definitions relate to the sphere of being and essence—are "metaphysical" in that sense—they require to be supplemented by others drawn from the moral and spiritual sphere. The highest manifestation of the Godhead of Christ is to be sought, all will agree, in the sphere of character and will—in that which makes the *human* in Christ the image and exponent of the divine. "We beheld His glory, the glory of the only-begotten of the Father, full of grace and truth."[1] Here, unquestionably, modern theology comes in to supplement defects in the Nicene theology. But modern theology can never dispense with the foundation laid in the witness of the Nicene theology to Christ's essential divinity.

III. The supreme divinity of the Son had been established, but the circle of Trinitarian doctrine was not yet complete. It could not be till similar expression had been given to the Supreme Deity and Personality of the Holy Spirit. This was a phase of controversy which could not but arise as a sequel to

thing" (p. 33). He attaches little importance to the term ὁμοούσιος where the thing itself is retained (p. 36). Harnack complains that the Nicene Creed separated dogmatics "from clear thinking and defensible conceptions" (p. 49). It is something to have it recognised that after all reason has some right to be heard in theology. But this is not easy to reconcile with the assertion that Nicene dogma is the product of Greek metaphysics.

[1] John i. 14.

the Nicene discussions, and at the same time was bound to be helped to a decision through them. The controversy, therefore, belongs to the fourth century, but earlier stages invite a moment's notice.

The earliest age of the Church shows little trace of reflection on the doctrine of the Holy Spirit. From the first the Church acknowledged the threefold name of Father, Son, and Spirit, and so, implicitly, may be said to have confessed the deity and personality of the Spirit. But there was no dogmatic treatment of the subject. The Church possessed the Spirit, and did not feel the need of discussing it. For long the wealth of material in the Apostolic Epistles lay unexplored. The Apostolic Fathers are for the most part content to use the Scriptural phrases. Hermas seems to confuse the Spirit and the Son.[1] The apologists are too exclusively occupied with the Logos to have much to say of the Spirit. They do not deny either His personality or His deity, but, just as in the case of the Son, do not regard His procession as eternal, and, in accordance with their subordinationist bent, place Him in a third rank in the Godhead.[2] Theophilus, one of the apologists, is the first to use the word *Trias*.[3] The Montanistic movement in the second century may be regarded as a reaction in favour of the recognition of the Holy Spirit ; but it passed into extravagance in its claim to inaugurate a new era of the Paraclete. The early Catholic Fathers carry the doctrine further. The deity and personality of the Spirit are fully recognised by Irenæus, Tertullian, Clement, and Origen. Tertullian expressly calls Him "God," and lays stress

---

[1] Cf. Sim. v.

[2] Justin, 1st *Apol.* 13 ; Athenagoras, 10.

[3] ii. 15. Elsewhere Theophilus tends to confuse the Son and Spirit (ii. 10).

on His unity of essence with Father and with Son.[1]
The Alexandrian Fathers (not Tertullian) acknowledge
His eternal origin ; but Origen, in line with his general
tendency, emphasises the subordination of the Spirit.[2]
As he calls the Son a δεύτερος θεός, so in one place he
speaks of the Spirit as γενητόν (originate), though
exalted in honours and dignity, as also in eternity, above
all γενητά.[3]   His language thus gave a point of connection to the loose views of the fourth century ; but
in reality Origen held strongly to the consubstantiality
of the Holy Spirit with God.[4]   The Monarchian
heresies, in both their Unitarian and Modal forms,
necessarily drew after them the denial of the Spirit as
a distinct Person.

It was, however, in the fourth century, as I have
said, and as a consequence of the Arian controversy,
that the doctrine of the Spirit came formally to be
discussed.   It had been decided in this controversy as
respects the *Son* that He was not a creature, but had His
personality in the sphere of the divine.   On this higher
and eternal side of His being He was ὁμοούσιος with
the Father.   But if Father and Son were divine Persons,
what of the Spirit—the third member of the sacred
circle ?   The Nicene formula did not pronounce on this
question, but only said briefly, as a kind of appendage to
the rest of the Creed, " And in the Holy Ghost."   It was
apparently taken for granted that, the personality and
deity of the Son being confessed, that of the Spirit would

---

[1] *Against Praxeas* (2, 25, 26), " The Spirit, although He is called
God " (26).

[2] *First Principles*, Preface, and ii. 2, etc.

[3] Com. on John i. 2.   The word is used in the sense of " derived."

[4] " Father, Son, and Holy Spirit," says Harnack, " form a triad to
which nothing may be compared ; they are equal in dignity and honour,
and the substance they possess is one " (ii. p. 358).

be acknowledged also, as, in fact, it had not hitherto been challenged by any section of the Catholic Church.[1] Nor till the middle of the century does there seem to have been much discussion on the subject. The Arians, denying the real divinity of the Son, naturally could not acknowledge that of the Holy Spirit, and appear to have regarded Him as a creature of the Son, even as the Son was of the Father.[2] After 350 A.D., however, the real controversy on the Spirit broke out.[3] The gradual approximation of the Semi-Arians to the acceptance of the *homoousion* formula did not imply that they were equally willing to extend this formula to the Spirit. Opinions, on the contrary, began to be freely broached unfavourable to the acknowledgment of the deity of the Spirit. He was declared by many to be a creature, and even to be a ministering spirit, similar to the angels, and differing from them only in degree.[4] Athanasius found this form of belief prevailing in Egypt, and wrote ir refutation of it a series of letters to Serapion, a bishop in the Delta.[5] The subject came up in a council held by Athanasius in Alexandria in 362 A.D., and the denial of the deity of the Spirit was there formally branded as heresy. From 360 A.D. the party found

---

[1] The language of Methodius, in the end of the third century, is specially strong and unequivocal, and evidently expresses general belief. To him the Spirit is ὁμοούσιον with the Father. Cf. Migne, xviii. 351 ; and E.T. in *Ante-Nicene Library*, pp. 209, 216, 230, etc.

[2] Epiphanius (69) says—"They say the Holy Spirit is the creature of a creature, for the sake of the making of all things by the Son." Cf. Athanasius, *Orat.* i. 6.

[3] Harnack states that "in the first thirty years after the commencement of the Arian controversy, the Holy Spirit is hardly ever mentioned," *i.e.*, in debate (iv. p. 111).

[4] Cf. Sozomen, iv. 27.

[5] He cites Scripture and appeals to catholic tradition (i. 28), but argues also that the principle of sanctification cannot be of the same nature as that which it sanctifies. As by Him we are made partakers of the divine nature, He must be divine (i. ii. iii.).

a head in the deposed bishop of Constantinople, Macedonius, a violent and unscrupulous man ;[1] and through his exertions the new views spread rapidly among the Semi-Arians. The Church was anew plunged into indescribable confusion. "What storm at sea," says Basil, "was ever so wild and fierce as this tempest of the Churches. In it every landmark of the Fathers has been removed ; every bulwark of opinion has been shaken ; everything buoyed up on the unsound is dashed about and shaken down. We attack one another, we overthrow one another ; if our enemy is not the first to strike us, we are wounded by the comrade at our side."[2]

It would be tedious to enumerate the synods and creeds to which the attempt to check this Macedonian ("Pneumatomachian") heresy gave rise. Treatises on the Holy Spirit, or against the Macedonians, now take their place in the writings of the Fathers with those against the Eunomians and other heretics. Amidst the distractions which they depict so graphically, the minds of the leaders never wavered as to where the truth lay, nor did the Church under their guidance waver in the public testimony it gave forth. Apart from other reasons, the defenders of the deity of the Spirit had always this great argument on their side, that if the *homoousion* of the *Son* with the Father is admitted, it is difficult to deny the applicability of the idea to the Spirit, who, whatever else may be said of Him, is always in the Scriptures recognised as in the fullest sense *divine*. Few seem to have denied the

[1] "The exploits of Macedonius," says Socrates, "on behalf of Christianity consisted of murders, battles, incarcerations, and civil wars" (ii. 38).
[2] *On the Spirit*, 30. Gregory of Nazianzus says some regarded the Son as an influence, others as a creature, others as God Himself, and others did not know what to decide (31*st Orat.*).

personality of the Spirit, though, as we learn from Gregory, some did. In modern times, on the other hand, it is usually the personality, not the deity, of the Spirit men deny. If, however, the first two members of the Trinitarian circle are admitted to be personal, the third, for that very reason, may be presumed to be so also. It is this logical implication of the one doctrine with the other which makes it rare for those admitting the personality and deity of the Son to deny a like personality and deity of the Spirit. The same logical implication accounts for the fact that the controversy on the supreme deity of the Spirit, if sharp, was also short. The Macedonian heresy was definitely condemned along with the Arian at the Council of Constantinople in 381 A.D. After this it seems to have died down—at least is little heard of. It has left its memorial in the enlarged clause in the Nicene Creed to which reference was formerly made. I quote the whole of this new portion, which makes explicit the divinity of the Spirit, and reaffirms certain articles already embraced in the Apostles' Creed. "And [we believe] in the Holy Ghost, the Lord and Giver of life ; who proceedeth from the Father ; who with the Father and the Son together is worshipped and glorified ; who spake by the prophets. In one holy, catholic, and apostolic Church. We acknowledge one baptism for the remission of sins ; we look for the resurrection of the dead, and the life of the world to come." [1]

It will be observed that the controverted word ὁμοούσιος does not occur in this addition to the Creed. It possibly was designedly omitted to avoid giving offence ; but the assertion of the supreme divinity of the Spirit is sufficiently plain, and the clauses may be

[1] The Prayer-Book (Western) version has the singular, "I believe."

regarded as ruled by the statement regarding the Son. The Church never hesitated in the interpretation to be put upon it.   It will be hard also to point to anything in these clauses that can justly be described as "metaphysical," or as having any analogy to Greek philosophy.   Even the term "proceedeth" has not the fixed theological sense it acquired later.   Its use is based on the etymological idea of spirit as something breathed forth, and it is employed to distinguish the mode of origin of the Spirit from that of the Son, who, in harmony with the filial relationship, is spoken of as "begotten."   There is doubtless a distinction covered by the difference of terms, but it should freely be acknowledged that we pass here into the region of the ineffable.

Supplementary

The only important addition to the Nicene-Constantinople Creed since 381 A.D. has been the insertion by the Synod of Toledo in 589 A.D. of the "filioque" clause, which marks the difference between East and West on the subject of the "Procession" of the Holy Spirit.   The Eastern Church reads the Creed—"proceedeth from the Father," while the Western Church has it, "proceedeth from the Father *and the Son*."   The dispute indicates a difference which has existed in these Churches from the first, and is easily explicable out of their respective conditions.   The Eastern Church had to do with Arians and Macedonians, who made the Spirit a creature of the Son, or viewed Him at least as inferior in dignity, because brought into being through the mediation of the Son.   It sought, therefore, to safeguard His full divinity by representing Him as proceeding solely and immediately from the Father—

the one principle (ἀρχή) or fountain (πηγή) of the
Godhead.   The Westerns, on the other hand, started
with the identity of the substance of Son and Father,
and, wishful of conserving the truth that the Spirit is as
truly the Spirit of the Son as of the Father—else the
two were held not to be equal — expressed this by
saying that the Spirit proceeds from *both* the Father
and the Son.   The Easterns rejected this formula
absolutely, and the division thence originating has
never been healed.   Augustine may be named as a
chief upholder of the "filioque" view.   The Synod of
Toledo, at which ecclesiastical sanction was given to it,
was held on occasion of the conversion of the Goths
to the Catholic faith.

V

THE DOCTRINE OF MAN AND SIN; GRACE AND PREDESTINA-
TION—AUGUSTINIAN AND PELAGIAN CONTROVERSY
(FIFTH CENTURY)

" His (Augustine's) appearance in the history of dogmas forms a distinct epoch, especially as regards anthropological and soteriological doctrines, which he advanced considerably further, and brought to a greater clearness and precision than they had ever been before in the consciousness of the Church."—SCHAFF.

" We can observe here, if anywhere, the 'logic' of history. . . . The inner logic of events is proved by the simultaneous and independent emergence of Augustinianism and Pelagianism."—HARNACK.

" One such writer is in himself a whole age, and more than an age of authorship; a complete school, and more than a school of divinity."—MOZLEY.

LECTURE V

The Doctrine of Man and Sin : Grace and Predestination—
Augustinian and Pelagian Controversy (Fifth Century).

THE next important step in the development of
doctrine is that associated with the name of Augustine.
With Augustine theology passes from East to West,
and from the region of theology proper to that of
anthropology. Not that this great Father was not a
theologian in the stricter sense as well. No man
plunged deeper than he into the mysteries of the
divine nature in his discussions of the Trinity ; or
soared higher in the apprehension of the speculative
questions involved in the relation of God to the world
and to time. He stood firmly in the paths marked
out by the Nicene decisions ; but, through his profounder studies of sin and grace, was able to carry his
inquiries into the doctrine of God into regions yet
unexplored. Greek theology had occupied itself mainly
with what are sometimes called the " metaphysical "
determinations of the Godhead—the Trinity and the
relations of the divine Persons to one another. But
there are deeper, more baffling questions than even
those of the Trinitarian relations — questions which
arise the moment we begin to reflect on man and
freedom in their relations to God, and on the problems
of sin and grace,—which also, because bound up with
the practical interests of our salvation, touch us more

vitally, and evoke emotions which the speculative
contemplation of the inner life of the Godhead does
not stir.   It is plain that these questions could not be
satisfactorily investigated till the general doctrine of
God had been firmly established—that, in logical order,
they come later than it.   It is equally plain that till
they had been raised, no satisfactory progress could be
made with either Christology or Soteriology.   For the
former calls for investigation of the nature of man as
well as of the nature of God ; and the latter has for its
presuppositions adequate conceptions of sin and grace,
and of God's relation to both.

This anthropological group of questions it is,
accordingly, which now, in the providence of God, is
brought to determination in the Church ; and that the
" hour " had come for them—that they were " in the
air," waiting to be discussed—is seen in the simultaneous emergence of the two men who represent the
opposite poles of doctrine on this subject—Augustine
and Pelagius.   What Athanasius and Arius were in the
Arian controversy ; what Anselm and Abelard were in
the Soteriological controversy; what Calvin and Arminius
were in post-Reformation controversy on the application
of Redemption—that Augustine and Pelagius were in
this Anthropological controversy.   It is therefore a sign
of weakness in a theologian to belittle the significance
of the Western or Augustinian theology in comparison
with the Eastern.[1]   The fact that the working out
this side of theology was given to the Latin Church

---

[1] As is done, *e.g.*, by Dr. Allen in his *Continuity of Christian Thought.*
The greater teachers, such as Harnack, do not fall into this mistake.
Harnack's appreciation of Augustine, however, squares ill with his theory
of the Greek origin of dogma.   His exposition of Augustine, as formerly
observed, is one of the most powerful parts of his work, though in many
places the lights are badly crossed.

and in it specially to Augustine, connects itself with the difference of bent in West and East respectively. In general, Latin theology distinguishes itself from Greek by its less subtle and speculative character,—though in Augustine the speculative faculty is combined with the practical in a remarkable degree, — by its stronger adherence to tradition, and by its preference for the treatment of the class of doctrines I have called anthropological—the doctrines of human nature, and of sin and grace; instead of, as in the Greek Church, those of the Trinity and of the Person of Christ. The Augustinian theology never took deep hold upon the Greek Church: hence in great measure its sterility and unprogressiveness. On the other hand, the rich progressive movement of theology on European soil—its vitality and productiveness—are in a large degree due to the upturning of the depths of human thought through the Augustinian theology, and the impregnation of the Western mind with its ideas. The way was prepared, no doubt, for Augustine by the Latin Fathers who preceded him—especially by Tertullian, Hilary, and Ambrose. Tertullian had early laid emphasis on the facts of sin, of hereditary depravity, of moral bondage, and of the need of divine grace to redeem from these; while, like Augustine after, he did not fail to insist on the soul's inherent and indestructible relation to God, and capacity for salvation.[1] But the thoughts which in these Fathers frequently lack in depth, and are only imperfectly unified, are in Augustine developed into a system of marvellous completeness, every part of it instinct with life and power through

---

[1] Cf. Tertullian's tractate on *The Witness of the Soul*, and his treatise *On the Soul*, 40, 41. Ambrose is repeatedly quoted by Augustine, *e.g.*, in his *Nature and Grace*, 75; *Grace of Christ and Original Sin*, i. 48; ii. 47, etc. On Hilary and Ambrose, cf. Neander and Harnack.

connection with his own experience. That system has, as we shall see, its sides of limitation and inconsistency, but it is none the less a vast, epoch-making effort, which secured for this Father a well-deserved supremacy over men's minds in the Middle Ages, and won for his conceptions a revival in yet more vigorous form at the Reformation.[1]

I. Augustine's theology, as just hinted, is only to be understood by reference to Augustine's experience. Biography here is more than information ; it is commentary and key. Happily, for Augustine's experience we do not need to travel farther than his own wonderful *Confessions*—a record in which the secrets of his heart and life are laid bare with a fidelity without parallel in literature. There is no ostentation, no morbid love of display or self-posing, in these disclosures of a soul's wanderings and recovery, but the most complete humility, blending with adoring praise of the grace that rescued him from the well-nigh hopeless labyrinth of his moral and intellectual errors, and restored him to the source of all good. The story of his early years and youthful aberrations ; of his saintly mother's prayers—a mother who never lost her confidence in God that her son would yet be given back to her ; of his disquiet of heart in the midst of his excesses ; of how, even in Cicero, whose polished periods seemed to him finer than the Scriptures, he missed the savour of the name of Christ—" for this name," he tells us, " according to thy mercy, O Lord, this name of my Saviour, thy Son, my tender heart,

[1] Cf. Harnack's striking tribute, commencing, "If we Western Christians are shut up to the conviction that religion moves between the poles of sin and grace—nature and grace," and concluding, "then we feel with the emotions, think in the thoughts, and speak with the words of Augustine " (v. p. 73, E.T.).

even with my mother's milk, had drunk in, and deeply
treasured, and whatever was without that name, though
never so learned, polished, or truthful, took not entire
hold of me ";[1] of how he fell into the snares of the
Manichæans in his search for a solution of the problem
of evil, and for nine years was held captive by that
sect; of his gradual disillusionment, and attraction for
a time to Platonism;[2] of his removal to Milan, and
contact with Ambrose, whose personal influence and
preaching, and not least the sweet music of his Church,[3]
broke down his prejudices, and won him back to faith;
of the marvellous crisis of his conversion in the garden
of his villa at Milan, where, in deep agitation at the
narrative of the conversion of two others, he flung
himself beneath a fig-tree, and wept and wrestled for
forgiveness, and for strength to break with his sins [4]—
all this I must assume to be familiar to you. Baptized
in 387 A.D., when yet a young man of thirty-three
years; soon after made presbyter at Hippo; he was,
in 395 A.D., elected bishop of that city, and there
laboured till his death in 430 A.D., his years filled up
with incessant labours, and with controversies—first
with the Manichæans, then with the Donatists, finally
with the Pelagians. Of his other works, I mention
only his *magnum opus* on *The City of God*—one of the
most comprehensive, as it is the latest, of the Christian
apologies, and at the same time the first sketch of a
Christian philosophy of history.[5] The "City of God,"
in its then existing form, Augustine naturally identifies

---

[1] iii. 4, 5.
[2] vii. 20; cf. 9, 21; viii. 2. In another work he tells us that the
writings of the Platonists kindled in him "an incredible ardour" (*Against
the Academics*, ii. 5).
[3] ix. 6, 7.   [4] viii. 6-12.
[5] The occasion of the work was the terrible shock given by the sack of
Rome by the Goths in 410 A.D.

with the Catholic Church ; but his conception is really much wider, for the two cities—"two kinds of human society," as he describes them—go back to the beginning, and actually stand for what we would call the Kingdom of God in time, with its antithesis in that portion of mankind who live after the flesh and not after the Spirit.[1]

The question has often been discussed as to the degree of influence, if any, which Augustine's long connection with Manichæism had on the shaping of his theology. To this source many are disposed to attribute what they regard as his gloomy and exaggerated views of the evil of human nature.[2] But there is little doubt, I think, that they are wrong. It was not Manichæism which led Augustine into his sombre views of human nature, but rather his profound experience of the moral discord within himself which drew him into sympathy with Manichæan error ; just as, again, it was his growing insight into the *ethical* character of this opposition between the carnal will and God—*i.e.*, into its real character as *sin*—which turned him away from Manichæan dualism, to which evil is a thing of *nature*—substantial, eternal, unalterable—and forced him to seek a truer solution. There is nothing that Augustine holds to more strongly than that every nature, as created by God, is good, and that sin and corruption have a voluntary origin.[3] Nor—though this is often charged upon him—does he ever so

[1] Cf. bk. xiv.

[2] Harnack often comes back on this (v. pp. 102, 115, 187, 204, etc.). Neander says—"Very unjustly have Augustine's anthropological views been attributed to the influence of Manichæism" (iv. p. 290, Bohn). It should be noted that while evil has a substantial existence in Manichæism, to Augustine it is a privation—a defect. See below, p. 147.

[3] Cf. *Confessions*, vii.. 12-16 ; *Enchiridion*, 12-15, etc.

emphasise the corruption of human nature as to imply that this nature has altogether lost the traces of its divine original. It is, on the contrary, of the essence of his teaching that the soul can never so cut itself away from God, its true good, as to cease to feel the need of Him and have an instinctive longing after Him. His own experience was the convincing proof of this, and his words in the opening of the *Confessions* are the expression of it—"Thou hast made us for Thyself, and our heart is restless till it rest in Thee."[1] Evil, it is true, was a subject which exercised his profoundest thoughts, but we may rest assured that it was not Manichæism, but his own experience, which was the source from which, above all, his doctrine of sin was drawn.

On the other hand, it is not to be denied that Augustine's theology has drawbacks and limitations of another kind. His theology has, in fact, two sides— the one, a *Churchly*, or *Old Catholic* side, in which he stands tenaciously on Cyprianic ground in his views of the nature of the Church, of its unity, its episcopate, its authority, its sacraments, the necessity of connection with it for salvation; the other, a *doctrinal* side, in which Protestants may more lawfully claim inheritance in him, in his doctrines of sin and grace, with which are connected his views of the fall and corruption of human nature, on the one hand, and of predestination, on the other. These two sides of Augustine's theology are never fully reconciled—could not, indeed, be. As respects the first, Augustine is a churchman of the churchmen, and Catholicism may fairly claim him as its own. This comes out peculiarly in the Donatist controversy. The line of his experience here was

[1] i. 1.

probably not unlike that of John Henry Newman in our own day, in his yearning for an objective authority, capable of being known by sure marks.[1]   Even so, we should greatly mistake if we supposed—what his whole history belies—that it was subjection to an external authority, and not inner experience, and irresistible conviction of the truth itself, which really decided Augustine to become a Christian, or gave his theology its distinctive colour.   We have seen what his struggles were ; how actively his mind was at work in searching out the true and false ; and how at length decision came in the throes of a mighty spiritual crisis.   It certainly cannot be said that what is peculiar in his theology was imposed on him by the authority of the Church ; for it is precisely in the region in which he worked—the doctrines of sin and grace—that previous theology had been weak and halting.   Augustine *gave* to the theology of the Church infinitely more than he took from it.   The truth is, Augustine's positions on the subject of Church authority are far from harmonious. When arguing with the Manichæans (this, however, in his first years as a Christian), it suited him to base his acceptance of Scripture on the authority of the Church ;[2] but afterwards, in conflict with the Donatists, who themselves claimed to be the true Church, he would allow no evidence to settle this claim but that drawn from the Scriptures.   The opponents must prove the genuineness of their Church, not by appeals to councils or bishops or miracles, but by the law and the prophets, and the word of Christ alone.[3]   In his theological controversies, appeal to the authority of the Church plays a very subordinate part.

[1] Cf. Neander, iii. p. 288 ; Harnack, v. pp. 78-82 (E.T.).   Harnack's remarks on "authority" here have a strange look from a Ritschlian.

[2] *Against the Epistle of Manichæus*, 6.

[3] *On the Unity of the Church*, 49, 50.

If Catholicism can claim Augustine on the side of his theory of the Church, it is different on the side of doctrine. Here, as I have said, he much more nearly approaches Protestantism—especially in its Calvinistic type—while Catholicism has largely abandoned his ground as inconsistent with its sacerdotal scheme, and receded into a vague Semi-Pelagianism. Yet there are characteristic differences. In two respects, particularly, we may note a difference in Augustine's theology from the later Protestant doctrine, both results of the crossing of the sacramentarian principle.

First, Augustine differs from the ordinary Protestant view in extending, with Catholicism generally, the meaning of " justification" to include, not merely the free forgiveness of sins, and acceptance of the sinner for Christ's sake, but the inward change, or impartation of a new nature or life, which he supposes to take place in baptism. It is not that Augustine means to overlook or deny what Protestants mean by " justification" ; on the contrary, he strongly affirms it.[1] In his controversy with the Donatists, *e.g.*, he boldly says, " No one makes me free from guilt but Him who died for our sins, and rose again for our justification ; for I believe, not in the minister by whom I am baptised, but in Him who justifies the ungodly, that my faith may be counted to me for righteousness."[2] Many such utterances might be quoted. It is none the less true that the ideas of justification and of regeneration and sanctification are not kept clearly distinct in his teaching ; and his confusing of them, and binding up

---

[1] Harnack says, " He who disregards the formulas, but looks to the spirit, will everywhere find in Augustine's works a stream of Pauline faith " (v. 88).

[2] *Against Petilian*, i. 8. Cf. A similar and striking passage from Ambrose in Harnack, v. 51.

of both with baptism, had a further obscuring influence on his treatment of the forgiveness of *post*-baptismal sin.[1]

A *second* point of difference between Augustine's theology and later (Calvinistic) Protestantism is in his doctrine of predestination. Both Augustine and Calvin (most of the other Reformers likewise) were strict predestinarians. But it is evident that Augustine was involved in a difficulty here by his acceptance at the same time of the Church doctrine of baptismal regeneration. For if all the baptised are regenerated, and if baptism is administered at the will of man, what becomes of the sovereignty of divine grace, or of the certainty of election? It seems difficult to combine a doctrine of election with another which makes every properly baptised person a child of God. The way in which Augustine got over this difficulty was by making the test of election to be, not *regeneration* simply, but *perseverance*. All the baptised are regenerate, but only the truly elect have the grace of perseverance.[2] This clearly is not satisfactory; for if there is to be a distinction between elect and non-elect at all, it ought surely to be made to turn on the reality of regeneration in the one as compared with the other; whereas Augustine allows both to be regenerated and justified,[3] only the one receives the grace of perseverance, and the other does not. The truth is, no *consistent* theory of predestination can ever be united with a

---

[1] Cf. Lect. VIII.

[2] Cf. especially the treatises on *Rebuke and Grace*, on *Predestination*, and on *Perseverance*.

[3] Dr. Mozley, in his *Primitive Doctrine of Baptismal Regeneration*, supposes that Augustine speaks of the baptised as regenerate only *hypothetically*, and regards the elect alone as actually regenerated. This seems to me to strain Augustine's language; still passages may be pointed to, as in *Rebuke and Grace*, 22, in which a difference of spiritual state seems implied from the first.

consistent theory of baptismal regeneration,[1] and churches which hold to the latter are compelled to modify, or give up, Augustine's view on the former.

II. I proceed now to the direct consideration of the Augustinian system, which has had so remarkable an influence on subsequent theology. Augustine's system was matured in his own mind fully ten years before the Pelagian controversy broke out. It will be convenient, therefore, that I should exhibit the main positions of his theology, at the outset, apart from the Pelagian opposition ; then that these should be looked at in connection with this controversy, in which the real bearings of his principles first became completely manifest.

The starting-point for a right comprehension of Augustine's system undoubtedly lies in his *doctrine of God, and of the soul's relation to Him.* Augustine does not start, as the Eastern Church did, with a speculative doctrine of the Godhead,—though he agrees with that church in its decisions on the Trinity,—but with him God and the soul are always viewed in relation to each other. God is the chief good of the soul ; the soul is made for God ; and even in its unfallen state was never intended to subsist apart from Him, or otherwise than in continual dependence on Him. Whereas the Pelagian doctrine, as we shall see, would represent man as holding naturally a middle ground between good and evil, and capable of realising his destiny through reason and free-will, without further help from God, Augustine laid stress on the fact that, even as sinless, man could only realise his destiny through a habitual dependence on God — the constant drawing of the supplies of his life from Him. Communion with God

[1] This Mozley would admit.

was the condition of all true blessedness and freedom. The soul is not a self-acting unit, but a receptive vessel ; and its life consists in God continually imparting Himself to it, sustaining it, and informing it with goodness.   This is, no doubt, a very different conception from that of our modern evolutionary philosophy :   but the acceptance or rejection of it will be found vitally to affect the character of a theological system all through.

But, *second*, from this fundamental position Augustine derives, next, his *doctrine of sin*.   In opposition to the Manichæans, he emphasises the voluntary nature of sin ;[2] that is, he takes it, as I have said, from the *nature* basis on which the Manichæans put it, and places it upon an *ethical* one.   The act of sin, he nevertheless holds, in breaking up the original communion of the soul with God, and cutting it off from its source of life and sustenance in Him, brings it under the dominion of an evil necessity.[3]   It can no longer realise its destiny, or will that true good which has its principle in love to God.   This does not mean that the soul loses all sense of its original relation to God, or ceases to long and sigh after Him.   But it means that it has no longer the power to realise the true end of its being, and, through ignorance and evil habit, sinks constantly deeper into bondage.   Augustine's analysis of the origin and nature of sin is very subtle.   Its essence lies, he holds, in defection from God—the Supreme

---

[1] This is the keynote of the *Confessions* (cf. i. 1-5, 20 ; ii. 5, 6 ; iii. 6 ; vii. 17, etc.) and *Letters* (Harnack emphasises the expression in Ep. 155, "It is good for me to cleave to God"). See also his *Christian Doctrine*, i. 5, 22, etc. ; *Enchiridion*, 106 ; and the Anti-Pelagian works generally.

[2] *Confessions*, vii. 16 ; *Rebuke and Grace*, 28, 31 ; *Enchiridion*, 105.

[3] *Grace and Free-will*, 31 ; *Rebuke and Grace*, 2, etc.

Good and Source of life. It is not, therefore, as he thought in his Manichæan days, something positive, but is negative—a *privation*, or the result of a privation ; not an addition to existence, but a subtraction from existence, which issues in positive corruption. We have an analogy in the living organism, which, while the vital functions are healthily performed, is sustained in integrity and beauty, but, when the vital principle is withdrawn, falls a prey to the forces of decomposition. In one sense the decomposition—corruption—which ensues is something positive; in another, it is the result of the withdrawal, or subtraction, of a force essential to the being. As disease and death, it results from *privation*.[1] The root-principle of sin Augustine finds, not in the solicitations of sense, but in *self-love ;* for only when the soul has already *inwardly* fallen through substitution of the love of self for the love of God have the solicitations of sense power over it.[2] In Kant's phrase, sin results when a " maxim " contrary to the love of God is taken into the will. The general result of defection from God is *concupiscence*, or the inordinate power of sensuous desire, as against the law of reason in the soul. From sin, and the disturbance it introduces, comes *death*. For man, Augustine held, was created by God, as became a moral intelligence, not in a neutral condition, but in possession of holiness and freedom, yet capable of abusing that freedom to his own hurt. He was not, as created, immortal, in the sense of being raised above the power of death, but he had the capacity of (bodily) immortality.[3] Had he proved obedient, he would have

[1] Cf. *Enchiridion*, 11.

[2] Cf. on *Forgiveness of Sins*, ii. 30 ; *Grace of Christ*, i. 17-22. As shown below, Augustine could not admit a *neutral* position of the will. A will in principle must be either good or bad.

[3] Cf. *Forgiveness of Sins*, i. 2-6.

been confirmed in holiness — would, in Augustine's phrase, have passed from the state of " being able not to sin and die " (*posse non peccare et mori*) to the state of " not being able to sin and die " (*non posse peccare et mori*)—a state like that of the holy angels, or of the saints in glory, or of Christ, or like that of God Himself.[1] For, as these examples show, the highest freedom here is one with the highest necessity — if necessity that can be called which is so complete an establishment of the will in goodness that defection can be no longer thought of.   But man fell, and through the connection organically subsisting between him and his descendants, transmits his fallen nature, with the guilt and corruption adhering to it, to his posterity.[2] Augustine conceived of this relation of Adam to his posterity, not simply, as in the later theology, *federally*, but *realistically*, regarding the whole race as germinally present in its progenitor, and sharing with him in his guilt and ruin.[3] Adam's fall involves the race, not by any arbitrary constitution, but from the fact that potentially he *was* the race, and that what proceeds from a tainted and disordered source must itself be tainted and disordered.   It is easy in a *doctrinaire* way to criticise this theory of Augustine's, which yet has such singular support in the modern doctrine of heredity ; but it should be observed that the point which the criticism really touches is the justice of an organic constitution of the race at all. For good or for evil, the race is not constituted on a purely individualistic, but on an organic principle. Can this be justified ?   Few, I think, will question

---

[1] *Rebuke and Grace*, 27-33 ; *Enchiridion*, 105.

[2] *Enchiridion*, 26, 27 ; *Nature and Grace*, 3, 5.

[3] *Forgiveness of Sins*, i. 11. Augustine founds on Rom. v. 12, reading, " *in whom* all have sinned."   But his theory does not depend on this text.

that in itself such a constitution is good, and, working under normal conditions, is fitted to yield the maximum of benefit to individuals, and to the race as a whole ; that by means of it the gains of humanity are accumulated, and handed on as they could be in no other way.   But it is by its working under normal conditions that a constitution must be judged.   Reverse its working : convert it into a system working *abnormally* in contrariety to its true ends ; its effects will be proportionally disastrous to the posterity it was designed to bless.   But does this prove it unjust ?   Is not the vindication of the Creator complete when its original beneficence is shown ?

This leads, in the *third* place, to Augustine's *doctrine of grace*.   We have seen that Augustine refuses to contemplate the creature, even as unfallen, as independent of God.   Grace is needed, therefore, even by the sinless.   Much more is grace needed now that the creature is fallen, and its original freedom to good is lost.   Augustine does not deny—here again I touch a common misrepresentation of his system — that the will has still a certain natural freedom ; " is free," as he says, but not " freed," [1] *i.e.*, is capable of acts civilly good, nay, from a lower standpoint, morally praiseworthy.   Still, as separated from God, and lying under guilt and the dominion of evil, man cannot will that which is good in *God's* sight.   For that only is good in God's sight which springs from the principle of love of Himself.[2]   Man's will stands in need, therefore, not only of aid and reinforcement, but of *renewal*,

---

[1] *Rebuke and Grace*, 42.

[2] Hence the paradox of speaking of the virtues of the heathen as "splendid sins," *i.e.*, acts relatively good, but wrong in ultimate principle.   The phrase, however, though commonly attributed to Augustine, does not appear to be found in his writings.

and this God alone, in the omnipotence of His grace,
can give.   Further, this work of renewal, in the nature
of the case, is *wholly* of God—is a work of grace from
first to last.   There is nothing in it which man's own
will is entitled to take credit for.   It is necessary to
understand Augustine properly here, to avoid doing
injustice to his conceptions.   For when Augustine
speaks of divine grace as alone concerned in the work
of human renewal, and above all as " irresistible "—*i.e.*,
as certainly effectuating its result [1]—we are apt to feel
as if human freedom were annihilated.   And so it is
often represented.   But this is by no means Augustine's
intention, nor is it really the effect of his doctrine.
When Augustine speaks of grace as " irresistible," what
he has in view is not a grace that overpowers the will, or
puts any foreign force or pressure upon it, but a grace
which *renews* the will, and restores to it its true
freedom [2]—which so acts on it that it *freely* chooses the
good—which, in familiar words, " persuades and enables "
it to do that which otherwise it would be unwilling or
powerless to do.[3]   As little does " irresistible grace "
mean that God can, or does, override the laws of
human nature He has Himself ordained, or, by a
sheer act of power, can convert the individual at *any*
time or under *any* circumstances.   On such a supposi-

[1] Not " irresistible " in the sense that the natural will cannot resist
grace, for this is what *qua* unregenerate it is constantly doing.   Cf.
Lecture IX.

[2] It is therefore an incorrect representation when the writer of the
article on Pelagius in *Dict. of Christ. Biog.* says (iv. p. 295) : " The
Augustinian theory made the action of grace entirely independent of the
will ; it was an irresistible power which forced the will."

[3] " The freedom of the will is defended in accordance with the grace
of God, not in opposition to it ; because the human will does not attain
grace by freedom, but rather attains freedom by grace. . . . Because by
the Holy Spirit their will is so much enkindled that they therefore *can*,
because they so *will*, they therefore so *will* because God works in them
to will."—*Rebuke and Grace*, 17, 38 ; cf. *Grace and Free-will*, 33.

tion it would be difficult to explain why means are used at all, or why all are not converted. But what Augustine holds is that God can use *such* means, can *so* deal with the individual in providence and grace, can bring him under *such* outer and inner disciplines, as, in harmony with, nay, through the laws of human freedom, to overcome his resistance.[1]   Grace, thus, does not enslave the will, but frees it.   Here comes in Augustine's great saying, " Give what Thou commandest, and command what Thou wilt." [2]   If it be said that the possession of freedom implies that, even when grace has done its utmost for a soul, there is still a possibility of resisting it, Augustine would reply that there is a higher freedom still—that in which even the desire to resist the good is overcome, and which therefore *certainly*, but not the less freely, chooses God.   Grace, accordingly, with Augustine, as with Paul, is the first as well as the last word in our salvation.   It is the source of everything good in us.   Through this conception, while accepting the Catholic doctrine of merits, he succeeds in transforming it in an essentially evangelical sense. In bestowing eternal life as a reward, God, he says, "crowns His own gifts, not thy merits." [3]   And, in another place, " It follows, then, beyond all doubt, that as your good life is nothing else than God's gift and grace, so also the eternal life which is the recompense of a good life is the gift and grace of God ; moreover,

---

[1] See specially his answer to questions in his two books addressed to Simplician of Milan, bk. i. quest. 2.   Neander says, " The Almighty and all-wise God could find, in reference to the different states of men, those means of influencing them which must make an impression on them with inward necessity, so that, awakened, drawn, touched, and enlightened, they would follow, without being conscious of any resistance against the grace operating " (iv. p. 297).

[2] *Confessions*, x. 19, 31, 37 ; cf. *Grace and Free-will*, 32 ; *On Perseverance*, ii. 53, etc.

[3] *Grace and Free-will*, 15.

it is a free and gratuitous gift of which it is the recompense. But the good life, thus rewarded, is solely and simply grace ; therefore the *eternal life* which is its reward—and because it is its reward—is grace *for* grace, as if it were the remuneration of righteousness ; in order that that may be realised, because it is true that God 'shall reward every man according to his works.'"[1]

From the preceding doctrines as premises follows now, *fourth*, Augustine's *doctrine of predestination*. Reduced to its essence, this doctrine is simply the assertion that what God does in time in the salvation of the believer, He willed to do in eternity. In his earlier writings, Augustine was disposed to regard predestination as conditional on man's free-will and faith, and thus he endeavoured to interpret Romans ix. God elected the person whom He foreknew as one that would believe on Him.[2] But soon after, as his thought matured, he saw that consistency with his doctrine of grace, equally with the fair interpretation of Scripture, required him to regard good willing as itself the effect of grace—God working in us to will and do of His good pleasure—and his doctrine of predestination was modified accordingly. Always and everywhere predestination is viewed by him in this strict connection with salvation. It is the salvation of the believer viewed, if we may so say, *sub specie æternitatis*. It is always predestination to life and salvation, never to sin and death. Thus regarded—whatever speculative difficulties may attend it—it is simply the expression of an experience which lies at the root of all genuine Christian consciousness, viz., that in this matter of

---

[1] *Grace and Freewill*, 20 ; cf. Calvin, *Instit.* iii. 15.
[2] Cf. his retractation of these views in his treatise *On Predestination*, 7.

personal salvation, the last word is always grace, not
nature ; that it is not *our* willing and running which has
brought us into the kingdom of God, but *His* mercy ;
that it is He who first enkindled in us the desire after
Himself, who drew us to Himself, who bore with us in
our waywardness and resistance to His Spirit, who step
by step overcame that resistance, and brought us finally
into the number of His children ; and that all this was
no *afterthought* of God, but an eternal counsel of His
love which has now effectuated itself in our salvation.
This is the *religious* interest in the doctrine of predestination which gives it its abiding value.   As a
religious experience, no one would think of questioning
that the fundamental attitude of the Christian spirit is
one which ascribes *all* to grace in its salvation ; that
any thought of a divided claim—of a partitioning out of
so much to God, and so much to self—is abhorrent to
sound Christian feeling.   It is when this religious experience is turned round, and made, as the Ritschlians
would say, the subject of *theoretic* reflection, that difficulties arise.   What these difficulties are, and how they
may be dealt with, had better be postponed till we have
considered the Pelagian opposition.

III. It was in the Pelagian controversy that the
principles laid down by Augustine were tested by being
confronted with their logical opposites.   It was inevitable in the nature of things that such a conflict as that
represented by this controversy should arise.   No such
profound treatment of the problems of sin and grace
had before been attempted, and some of Augustine's
positions were new to the Church.   The Eastern branch
of the Church, in particular, had never gone deeply into
this class of questions.   It laid hold by preference of
the element of *freedom* in human nature, and gave

prominence to that in opposition to pagan ideas of fate and destiny. That human nature had been *weakened* by the fall—had become subject to sensuous temptation, to the dominion of Satan, and to death—was indeed acknowledged, and the impartation of a new and supernatural life in baptism was held fast. But it was deemed sufficient, as Neander remarks,[1] to affirm grace and free-will side by side with each other, without attempting exactly to define their relations. Augustine's more thorough-going treatment, which derived everything in salvation, free-will included, from grace, could not but come into collision with this undue exaltation of the powers of human freedom, with the result of bringing the issues clearly into view, and compelling a decision between them. This is what took place in the Pelagian controversy, and bestows on that controversy its importance as one of the great landmarks in the history of doctrine.

Pelagius, who gives his name to this controversy, was not, however, from the east, but from the west. He was a monk of Britain, a man of austere life and blameless character, but without any of those conflicts with sin, or deep experiences of an all-renewing grace, which moulded the theology of Augustine. He had come to Rome, and hearing Augustine's words quoted, "Give what Thou commandest, and command what Thou wilt," was very angry, and, says Augustine, "contradicting somewhat too excitedly, nearly came to a quarrel with those who had mentioned them."[2] He held, as Kant did after, that the giving of a command presupposes in him who receives it the power to obey ; and believed that it was of the utmost importance in the interests of holiness to lay stress on man's full and

---

[1] iv. p. 279 (Bohn).   [2] *On Perseverance,* 53.

complete power in his natural strength to obey the whole law of God. Sometime before 409 A.D., he won to his side the advocate Cœlestius, a man more logical and skilful in debate than himself, by whom the system known as Pelagianism was really formulated.[1] This Pelagian system was in every respect the direct antithesis of that which I have described as Augustine's. It will conduce to clearness if I draw out some of the principal contrasts.

A first contrast relates to the *nature of God and man.* Augustine, as we saw, made man, throughout his whole existence, dependent on God and on the impartation of His grace. Pelagius, on the contrary, viewed man as endowed by His Creator with reason and free-will, and as capable thereafter of pursuing his course, and realising his destiny, independently, in virtue of his natural powers.

A second contrast is as to the *nature of the will and freedom.*[2] Augustine held that there can be no such thing as a morally neutral condition of the will. A will must be either good or bad, according as it has for its principle love of God or love of self. Pelagius viewed the will as a natural faculty of choice, maintaining itself unimpaired in the middle point between good and evil, and able freely to choose either. Freedom, in accordance with this, is reduced to the bare power of choice, and is held to involve at every point the possibility of a contrary election. Augustine, on the other

---

[1] Pelagius afterwards repudiated some of the positions of Cœlestius, but, as Augustine shows, disingenuously (*Original Sin*, 11, etc.). It would be more correct to say that Pelagianism owes its systematic form to a third and yet abler representative, Julian of Eclanum, against whom Augustine latterly wrote elaborately.

[2] The treatise of Pelagius on *The Freedom of the Will* is criticised, and the opposite view defended, by Augustine in his *Grace of Christ.*

hand, placed the essence of freedom in the power to will the *good* and *right ;* and held that the highest freedom is that in which the will is confirmed in goodness, and raised above the possibility of sinning.[1] The truly free man is the virtuous man ; and the perfection of virtuous character is not a liberty of indifferentism, but formed habits of goodness. Good character is character on which one can *depend*—on whose action in things moral one can rely with the certainty of reliance on a law of nature.[2]

A third and weighty contrast in the systems is as to the *nature of virtue and vice*—whether, that is to say, these consist solely in *acts*, or do not reside also in *dispositions ;* above all, whether good or evil quality can attach to inborn or hereditary dispositions. Pelagius took the view that responsibility cannot attach to man for anything that is not the free product of his own will—for anything, therefore, that is hereditary. This excludes the possibility of original or hereditary sin. Augustine held, on the contrary, that good or evil inheres in dispositions as well as in acts—nay, that good dispositions must *precede* good volition, and that it is they which give their moral quality to the acts. The supreme command of the law, *e.g.*, is that we love God. But we do not create love to God by our acts ; we must have the love of God before we can do the loving acts. The tree must be good before it can produce the good fruit.[3] It is the old question raised by

[1] Cf. Mozley's *Augustinian Doct. of Predestination*, p. 62. Valuable suggestions will be found in this work on the whole subject.

[2] In common judgment also the truly free man is not the man on whose consistency of action no dependence can be placed—the *unreliable* man— the man who may be truthful to-day, untruthful to-morrow, etc. It is universally recognised that as character becomes established in virtue, it can be the more surely *reckoned* on. This is not a detraction from freedom, but the excellence of it.

[3] Cf. *Grace of Christ*, 20.

Aristotle—Is a man virtuous because he does virtuous acts, or are the acts virtuous, because they are the acts of a virtuous man?[1] It is more frequently, however, with regard to *vicious* dispositions than to *good* ones, that the question is raised, whether they can be hereditary, and, if they are, whether men can be held responsible for them. We naturally give men credit for their good dispositions, whether inborn or not. But are there inborn vicious dispositions? Augustine would unhesitatingly answer "Yes," and would point in proof to the mean, spiteful, selfish, malevolent traits in human character, which often display themselves from childhood—qualities which we instinctively reprobate and condemn.[2] These qualities, as ethically evil, must, he would grant, have a *voluntary* origin ; but the origin goes back beyond our personal wills—goes back to the beginning of the race. There is, in other words, a race-life, as well as an individual life, in the evil of which we are involved. The presence of a moral disturbance in the nature—of an unholy dominance of the fleshly over the spiritual—of inborn qualities which we are compelled to pronounce evil, is, he would say, a fact of experience, whatever explanation we may give of it. Will, no doubt, early begins its work on this natural basis, converting it into the material of *personal* life, but this does not prove that original disposition is without moral quality as good or evil.

It is implied in what has been said, as a *fourth* contrast, that the systems go widely asunder in what relates to *the fall of man,* and *its effects on human nature.* Augustine, we have seen, regards the fall as issuing in the loss of the power for spiritual good, and in a corruption of nature which, with a mortal state of the body,

---

[1] *Nic. Ethics,* ii. 4 ; cf. Luther's *Galatians,* iii. 10.
[2] Cf. Mozley, pp. 63-70.

descends to every child of Adam. Pelagius, on the other hand, views the powers of human nature as un-impaired by the fall, and traces the prevalence of sin in the world to evil education and example. There is no "original sin," or injury to the moral nature derived from Adam. Children are born into the world as pure and perfect as Adam was.[1] Every human being has natural ability to fulfil the law of God, and there have, in point of fact, been instances of sinless lives.[2]

The *last* contrast between the systems relates to *the idea and operations of grace.* We have seen that with Augustine grace is all in all in the spiritual life : the source of all goodness, and of spiritual freedom. Pelagius cannot, in consistency with his principles, admit the *necessity*, but he grants the *advantage* of grace, as an aid to man in the fulfilment of his destiny. When brought to the point, however, he can only explain grace in the sense either of the natural faculties themselves, as gifts of God, or of law and doctrine, or of the teaching and example of Christ. Only rarely does he use expressions which might imply an inner illumination and assistance of the Spirit, and such a conception does not appear to have any real place in his system. As Augustine says, he speaks much of grace, but when you get to the bottom of his meaning, you find only "law and doctrine." [3]

The main features of the Pelagian theory can now be briefly sketched. Adam, it is taught, was naturally mortal, and death is not the result of his sin. Adam's

---

[1] See the treatises on *The Proceedings against Pelagius*, on *Original Sin*, etc., in which these views are contested by Augustine ; and cf. Mozley, pp. 57, 58.

[2] *Nature and Grace*, 42. Augustine is disposed to make an exception as regards actual (not original) sin in the case of the Virgin.

[3] *Grace of Christ*, 11, etc.

fall injured no one but himself, and leaves the power of human nature unimpaired for good. Children come into the world as perfect as Adam was before his fall, *i.e.*, there is no hereditary transmission of a sinful nature or of guilt. Man, in his existing condition, is able perfectly to keep the commandments of God, and the seeming universality of sin is the result of education and bad example. Pelagius, nevertheless, acknowledges the advantage of grace as a help ; but grace is interpreted of natural gifts, or is made to consist wholly, or mainly, in something outward, as teaching or example. In accordance with the usage of the Church, he granted that infants were to be baptized (a clear difficulty on his theory) but he explained baptism as a rite of consecration, or as anticipative of future forgiveness. Yet he illogically held that children dying unbaptized were excluded from the kingdom of heaven, though not from a state of lower happiness, which he still called "eternal life."[1]   Finally, as there is no fall or death in Adam, so there is no resurrection in Christ.

IV. It is evident that no two systems could be more absolutely opposed in principle than those now delineated. The controversy which ensued in the Church respecting them had three short stages. The first was at *Carthage*, in 411-12 A.D., where the opinions of Cœlestius were condemned by a council ; the second was at Palestine, in 414-16 A.D., where two synods sat in judgment on Pelagius, but were misled by his specious explanations to look favourably on his cause—the latter

---

[1] This phase of the Pelagian theory is dealt with in the treatise on *Forgiveness of Sins and Baptism of Infants*.   Augustine held, in accordance with his theory of baptismal regeneration, the condemnation of unbaptized infants—a doctrine as unchristian as that of Pelagius

even to acquit him entirely ;[1] and the third, in 416-
418 A.D., was at *Rome*, whither the cause had been
referred by the former of the Palestinian synods.   The
vacillation of the Roman bishop Zozimus in this case
of Pelagius is a curious commentary on the doctrine of
Papal Infallibility.   In the first instance Zozimus
cleared Pelagius, giving him a certificate of orthodoxy,
and censuring his accusers.   " Scarcely could I refrain,"
he says, " from tears to find men so thoroughly orthodox
could yet be made objects of suspicion.   Was there a
single passage in the letter (of Pelagius) where grace or
the divine assistance was not mentioned ? "   Afterwards,
on a strong protest being made by a Council at
Carthage, he reversed this decision, and gave judgment
with equal emphasis *against* Pelagius and his adherents,
anathematising their doctrine, and deposing and banish-
ing those who refused submission to his decrees.   Finally,
as a fourth and supplementary stage in this controversy,
it may be mentioned that the doctrines of Pelagius
and Cœlestius were condemned, with those of Nestorius,
at the so-called ecumenical Council of Ephesus in
431 A.D.[2]

Between the extremes of these two systems—
Augustinianism and Pelagianism—it was natural that
a conciliatory or mediating movement should arise,
and this is the nature of the system known as *Semi-
Pelagianism*.   It needed such a system to make it
clear that the Augustinian view alone, with its strong
logical cohesion, could hold the ground successfully
against Pelagian attack.   Semi-Pelagianism denotes a

---

[1] At this Council of Diospolis (Lydda) Pelagius said, " I anathematise
those who hold these views."   " With these words," Harnack remarks,
" he pronounced judgment on himself! they were false" (v. p. 180, E.T.).

[2] Each of the above stages drew forth important works of Augustine
on the whole merits of the controversy.

view which sought to steer clear of difficulty by giving
a place in conversion to both divine grace and human
will as *co-ordinate* factors ; and by basing predestination, as Augustine did earlier, on foreseen faith and
obedience. It did not deny human corruption, but
regarded man's nature as weakened, or diseased, rather
than as fatally injured, by the fall. Fallen human
nature retains an element of freedom in virtue of
which it can *co-operate* with divine grace, and conversion is the joint-product of the two factors.[1]
Augustine, on the other hand, as we saw, views the
will in conversion as set in motion, and spiritually
liberated by divine grace. These views, arising in
Augustine's later years, spread specially in southern
Gaul. Their chief representative was John Cassian,
Abbot of Massilia (Marseilles), whence the party are
sometimes called Massilians. The system had able
defenders during the remainder of the fifth century (*e.g.*,
Faustus of Rhegium, Gennadius of Massilia), but it was
too vague, lacked too much in internal coherence, to
stand permanently against the compactness of the
Augustinian doctrine.[2] Next century (529 A.D.) it was
condemned, and a moderate Augustinianism vindicated,
at the important Council of Orange, the decrees of
which were sanctioned by the Pope, Boniface II. (530
A.D.). On the other hand, Augustine had trouble
towards the end of his life with a section who sought
to push his predestinarian doctrine to an extreme of

---

[1] On the logical difference of the two views, see Mozley, pp. 47, 48.

[2] Baur judges Semi-Pelagianism very unfavourably. "This halving
and neutralising," he says, "this attempt at equal distribution of the two
complementary elements, not only setting them apart, but also balancing
them with each other, so that sometimes the one, sometimes the other, is
preponderant, and thus within the whole sphere everything is casual and
arbitrary, varying and indefinite, according to the diversity of circumstances
and individuals, this is characteristic of Semi-Pelagianism throughout,"
etc. (quoted by Schaff, *Hist.* ii. p. 858).

fatalism, and convert it into an excuse for sin. Against these troublers he wrote two important works ; his view found defenders also in writers like Prosper Aquitanus, and the author of an anonymous book on the *Calling of the Gentiles* (*De Vocatione Gentium*), who, with great skill, and no little success, endeavoured to present the predestination doctrine in a form which would soften its apparent harshness, and conciliate Christian feeling. The impulse given by Augustine to theology lasted, as already stated, through the whole of the Middle Ages. Most of the greater schoolmen, as Anselm, Bernard, Peter the Lombard, Aquinas, Bradwardine, with earlier scholars, as Bede and Alcuin, were his disciples. The predestinarian controversy had a brief revival in the ninth century in the dispute between the monk Gottschalk and Hincmar, Archbishop of Rheims. Gottschalk outdid Augustine himself in the rigour of his advocacy of predestination, while Hincmar was Semi-Pelagian. The views of the latter were condemned at two Synods —a proof of Augustine's influence—but Gottschalk's extreme and intemperate opinions caused his own friends ultimately to desert him.

V. Of the massive system of Augustine, we shall see afterwards that the best elements were taken up by the Reformers, and incorporated in the Protestant creeds. There, I am convinced, in substance they will remain. In proportion to the thoroughness of our views of the evil of sin, and its effects on human nature—of the essential nature of man, and of the ruin sin has wrought in his constitution and condition —will be our estimate of their value and importance. I shall only at this stage briefly refer to that part of the Augustinian system which has been the special object of hostile criticism—its doctrine of *predestination.*

Criticism of this doctrine may take the form of a criticism of the doctrine of predestination in general, or a criticism of the particular shape in which it was held by Augustine. Some remarks on the latter aspect have already been offered,—especially on the inconsistency arising from the combination of it with sacramentarian doctrine. Of the more fundamental objections, some will be found to rest on misconception ; others would seem to suggest the necessity of an alteration in our point of view in dealing with the scope of the divine purpose,—an alteration which our modern ways of thinking, and fuller insight into Scripture, should make easier for us.

A common objection to the Augustinian doctrine is that it represents predestination to salvation as a perfectly *arbitrary* act of God—the decree of a will acting on no ground but its own good pleasure.[1] This certainly is not correct. Augustine, as everyone must see who apprehends his fundamental positions, knows nothing of arbitrary acts of God. The grounds of the divine action in providence and grace, the last reasons of the divine determinations, may be, doubtless are, to us inscrutable, but they are none the less assuredly the outcome of an eternal wisdom, righteousness, and love. Faith cannot falter in the conviction that God governs the world, and orders all things in it, for the best. What Augustine would say is, that on *any* theory of the universe, the last reasons of the constitution and course of the world must always be sought for in the counsel of an eternal wisdom which it is beyond our capacity to fathom.[2] We all recognise this in

---

[1] " Good pleasure " is an ambiguous phrase. The εὐδοκία of Eph. i. 5 has no suggestion of arbitrariness.

[2] Augustine invariably falls back on this " inscrutability " in the divine counsels, while maintaining that there can be no injustice or partiality in

external providence—in the history and distribution of peoples, and their providential functions in the world ; in the diversities of rank, fortune, privilege, opportunity, gifts of individuals ; in the torturing enigmas of life, which often so baffle and oppress us. But faith holds fast by the certainty that behind it all, if we could only see it, there is a will of righteousness and love. The same sovereignty is witnessed in the history of revelation and salvation—in the call of Abraham, *e.g.*, and the election of Israel ; in the distribution of privilege under Christianity—some nations favoured with the Gospel, others still in the darkness and death of heathenism ; in the diverse results which follow from apparently the same enjoyment of privilege. In consistency with his doctrine of grace, Augustine could not but hold that the last grounds of all this, and of individual salvation, must be found in the counsel of God ; but this is a counsel of eternal wisdom and goodness.[1]

A deeper criticism, but one still resting, to a certain extent, on misapprehension, relates to the bearings of this doctrine on *free-will and responsibility.* Here also the Augustinian doctrine is frequently burdened with consequences which by no means rightfully belong to it. As respects predestination proper, it should be remembered that in Augustine's system predestination only comes into view in connection with a race which already has *lost* its spiritual freedom, and has for its end the restoration of that freedom, and through this the accomplishment of the divine purpose in salvation.

God. Cf. *Rebuke and Grace,* 17, 18, 19 ; on *Perseverance,* 18 ; *Forgiveness of Sins,* i. 29, 103 ; *Nature and Grace,* 66, etc.

[1] God to Augustine is supremely and essentially Love. Cf. the remarks of Harnack, v. 118, 119 : "as God is in all being, so He is also in love ; nay, His existence in being is ultimately identical with His existence in love," etc.

Augustine, however, goes deeper than this, and retorts on the objector that no tenable view of human freedom relieves him of difficulty on this subject.[1] It is an easy word to use—freedom ; but those who use it do not always see that they are playing with an unanalysed notion, and that, if they did analyse it, they would find most of their old difficulties returning. It is thought by many, *e.g.*, to get rid of this difficulty by basing predestination on foreknowledge.[2] The truth is, as has often been demonstrated, the difficulty returns here in as acute a form as ever. For the question immediately recurs, how a free act can even be foreknown. A free act, in the sense of the objector, is one which springs solely from the will of the creature ; it has no cause beyond that will ; it rests with the agent alone to say what it shall be. This raises the difficulty of supposing it to be foreknown what an action shall be *before the creature who alone is to determine what it shall be has so much as been brought into existence.*[3] On the other hand, granted that such acts can be foreknown, no insuperable difficulty attaches to the supposition that they can be taken up as elements into an all-embracing divine plan.[4]

A graver objection which may be urged against this

[1] Cf. his *City of God*, Bk. v., and his treatise on *Grace and Freedom*.

[2] Thus Augustine earlier, the Semi-Pelagians, the Arminians, etc. Cf. Lecture IX.

[3] Some theologians, accordingly, *e.g.*, Rothe, Martensen, Dr. James Morison, go so far as to deny the foreknowledge of free acts. Augustine more philosophically confesses and maintains both (*City of God*, v. 9, 10).

[4] I have said elsewhere—"One thing is certain, that neither the materialist nor the idealist of our day can logically take up the stone against the doctrine. Not the school of Huxley, Tyndall, Maudsley, or Galton, who deny free-agency from the physical side ; not the school of Mr. Spencer or Mr. Bain, who are necessitarian on the metaphysical side ; not even the Hegelian school, which, with a higher aim, yet sees in all things the working out of an eternal necessity."—Lecture on Calvin in *The Reformers* (1885).

doctrine is, that, even if freed from the charge of arbitrariness, it conflicts with just ideas of the divine *love*, and, in particular, is incompatible with the Christian belief in the divine *Fatherhood*. Augustine meets the charge of injustice by the plea that, seeing the whole race is justly involved in condemnation—a *massa perditionis* [1]—there can be no injustice to those passed by in the fact that, in God's inscrutable purpose, some are chosen to salvation, and others rejected. But even supposing this granted (and I do not suppose it can quite satisfy anyone), the question recurs — If no injustice, what of the love? The more modern turn given to the objection is—What of the divine Fatherhood? Even this argument, however, may be over-driven, through not observing the difficulties which the doctrine of the divine Fatherhood has in any case to face from the actual constitution of the universe. It is not always considered that predestination, in any form, does not alter in one whit or degree the actual constitution of things as history and experience reveal it to us—does not add one anomaly to those already existing in the universe—does not make one soul more to be saved or lost than actually is saved or lost. If the actual constitution of things is ultimately reconcilable with the love or Fatherhood of God—which ultimately it must be—it may be fairly urged that predestination, which simply carries back this state of things to its last ground in the holy, wise, and good will of God, must be so also.[2] It is but the existing condition of things,

---

[1] *Rebuke and Grace*, 16 ; and repeatedly.

[2] Reflection will make it clear that, seeing it rests ultimately with the divine wisdom to determine what, out of the infinite possibilities of things, the actual course of the world shall be, it also rests ultimately with the divine will which of the infinity of possible free acts shall be allowed to eventuate, or become actualities, and under what conditions. It is obvious that the slightest change in the *outward* course of providence at any point would intercept and alter the whole line of free acts, with their

with all its existing anomalies, inequalities, and results in salvation or loss, carried up, as already said, into the light of eternity, viewed *sub specie æternitatis*.

Still, it is frankly to be granted that so long as this doctrine is confined to the form which it has in Augustine, it is impossible to free it wholly from the appearance of conflict with that love of God which is at the same time asserted to be of God's essence. An indication of this is seen in the necessity felt by Augustine of limiting to the elect the force of the passages which speak of God's will of love to the world.[1] Where then is the defect, and wherein lies the possibility of solution? The fault of Augustine's doctrine, I would venture to say, lies in its regarding the subject too exclusively in its relation to the individual salvation, and not sufficiently in connection with an *organic view* of the divine purpose in its relation to the world and history. So long as we abide by the view of the human race as simply a *massa damnata*, out of which, for whatever holy and wise reasons, a selection is made of a certain number of individuals for salvation, we cannot free this doctrine from an aspect of harshness and partiality. But this is not the full or Scriptural view of the doctrine. Election there stands always in connection with a developing purpose of God, and has for its aim, not the *exclusion* of others, but the ultimate larger blessing and salvation of others. A typical example is furnished in the choice of Abraham. God

consequences, proceeding from that point. But so also at *every* point. Freedom, therefore, does not supersede foreordination but demands it.

[1] Cf. his *Rebuke and Grace*, 44. It is noteworthy that Calvin, with his sounder exegetical sense, does not explain away the natural larger sense in such passages. Cf. his Com. on John iii. 16 ; and *Instit.* iii. 24, 16, etc.

chose Abraham, and made His covenant with him. But this was done, not for Abraham's own sake only, but in order that in him all families of the earth should be blessed.[1] It was election with a view to ultimate comprehension—the choice of one with a view to the blessing of many. Only in this way, by starting at one point—with one person—and working out to a wider result, could the divine end be accomplished. It is the same with the elect nation—the people of Israel. It alone was chosen of the families of the earth, but it was not as an act of partiality, but with the view that it might, in the fulness of time, be a light to the Gentiles, and the means of spreading the glory of God throughout the earth. Augustine, perhaps, comes nearest this point of view when he speaks, as he frequently does, of Christ Himself as the highest example of predestination.[2] But Christ—the elect one —is the crowning proof that election does not bear an *exclusive* aspect to the world, but is a means of bringing blessing to it.

We must, therefore, in considering this subject, dismiss absolutely from our minds all idea of arbitrariness, and bring the divine purpose in election *dynamically* into the closest connection with the *history* in which it is realised. Only a foolish person will ask, Why did not God, by a simple stroke of omnipotence, change the hearts of all men, instead of selecting *one* Abraham, or choosing *one* nation to be the recipient of His training, or sending *one* Christ to a particular people in one age of the world? Why this leaving of His kingdom to the slow and unequal progress it

---

[1] Genesis xii. 3.

[2] *E.g.*, *On Predestination*, 30, 31 ; *On Perseverance*, 67, etc. Thus also Calvin, *Instit.* ii. 17. 1 ; iii. 22. 1.

has had through the centuries? It is safe to say that, to anyone who has even an elementary conception of God's methods of working in providence and grace, such a simultaneous conversion of all peoples, by a simple exercise of divine power, is an impossible idea. Such an one will see at once that the only way in which the high ends God has in view could be attained in harmony with the laws of nature and freedom is the way which has been actually adopted—that, viz., of working from one point to another in the line of historical development—ever new vantage-points being established as the way is prepared for them. Election means that it is not of man's own doing, or deserving, or of aught but grace, that along the whole line of development, such points are found provided, and centres of new influence established. Here another error has to be avoided. It is a shallow view of the divine election which regards it as simply availing itself of happy varieties of character and temperament spontaneously presenting themselves in history; as a workman, for instance, might select from a set of ready made tools those best suited for his purpose. There is a sentence somewhere in Lange's *Dogmatics* which acutely says—" Election presides at the *making* of its objects." The appearance of great men at particular junctures of history, *e.g.*, is not to be attributed to chance. The question is not simply how, a man of Abraham's or Moses' gifts and qualifications being given, God should use him as He did; but rather, how a man of this mould came at that precise juncture to be there at all—broke out at that precise point in the genealogical tree. This is the true problem, and the solution can only be found in the working of that self-same divine purpose which, from " the foundation of the world," has been preparing the means for its own realisation.[1]   The same principles apply to the humblest soul that God calls into His Kingdom.   Difficulties can never be altogether removed, but if these principles are firmly grasped, they afford us, I believe, a clue by which we may find our way through many intricacies of this perplexing subject.   The one thing to be held fast is, that, whether we can explain the mystery of God's dealing with others or not, our own salvation, if we have been brought into His Kingdom, and the salvation of all who share this divine calling, is due to an unsought and undeserved grace.[2]

[1] Cf. Gal. i. 15.   It is due to Augustine to say that in his *City of God* he shows more than a glimpse into this organic character of the divine purpose.

[2] This subject is resumed in Lecture IX., in connection with Calvinism and Arminianism.

VI

THE DOCTRINE OF THE PERSON OF CHRIST—THE CHRISTO-
LOGICAL CONTROVERSIES : APOLLINARIAN, NESTORIAN,
EUTYCHIAN, MONOPHYSITE, MONOTHELITE (FIFTH
TO SEVENTH CENTURIES)

"Faith is discovered by us to be the first movement towards salvation ; after which fear, hope, and repentance, advancing in company with temperance and patience, lead us to love and knowledge."—CLEMENT OF ALEXANDRIA.

"Far be it from us to suppose that God should hate in us that by means of which He has made us superior to all other creatures. Far be it from us to suppose that we are to believe in order that we may be under no necessity of receiving, or of seeking, rational knowledge, since we could not even believe, unless we were possessed of rational souls. Even this, too, is beyond all question in conformity with reason, that in some things pertaining to the doctrine of salvation, which we are as yet not able to penetrate by our reason, faith precedes rational knowledge, that so the disposition may be purified by faith, in order to be in a condition, at some future period, to receive the light of so great a truth."—AUGUSTINE.

"Not God converted into man, but man glorified in God."—ALCUIN.

LECTURE VI

The doctrine of the Person of Christ—the Christological Controversies: Apollinarian, Nestorian, Eutychian, Monophysite, Monothelite (Fifth to Seventh Centuries).

As the next chapter in the history of doctrine we come to the long series of controversies we call Christological. The doctrine of the Person of Christ may be approached either from the side of Theology, the doctrine of God, or from the side of Soteriology, the doctrine of redemption. It has manifest relations with both. The Nicene affirmation of the oneness of essence of the Son with the Father at once raises the question of how this divine, co-essential Son is related to the humanity in which He appeared on earth. On the other side, the doctrine of redemption compels us to move back on the Person of the Redeemer as One who, for the adequate accomplishment of His work, must be divine as well as human. It is from this soteriological side, as we shall see, that the subject is approached by Anselm. While, however, the soteriological aspect is far from overlooked in the ancient church,[1] it is naturally by the other pathway that we enter on the controversies which concern us here. These arose primarily as the sequel of the discussions the Church had been engaged in on the doctrine of the Trinity,

---

[1] Cf., *e.g.*, Athanasius in his *Incarnation of the Word*, and the Epistle of Leo in the Chalcedonian disputes.

and, through the exhaustive consideration of the class
of questions which they involved, prepared the way for
the soteriological problem.

I said in the first lecture that the Christological
controversies are among the most unlovely in the
history of the Church—the most confusing also, and
perplexed.   One's heart well-nigh fails at the spectacles
of passion, intrigue, fanaticism, and rancorous violence
which they exhibit.   How easy to conclude that
doctrines engendered in such an atmosphere, having
reference, too, above all things, to the Holy Person of
the Saviour, so far from aiding the apprehension of
the truth, must infallibly bear on them the stamp of
error!   Yet this would be a hasty judgment.   The
Spirit of God had not left His Church, even in the
midst of these confusions, but was guiding it, at heavy
cost to its own peace, to a sure understanding of the
meaning of its own beliefs.   It soon becomes evident
that there were deeper principles and more vital issues
involved in these controversies than at first sight
appear.   And there were strong men at every stage
who had the power of discernment of these larger
issues, and the wisdom to guide the Church to sound
decisions regarding them.   I shall best consult the
ends I have in view, if, neglecting the elements of
strife and passion which disfigure the outward course
of the history, I seek to fix attention on the real logic
of the movement, and on the ideas and aims of the men
who most worthily represent it.

For there can be no reasonable question that the
controversies we call Christological had their true
origin, not in caprice, but in the necessary course of
the doctrinal development—that their rising or not

rising was not a matter dependent on individual will. The Arian and Macedonian controversies had established once for all the essential oneness of the Son and Spirit with the Father. It was also an integral part of Christian faith that Christ had a true and perfect humanity. But this immediately raised the question of how this union of the divine and human in a single Person was to be positively conceived. Christ is divine, and He is human (θεάνθρωπος, God-Man); how are these two sides of His personality to be thought of as related to each other? This is the question of Christology proper, and it was inevitable that, in dealing with it, various solutions should be attempted, the admissibility or inadmissibility of which could only be discovered after exhaustive trial. One easy mode of solution, of course, was the suppression of one or other of the sides altogether—either the *human* side, as with the Docetists, or the *divine*, as with the Unitarians.[1] But this was precisely what the Church of the day, in light of its previous decisions, refused to do. It would neither give up Christ's true humanity; nor would it consent to sink the truth of His divinity, or allow that He was divine only in a metaphorical or dynamical sense. It held fast to the central confession of a *real incarnation of the eternal Son*, and the problem was, how, on this assumption, to exhibit the union of the real humanity with the true divinity in one Person. One thing which undeniably made the solution of this problem more difficult for the ancient Church, was the tendency inherited from Platonism to regard humanity and divinity as in a sense *strange* to each other—two magnitudes, foreign and disparate—which,

[1] So Harnack finds the root of the difficulty in the doctrine of the two natures which, accordingly, he rejects.

therefore, could never truly be brought together. Even Cyril of Alexandria regards the divine and human as separated by an infinite gulf, and defines them by opposite predicates.[1] It is evident that on this footing any union that is postulated will always be more or less external. This may be said to be the radical weakness of the old Christology, and probably the chief gain of our modern way of thinking on Christological questions is that it transcends this older dualism, and starts rather from the side of the affinity of the divine and human— from the idea of man as *capax infiniti*—recognising a God-related element in human nature, as created in the divine image, which furnishes a starting-point for the conceivability of the incarnation. On the other hand, it is possible to make too much of this. Attempts were made also in the ancient Church to overcome this dualism ;[2] and, even when we have stated the matter most favourably for ourselves, the essential difficulty remains of how a true manhood and a true godhead are to be conceived of as united in one historical personality. And when the subject is well considered, we shall perhaps find reason to admire the tact by which the Church was guided, if not to a complete solution of the mystery, at least to the rejection of the principal errors by which such a solution is imperilled.

This leads me to observe that, to do justice to the Christological findings of the ancient Church, it is necessary to keep in view what precisely it was which the Church set before it as its aim in these decisions. Blame is frequently attached to it for attempting to define metaphysically by a series of subtle distinctions

---

[1] Cf. Dorner, *Person of Christ*, iii. p. 65 (E.T.). God, *e.g.*, is represented as infinite, unchangeable, impassible, etc. Man is the opposite of all this—finite, changeable, corporeal, passible, etc.

[2] Cf. below, *e.g.*, in Apollinaris and Theodore of Mopsuestia.

what in the nature of the case must always transcend definition. In truth, however, what the Church aimed at was not so much to furnish an exhaustive definition —metaphysical or other—of what it always recognised to be an ineffable " mystery of godliness," [1] as rather to maintain the integrity of the Christian fact against theories and speculations which *did* profess to explain it, but in reality impinged upon and mutilated it in a variety of directions. Christian faith may not be able to solve the mystery of the incarnation, but it may recognise that certain theories do conflict with vital religious interests, and may feel called upon to contend against them very earnestly on that account. We may be conscious, for example, of our inability to see into the depths of this great subject, and yet be able to perceive very clearly that the integrity of Christ's humanity is compromised by the denial to Him of a true human soul—which was the error of *Apollinaris ;* further, that it does not comport with the Christian fact to resolve Christ's single person into two —which was the error of *Nestorius ;* again, that there is something wrong in representing the nature of Christ as a mixture or fusion of deity and humanity— a *tertium quid,* which preserves neither nature in its integrity—which was the *Eutychian* and *Monophysite* error ; or, finally, that it is erroneous to restrict this fusion even to the element of will in Christ—which was the *Monothelite* error. In opposing these various errors, the Church did not profess to be giving a *rationale* of the incarnation on its own account, but only to be warding off theories on one side or the other by which the integrity of the fact was threatened ; and it will be

---

[1] The watchword of the Alexandrians, Neander says, was " the ineffable, incomprehensible, transcendant union of natures " (iv. p. 120). Cf. Harnack, iv. p. 174.

exceedingly difficult for any one who truly believes in the incarnation, and reflects on the meaning of his own assertions, to show that it went seriously astray in so doing.[1] At the same time it is evident that a work of this kind, unavoidable as it may be, is fraught with drawbacks and dangers. Around a fact originally apprehended in the simplicity of Christian faith there gradually grows up, as the result of this process, a scaffolding or encasement of protective formulations— abstruse, complex, scholastic—and the temptation is great to make the acceptance of these a substitute for faith itself. This is the real peril of intellectualism to which the Church is constantly exposed ; and the remedy for it is the continual reversion to, and habitual contemplation of, that living image of Christ in the Gospels in which all contrasts are harmonised,— where the divine and human are seen in their *actual* union. But it would be as foolish to make this an objection to the work of definition as it would be to complain that, in our attitude to truth generally, we cannot remain always at the naïve, irreflective stage of childhood. For good or evil—doubtless for good rather than evil—questions emerge which force doctrinal reflection upon us, and, when they do arise, there is no alternative for the Church, any more than for the individual, but honestly to face and deal with them.

Christological speculation had of necessity a place in the Church from the commencement. Ebionitic, Gnostic, Patripassian, Sabellian theories, not less than the theories of Paul of Samosata and of Arius, involved the elements of a Christology. The name " Christological," however, is specially appropriated to that series of post-Nicene discussions which issued in the

---

[1] Cf. an interesting passage in Mr. Balfour's *Foundations of Belief*, p. 279.

dogmatic affirmations of the Creeds. They embrace the five controversies already named ; the Apollinarian, the Nestorian, the Eutychian, the Monophysite, and the Monothelite. I have now to ask you to look at these in their historical, which will prove also to be their logical, connection.

I. The first, or *Apollinarian*, form of Christological heresy goes back to the fourth century, and is, in a manner, a prelude to the greater disputes. The simplest solution of the unity of the divine and human in one Person which suggests itself, is obviously that which supposes that in the constitution of this Person the divine Son or Logos takes the place of the rational soul in the ordinary human being. The Son of God takes to Him our entire humanity, saving only that in it which constitutes man a *self*. But the personal self-determining centre in man is his rational soul. This, therefore, it is contended, Christ cannot assume ; else we would have two personal centres, or selves, in Christ, which is not to be conceded. There appears no alternative but that the Logos should take the place of the rational soul in Christ, and this He is supposed to have done. This view has affinities with both Arian and Sabellian speculation ;[1] but the person by whom (about 375 A.D.) it was brought to formal expression was Apollinaris, Bishop of Laodicea,[2] a worthy man and follower of Athanasius, well versed in Greek learning. Apollinaris did not deny to Christ the

---

[1] The Arians taught that the Logos took the place of a human soul in Jesus. The opinion was evidently current in the middle of the fourth century. It was condemned by the Council of Alexandria in 362 A.D. (before Apollinaris).

[2] Commonly called Apollinaris the Younger, to distinguish him from his father of the same name. The remains of his writings were collected by Draseke in 1892.

possession of a human soul in every sense. He was a trichotomist in his psychology, *i.e.*, distinguished in man the *three* elements of body, animal soul, and spirit; and he granted that Christ had assumed into union with Himself a true body and an *animal* soul (ψυχή), the seat of appetite, passion, and desire. But the place of rational and self-determining element (πνεῦμα) in man, was taken, he contended, by the Logos Himself. It could not be otherwise, he thought, if Christ was to be raised above mutability, and if duality was not to be introduced into His consciousness. It is plain that there is here a mutilation of the idea of Christ's true humanity against which the Church did right to protest,—the introduction of a docetic element, as if, in respect of the soul, Christ were only *seeming* man, and were withdrawn from the conditions of a true human development.[1] Yet it would be a mistake to think too lightly of Apollinaris and his theory. Apollinaris was really an able thinker, and there is at least one element of truth in his speculations to which the Church of that time was not fitted to do justice. In meeting the objection that he denied a true human soul to Christ, Apollinaris took the ground that this was not the real purport of his doctrine. The Logos, he held, does not stand apart from man, as something foreign to his essence, but is rather Himself the archetype of humanity —has the potency of humanity eternally within Himself. In realising, therefore, this eternal determination of His nature, and becoming man in Christ, the Logos does not simply *take the place of* a human soul; He *becomes* a human soul—is more truly human than any individual of the species. In Dorner's words—

---

[1] Athanasius argued against this doctrine that Christ could not redeem human nature in its completeness if His nature was not entirely homogeneous with ours. Cf. Neander, iv. p. 104 (Bohn).

" The Logos, so far from being foreign to, constitutes rather the perfection of, the humanity. This he expressed as follows : ' The πνεῦμα in Christ is human πνεῦμα, although divine.' " [1]   There is here a step towards the recognition of that inward kindredness of God to the human spirit—that natural grounding of the soul of man in the Logos as the light and life of man [2]—which must be taken account of in any adequate doctrine of the incarnation.   Since, however, the avowed aim of Apollinaris in identifying the soul with the Logos was to lift Christ above human mutability and weakness, it is evident that the idea of " becoming man " is very imperfectly carried out.   There is an important difference, besides, between a soul which is grounded in the Logos, as every human soul is, and a soul *replaced* by the Logos in Christ, which is the Apollinarian point of view.   In this latter assertion, the Church, in its great teachers, and formally at the Council of Constantinople (381 A.D.), rightly recognised a note of error, and affirmed against it the possession by Christ of a complete humanity — rational soul included.[3]

II. By the rejection of the Apollinarian view the Church declared that Christ was possessed of a true and unimpaired humanity—had as truly a human soul as a human body.   But this only raised in a more

---

[1] *Person of Christ*, ii. p. 371 (E.T.).   Dorner possibly reads rather much into some of the expressions of Apollinaris, but in the main his exposition seems justified.   He shows also that strange theories were afloat at the time, with some of which Apollinaris has been unjustly connected.

[2] John i. 4.

[3] Harnack admits, while regarding the Church doctrine of the two natures as contradictory, that in this controversy, " by preserving the thought of the perfect humanity of Christ, it did an inestimable service to later generations " (iv. p. 163, E.T.).

acute form the question of how this union of the divine
and human in His Person was to be conceived. And
the solution which next in order naturally presented
itself was that connected historically with the name of
Nestorius, viz., that the Logos united Himself in the
closest form of *moral fellowship* with the man Christ
Jesus, without the latter thereby losing His independent personality, or becoming, as was alleged to be the
case on the opposite view, a mere " accident " of the
Logos. In the Nestorian controversy, no doubt, many
secondary and often condemnable factors were at
work. Among them we may notice the deep-seated
jealousy which subsisted between the rival patriarchates
of Alexandria and Constantinople, and the growing
veneration of the Church for the Virgin Mary—a
veneration that found its expression in the epithet θεοτόκος (Mother of God), which became in a manner the
watchword of this controversy. But these were after
all but straws upon the surface. The real explanation of the dispute is to be sought in the trend of the
theological development, and specially in the opposed
tendencies of thought which now reveal themselves in
the schools of Alexandria and Antioch respectively.
The Alexandrian school—from the first, as we saw,[1]
of an idealistic and speculative character — received
about this time a mystical tinge from Syria which disposed it to look predominatingly at the divine, or
transcendental, side of Christ's Person, and to view the
humanity as merged in, if not absorbed by, this higher
side. The Antiochian theology, on the other hand,
in accordance with its more rational bent, made careful
discrimination of the natures, and laboured to preserve
each in its independence and distinctness, with the
opposite peril of separating them too far, and destroy-

[1] See above, p. 83.

ing the unity of the Person. It is in the conflict of
these two tendencies, each of which had its providential
place and side of truth, that we are to seek the key
to the controversies that followed. The tendency of
the Antiochian school is seen nowhere more clearly
than in the theology of its most distinguished representative, Theodore of Mopsuestia, fellow-pupil with
Chrysostom of Diodorus of Tarsus, and master of
Nestorius. To his views, for clearness' sake, I must,
in the first instance, devote a little attention.[1]

Theodore's system is one of the most original and
carefully thought-out of the period. Man he conceives
of as the visible image and representative of God on
earth—the bond of union of the whole creation. With
Augustine he holds that true freedom is only attained
when the soul is established in goodness, raised above
the possibility of sinning through union with God.
But this state he regards as only to be reached by a
process of moral development. As originally created,
man was fallible and mortal, and had to learn his
inability to stand in his own strength by the actual
experience of falling. The fall, therefore, with the
sin and death that resulted from it, is, in a sense, in
Theodore's system, a necessity of man's natural condition.[2] From this state we are restored by Christ,
the new Head of the race, in whom the image of God
in humanity is for the first time perfectly realised.
But even the union of the Logos with Christ does not

[1] Theodore died in 428 A.D. His works are known mostly in fragments. The chief in this connection are his treatises on the Incarnation
and against Apollinaris. His creed may be seen in Gieseler, i. p. 392
(E.T.). On his theology, cf. Neander, Dorner, Harnack, etc.
[2] Theodore, at the other end of his system, was a restitutionist—a
logical result of his views of human nature and the fall, if divine goodness
was to be vindicated.

exclude freedom and moral development. Human nature in its completeness, including personality, is united with the Logos from the beginning—is irradiated, strengthened, inspired, sustained by it, and for this reason grows and matures with exceptional rapidity—yet not without a free ethical development which appropriates the divine in all its stages.

This brings us to Theodore's view of the nature of the union of the divine and human in Christ. Theodore works this out from the point of view of "indwelling" (ἐνοίκησις). What, then, is the manner of this indwelling of God in Christ? He shows first that it is not the indwelling of mere immanence—of that omnipresence and energy by which God is present to and in *all* His creatures. It is not simply an *essential* presence (κατ᾿ οὐσίαν), or a presence in *energy* (κατ᾿ ἐνεργείαν). The Incarnation cannot be explained from the mere immanence of God, for God is immanent in everything. But there is another mode of the presence of God by which He draws nearer to some than to others, according to their *moral* dispositions—a mode of indwelling which Theodore describes as one of God's *good pleasure* (κατ᾿ εὐδοκίαν). It is the peculiar relation of moral fellowship in which God stands to those who are fitted for it by the spirit of trust and obedience. It is thus God dwells in believers; thus, in a unique and pre-eminent way, the Logos dwelt in Christ. The union here is of the most perfect kind conceivable. The human spirit of Jesus so perfectly appropriates the divine as to become entirely one with it. Christ's thinking and willing as man are truly the thinking and willing of God in Him, yet is human nature not thereby annulled, but rather raised to its highest degree of perfection. On the other side, the divine Son so entirely appro-

priates and unites the human nature with Himself as
to make it the organ of His personal manifestation.
Through this union, further, the humanity is made to
share, after the ascension, in all the glory and dominion
of the Logos. This, it will be felt, is an exceedingly
able attempt to solve the problem of the unity of the
divine and human in Christ—one, also, not without its
elements of value. It involves the recognition, elsewhere so often wanting, of the affinity of the divine
and human which makes true union possible, and is a
praiseworthy attempt to do justice to the ethical factor in
Christ's development. Yet, with all its ingenuity, it will
be felt also that it never really gets beyond the most
perfect form of moral union of two persons originally
distinct. Theodore practically admits this by the
term he uses to describe it. It is a conjunction (συνάφεια), or, again, is likened to marriage, in which two
become one. It can easily he understood, therefore,
how the Alexandrian school, with Cyril at its head,
should persistently oppose this doctrine as failing to
satisfy the conditions of a true incarnation, and that
the pupils of Theodore should in some instances
be disposed to go farther than he himself did,
and undisguisedly affirm a double personality in
Christ.

This, accordingly, is what we now see in the case of
Nestorius, patriarch of Constantinople, a well-meaning
man, and noted zealot against Arian and other heresies,
but convinced adherent of the Antiochian school, who,
in 428 A.D., drew down indignation on himself by his
vehement opposition to the term θεοτόκος (Mother of
God), applied to the Virgin Mary. *Christotokos* he
would allow, but not *theotokos ;* for the Logos, he said,
was not born of Mary, but dwelt in Him who was born

of Mary.[1] Nestorius went considerably farther in his separation of the divine and human in Christ than Theodore would have approved, though undeniably he was on the same lines. The "conjunction" (συνάφεια) of the two natures which Theodore taught becomes with Nestorius little more than a "relationship" (σχέσις) between them, an intimate moral fellowship of two persons. It is this doctrine which Cyril of Alexandria vigorously assailed. Cyril is a personage for whom, ordinarily, Church historians have hardly a good word to say. He seems to have inherited too faithfully the temper and method of his violent and domineering uncle and predecessor, Theophilus ; and, supported by his monks, and crowds of fanatical *parabolani*,[2] he used his position of high influence in the city with both pride and passion. We shall perhaps judge him more fairly if, acknowledging the grave faults into which ambition and love of power led him, we recognise with Dorner, Newman, and others,[3] that there were better traits in his character, and that, though frequently swayed by prejudice, he was actuated by a more sincere love of truth, and even by a more moderate and forbearing spirit, than he is usually credited with. His first letters to Nestorius are calm and temperate in tone ; and it is remarked that, after the banishment of Nestorius, no violent act is recorded of him. One thing certain is, that as a theologian Cyril is *facile princeps* in this controversy.[4] He had no equal in his day in firm grasp

---

[1] See passages from his sermons in Gieseler, i. p. 394 (E.T.), and cf. Dorner, Neander, etc. The Logos, he taught, dwelt in Christ as in a temple, the humanity was the garment of His divinity, etc.

[2] Originally a corps for the care of the sick. They became afterwards a sort of bodyguard for the archbishop, and caused great disorder through their turbulence. Cf. the picture in Kingsley's *Hypatia*.

[3] Cf. Dorner, ii. p. 55 ; Newman, *Historical Sketches*, ii. (under Theodoret) ; *Dict. of Christ. Biog.* art. "Cyril."

[4] Baur pays a high tribute to Cyril as a theologian.

of the issues involved, and in luminous and convincing reasoning on behalf of the positions he upheld. His views, as we shall see, are not free from defects. Certain of his expressions held within them the germs of a Monophysitism which is the justification of the opposition shown to him by Theodoret and others of the Antiochian school. But in his polemic against Nestorius, Cyril was unquestionably in the right. He justly argued that on the theory of Nestorius there was no proper incarnation, but only the juxtaposition of two beings, God and man ; that the Son of God was little more than the guest of the humanity ; that there existed between them only a relational conjunction (σχετική συνάφεια). When the question was pressed, How could Christ, according to His humanity, be called the Son of God, or as man be lawfully worshipped? the Nestorians could only reply by speaking of a transference (ἀναφορά) of the name son to the humanity, and suggesting that as a man Christ might be worshipped if the worship was directed in thought to the indwelling Logos.[1] The union of the humanity with Godhead was spoken of as union in worth (κατ' ἀξίαν), in will, in name, and so forth.[2] This plainly was not satisfactory.

The essential point in Nestorianism, then, is *the dissolving of the unity of the personality in Christ.* As against the view of the assumption of a human nature by a divine Person, the Nestorians held that there were *two* persons—a divine and a human—subsisting in the closest moral union. The Logos *inhabited* the humanity, which had a personality of its own. This was a type of doctrine which, however plausibly defended, could not permanently be maintained. Though

---

[1] Dorner, ii. p. 59 ; thus also Theodore.
[2] Cf. Bruce's *Humiliation of Christ*, p. 64.

supported for a time by imperial authority, the battle went steadily against it. Rome and Alexandria united in its condemnation; finally the Council of Ephesus—the third so-called ecumenical (431 A.D.)—was summoned to decide the question. It would be unprofitable to dwell on the confusions that attended and followed in the wake of that assembly. After a fortnight's waiting, due to delay in the arrival of John of Antioch and his Syrian bishops, Cyril opened the Council and proceeded to business. In a day's time Nestorius was condemned, excommunicated, and deposed. The imperial commissioner refused his sanction to the proceedings; on the other hand, popular feeling was overwhelmingly with the bishops, and the city was illuminated on the announcement of their decision. The Antiochians, when they came, were bitterly incensed, and held a rival council. Recriminations, mutual depositions, imperial vacillations ensued; but in the end things remained as Cyril's Council had left them, and the unfortunate Nestorius was silently abandoned by all parties. He died, after many hardships, in exile (440 A.D.). In 433 A.D. a reconciliation was effected between Cyril and some of the Antiochian leaders (others, including Theodoret, held aloof) on the basis of a mediating formula—the Antiochians accepting the *theotokos* and the Alexandrians the " unconfused union " (ἀσυγχύτος) of natures. Theodoret was really the author of this formula, but he refused to sanction the condemnation of Nestorius, which he held had been illegally obtained. Cyril would fain have included in the condemnation the person and writings of Diodorus and Theodore, but this proved beyond his power. We shall find Theodore condemned later at the *fifth* Council in 553 A.D.[1]

[1] The Nestorians, persecuted in Syria, took refuge in Persia, and

III. Nestorianism was condemned, but the controversy was not thereby ended. It only entered on a new phase—that known as the *Eutychian*. The Alexandrians took the decision of the Council of Ephesus as a victory for themselves, and the more extreme of them were fain to regard it as a condemnation of the whole Antiochian position, with its strong discrimination of the natures. Their own formula was "one nature (μία θύσις) of the Logos incarnate."[1] Cyril himself, though in words accepting the formula of the unconfused union (ἀσυγχύτος ἐνώσις), was far from unambiguous in his teaching. He maintained the difference of the natures, yet because of the "physical union" (ἐνώσις φυσική), could speak also of "one nature" in Christ incarnate.[2] In virtue of the union, he freely took over divine attributes upon the humanity, *e.g.*, omniscience, so that Christ's ignorance was held to be only seeming—a species of "economy."[3] After the Ephesian decision, these tendencies had fuller scope. The divine and human natures might be distinguished *in abstracto*, but after the incarnation they were held to be no more two, but one. The Alexandrians, accordingly, were fond of expressions which brought out this appropriation and interchange of the attributes of deity and humanity, as *e.g.*, "God was born," "God suffered," "God was crucified for us." The whole tendency of the Antiochian school, as contrasted with this, was

---

spread into India and China. From 498 A.D. they renounced communion with the Greek Church. The remnants of them are found in Kurdistan, Armenia, etc.

[1] "An expression," Harnack says, "taken from a work of Apollinaris, which Cyril considered as Athanasian, because the Apollinarians had fathered it on Athanasius" (iv. p. 176).

[2] Harnack, *ut supra ;* Dorner, iii. pp. 57, 68, 75, etc. The sources are Cyril's work against Nestorius, his dialogue on the Incarnation, his epistle to Acacius, etc.

[3] Cf. Bruce's *Humiliation of Christ*, pp. 71-75.

branded as Nestorian, and vehemently repudiated. Thus the controversy stood at Cyril's death in 444 A.D. Cyril was succeeded in Alexandria by the coarse Dioscurus, whose violence, unscrupulousness, and intimidation of opponents are unrelieved by any redeeming feature. With him, supported by the great body of the Egyptian monks, the doctrine of the "one nature" passed over into an undisguised blending of the divine and human, or absorption of the human by the divine. The Egyptian party had relations with bodies of monks in Syria ; had likewise the support of the monastic communities in Palestine and Constantinople. Above all, it was strong in the support of the imperial court—the feeble Emperor Theodosius being completely ruled by his empress, Eudocia, and the unscrupulous eunuch Chrysaphius,—and no pains were spared to crush the Antiochian leaders, and especially Theodoret.

The actual outbreak of the Eutychian controversy in 448 A.D., is connected, as the name suggests, with Eutyches, an abbot in Constantinople, and strenuous upholder of Alexandrian opinions. At a local synod, presided over by Flavian, the patriarch, who seems to have acted a fair-minded and independent part, Eutyches was accused of denying the distinction of the natures in Christ, and of declaring that Christ's body was of different substance from ours. On his admission that these were his beliefs, he was condemned, deposed, and excommunicated. His condemnation, as was to be expected, created immense commotion, and stirred up Dioscurus and his following to the most active measures. Eutyches complained of injustice, and clamoured for a council, and both he and Flavian sought to gain the support of the influential Leo, Bishop of

Rome. Leo, a man of strong practical judgment, gave his verdict decisively against Eutyches, and, in view of a general council which the emperor had now summoned, wrote to Flavian a long doctrinal epistle—his famous "Tome"—which became later the basis of the decision at Chalcedon. I need not dwell on the proceedings of the Council at Ephesus held in 449 A.D., which, from its unexampled unfairness and violence, earned for itself the name of the "Council of Robbers" (*Latrocinium*), by which it has been ever since known. At this Council, presided over by Dioscurus, Eutyches was cleared, Theodoret deposed, and Flavian so cruelly maltreated that he died a few days later.[1] The decisions of a Council of this kind, obtained by the grossest terrorism, could have no moral weight, and they were immediately repudiated by a synod held at Rome. There was difficulty in getting the matter re-opened, but a revolution at Court, which occurred at this juncture, altered the aspect of affairs,[2] and prepared the way for the summoning of a new Council—that which finally convened at Chalcedon (451 A.D.), and ranks as the *fourth* ecumenical. With this Council— the largest in point of numbers yet held[3]—we reach a distinct landmark in the history of dogma. Its importance arises from the fact that it was the first Council after Nicæa which ventured on the composition of a new Creed. Its initial proceedings, when the charges against Dioscurus were being inquired into, were sufficiently tumultuous. But Dioscurus speedily

---

[1] Harnack strangely constitutes himself the apologist of Dioscurus and his Council, and shows a bias against Flavian which seems unwarranted (iv. pp. 209-10). Cf. Neander's account.

[2] Chrysaphius was banished and Eudocia driven into exile. Pulcheria, the sister of Theodosius, gained the ascendency, and after the death of Theodosius gave her hand to Marcian, who became emperor. He summoned the Council of Chalcedon.

[3] 520 bishops were present.

found himself deserted by all save some thirteen Egyptian bishops. A Creed was ultimately framed on the basis of Leo's letter, and, apart from these dissentients, obtained universal approval. Shouts were raised, " This is the faith of the Fathers. This is the faith of the Apostles. We all agree to this." Dioscurus ended his unworthy career in banishment.

A few words are necessary on this Chalcedonian Creed, which marks the real turning-point in the Christological controversies, and has held its ground through so many centuries as of ecumenical authority. It is a lengthy document, but the essential sentence in it is that now to be quoted. After endorsing the Creeds of Nicæa and Constantinople, and accepting as valid Cyril's letters against Nestorius, and Leo's letter to Flavian, it goes on to define the true doctrine of Christ's Person in the following terms—" One and the same Christ, Son, Lord, only-begotten, confessed in two natures,[1] without confusion, without conversion, without division, without separation " (ἀσυγχύτως, ἀτρέπτως, ἀδιαιρέτως, ἀχωρίστως). The significance of these predicates will be readily perceived. The two former are directed against Eutyches, with his confusion or conversion of the natures ; the two latter against Nestorius, with his division or separation of them. The aim of the Creed, therefore, is to assert the unity of the Person along with the distinctness of the natures. In theological tendency, it will be seen that it has more affinity with the Antiochian than with the Alexandrian mode of thinking, and it indicates correctly enough the

[1] In the Greek text the words stand ἐκ δυο φύσεων, but this, it is generally recognised, is a misreading for ἐν δυο φύσεσι (*in duabus naturis*), the form insisted on by the Council. Baur and Dorner are nearly alone in thinking otherwise.

errors to be avoided. But this, which is its strength, is, from a theological point of view, its weakness. It states the factors for us, but gives us no help to a positive solution of the problem they involve. It puts the predicates alongside of each other, but does nothing to show their compatibility and mutual relationship. If I may say so, the formula resembles the statement of the terms in a proportion sum : it gives the ratios, but does not work out the sum. Perhaps it was better that it should do so ; should stop with the warding off of errors, and should leave the attempts at positive construction to theology. The curious thing is that this Creed, with its unspeculative character—a product of the *Latin* practical genius—should be held to be a creation of *Greek* metaphysics.[1] Metaphysics is the last thing you will find in it. It puts the factors, as I say, side by side, without any attempt at showing the possibility of their combination. There is one remark more that must be made on it. A perfectly true Creed in what it negates, there is yet an element of truth in the Alexandrian or Monophysite view to which it fails to do justice. It is the presence of this truth which is the vitalising element in the controversies that follow, for men felt it even when they could not state it properly, and would not let it be suppressed. There was the ineradicable conviction that, however the union of the divine and human in the Person of Jesus was to be conceived, it was something infinitely richer, more vital and penetrative, than the Chalcedonian formulation took account of. The fundamental error, I take it, in much of this controversy on both sides was the idea that by the union of the divine with the human—the presence and energising of the divine in the human—the human

---

[1] The non-Hellenic character of the creed is dwelt on by Harnack (iv. 222-3).

is *annulled*, or robbed in some degree of its integrity or perfection ;[1] the truth being, as a deeper psychology shows, that it is only as the human takes up the divine into itself, and assimilates it, that it realises the true and complete ideal of humanity.   The Eutychian (or Mono-physite) could only regard this union of human nature with the divine as a mingling, a mixture, a fusion, else as the absorption of the human in the divine,—and against this the Council of Chalcedon rightly protested.   But the Monophysite, on the other hand, felt that the Chalce-donian formula held the natures too coldly, too abstractly apart, too jealously shut out all intercommunion between them.   Hence the long fight which followed.   It is the perception of this element of truth in the Monophysite side which gives to these further conflicts, so dreary in their outward details, a measure of interest and profit.

IV. The *Monophysite*, or " one nature " controversy (μόνη or μία φύσις), to which we now turn, is simply in principle a continuation of the Eutychian.   The name denotes the new forms which that controversy assumed after the decisions of the Council of Chalcedon.   The Chalcedonian Creed, so far from meeting with uni-versal acceptance, proved, partly for the reason above mentioned, the signal for a general revolt of the adherents of the " one nature " doctrine, who defended their views with much earnestness and no incon-siderable ability.   The doctrine promulgated at Chal-cedon they regarded as rank Nestorianism, and would have none of it.   The chief centres of the Monophysite party were Egypt, Palestine, and parts of Syria, and its main strength was among the monks.   In all the regions named, immediately after the Council, tumults broke out, and opposition bishops were set up in

[1] See above, p. 176.

Alexandria, Jerusalem, and Antioch. As time went on the controversy only grew keener, sects were multiplied, and the relations of parties underwent the most curious changes. It is sometimes sought to distinguish the earlier or Eutychian form of Monophysitism from its later forms by saying that Eutyches taught an *absorption* of the human nature in the divine —its deification—while later teachers held rather a *fusion* of the divine and human in Christ—the production of a *composite* nature. This distinction, however, cannot be carried through. Certainly Eutyches did teach the assimilation or transformation of human nature—its merging in the divine—but so did many later Monophysites. On the other hand, the doctrine of a σύγχυσις or κρᾶσις of the divine and human, *i.e.*, of a fusion or mixture, is already condemned by the Council of Chalcedon.[1] The truth is, as hinted above, Monophysitism had its own *rationale*, its own element of truth to protect ; hence its ability to stand out so long against the rival view, and the fact that what Dorner calls its long " dialogue "[2] with the Church was not unfruitful of good. One of the strangest results of the development was that, in the course of the controversy, the parties, like Hamlet and Laertes in the play, came to change weapons ; so that we have Monophysites teaching so strongly the ignorance of Christ's human nature (Agnoetes), that they look like the advocates of an exaggerated Chalcedonianism ; and, on the other hand, we have advocates of the Chalcedonian view so exalting the human nature — attributing to it, *e.g.*, omniscience—that they are Monophysites in all but

---

[1] Those carrying out the idea of a conversion or transformation found an able representative in Julian of Halicarnassus ; the view of a composite nature had advocates in Philoxenus and in Severus of Antioch (about 500 A.D.). Cf. Dorner, iii. 122 ff.

[2] iii. 125.

the name. The hair-splitting that went on in all the parties was extraordinary, as if, says Dorner again, " it had been ordained that Christendom should make experiments in all possible directions " ;[1] and the names alone of the sects that resulted (Aphthartodoce-tists, Phthartolatrists, Actistetes, etc.) are enough to give one a cold shiver.

A situation already so difficult was made much worse by the injudicious interference of the emperors in their efforts to enforce unity. First we have the attempt made (482 A.D.) by the Emperor Zeno, a coarse, debauched man, in conjunction with the patriarch Acacius, to devise a formula of union—that known as the *Henoticon*—which might conciliate the Monophy-sites, or the more moderate section of them, but which in reality pleased neither party, and only aggravated the evils it sought to cure. Later on came the attempt of the Emperor Justinian (544 A.D.) to bring about a reunion of the Monophysite parties with the Church through his famous edict of " The Three Chapters," in which he condemns (1) the person and writings of Theodore ; (2) the writings of Theodoret against Cyril ; and (3) a letter of Ibas of Edessa, likewise reflecting upon Cyril.[2] It need not be said that, though enforced by deposition, these articles, instead of settling the con-troversy, only plunged the Church into worse confusion than ever. I may simply note two other influences which entered the history of Monophysitism in this period, destined considerably to affect it, though in

---

[1] iii. 121.

[2] It sought to steer a middle course, on the one hand condemning Eutychianism and Nestorianism ; on the other, setting aside the creed of Chalcedon, and adhering to Cyril's ἐνώσις φυσική. It further split up the Monophysites in Alexandria, and led to a rupture between Rome and Constantinople, which lasted for thirty-five years (484-519 A.D.).

opposite directions—one, a powerful reinforcement of the *mystical* tendency derived from the writings of the pseudo-Dionysius the Areopagite (fifth century); the other, the introduction into the controversy of the categories and distinctions of the *Aristotelian* philosophy by a learned Monophysite of the beginning of the sixth century, John Philoponus,[1] who found the technology of nature, essence, genus, species, etc., eminently suitable for the kind of disputation in which he was engaged.

Thus for a whole century the controversy went on till, finally, in 553 A.D. a new Council was summoned by Justinian—the so-called *fifth* ecumenical—at Constantinople, to judge upon it. This fifth Council was attended only by 165 bishops, all but five of them Eastern, and its decrees were so far a victory for the Monophysites that they endorsed the anathemas of " The Three Chapters," and so secured at length the end dear to Cyril's heart of the condemnation of the person and writings of Theodore, and, in part, the condemnation of Theodoret. But it saved the authority of the Council of Chalcedon by anathematising those who declared that it countenanced the errors condemned. The *persons* of Theodoret and Ibas were spared on the ground that they had recalled their erroneous doctrine, and had been received by the Council of Chalcedon. The Council failed, however, in reconciling the Monophysites; rather it sealed their final separation from the Church of the Empire.[2]

V. Last of all in this unlovely series came, a full

---

[1] On Philoponus, see Neander, iv. 274. He was accused of Tritheism. A predecessor was Leontius. Cf. Harnack, iv. 232.

[2] Most had already broken off, forming churches, of which representatives still remain in important communities in the East (Copts and Abyssinians, Armenians, the Jacobites in Syria, Mesopotamia, etc.).

century after the fifth council, the *Monothelite* controversy, on the doctrine of the *will* in Christ. This
speculation did not spring up outside, but had its
origin in an attempt of the Emperor Heraclius to win
back the Monophysites to the Church, and in Alexandria did succeed in winning back some of them.[1] The
germ of the new development is perhaps to be sought
in a passage in the Areopagite, in which he speaks of
a θεανδρικὴ ἐνέργεια—a divine-human energy—in Christ.
It is already evident that the doctrine of the natures
could not remain where the decisions of the Council of
Chalcedon had left it. To say that there is unity of
Person and duality of natures leaves a number of vital
questions unresolved. For, apart from the *how* of this
union, it is still left undetermined how much is included
in the Person, and how much in the nature. Does
will, *e.g.*, belong to the Person or the nature? How,
on the one hand, can there be a willing agent without
personality? If we say there are two wills in Christ,
does not this imply that there are two *personal centres*
or *egos*, and are we not thereby driven back upon a
form of Nestorianism? If, on the other hand, we say
there is but one will in Christ, viz., the divine, does not
this seem to rob Christ of true human volition, and
detract from the integrity of His humanity? The
Monothelite started from the unity of the Person, and
his doctrine, just as in the Monophysite controversy,
could take two forms. Either the human will might
be viewed as altogether *merged* in the divine, so that
the latter alone acts ; or the will might be regarded as
composite, *i.e.*, as resulting from a fusion of the human
and the divine. In either case the logical carrying

---

[1] The Emperor, who had recovered the provinces of the East from the
Persians, was naturally anxious to conciliate the Monophysites in Syria
and Armenia.

out of the doctrine view seemed to involve the denial of truly human volition to Christ. Thus, when Jesus says, " Not as I will, but as Thou wilt,"[1] or, " I seek not mine own will,"[2] etc., — language in which He appears to claim a will of His own,—his words were explained as a mere condescension for the purposes of instruction. The Dyothelites, on the other hand, starting from the duality of the natures, and attributing a will to each, seemed to create two will centres in the one consciousness, and apparently destroyed the unity of the personal life. The controversy, it will be seen, involved a real point of difficulty, and was not, as we might be tempted to think it, a simple piece of logomachy.

In the first form which the controversy assumed, however, the dispute was not so much about one *will*, as, in accordance with the phrase above quoted from the Areopagite, about one *energy* in the Person of Christ.[3] If we take the analogy of two streams, issuing from separate fountain-heads, but mingling their waters in their afterflow, we may see that there is conceivable a union or blending of the *energies* or *operations* of Christ's divine and human Person, though these proceed from two sources or wills. It was this idea of the union of energies which the Emperor Heraclius, supported by the patriarchs of Constantinople and Alexandria, now took up, and through it endeavoured to gain over the Monophysites (630 A.D.). But in the logic of the case, the controversy soon moved back on the question of the *one will*. Sergius of Constantinople sought to secure the favour of Honorius, the bishop of Rome, for this doctrine ; and here we come to another of

---

[1] Matt. xxvii. 39.   [2] John v. 30.
[3] θεανδρικὴ ἐνέργεια.

the curious lights cast by the history of the period on the doctrine of Papal Infallibility. Honorius gave his judgment quite unequivocally for the assertion of one sole will in Christ. "We confess," he says expressly, "one will of our Lord Jesus Christ."[1] This second stage of the controversy is marked by the publication of an imperial edict—that known as the *Ecthesis*, or Exposition of the Faith (638 A.D.), which sets aside the term "energy" (ἐνέργεια) as liable to mislead, and advances explicitly to the affirmation of one "will" (θέλημα) in Christ. This, it is evident, was simply carrying back Monophysitism into the region of the will, while granting in words the distinctness of the natures, and it necessarily revived in an acuter form all the old controversies. The decree was endorsed, of course, in Constantinople, but was stoutly resisted and condemned in North Africa and in Italy, where the successors of Honorius refused it their assent. Thus the matter stood till 648 A.D., when a new Emperor, Constans II., substituted for the *Ecthesis* another edict called the *Type*, which went on the futile idea of forbidding discussion altogether, ordaining that neither one will nor two wills should be taught. Severe punishments were decreed against all who should disobey. Pope Martin resisted, and had Monothelitism condemned at Rome in 649 A.D. For this offence he was taken, a few years after, in chains to Constantinople, and finally was banished to the Crimea, where he died literally of hunger. Another leading opponent, the aged Maximus (82 years old) had his tongue cut out, and his right hand cut off (622 A.D.), and died shortly after from the effects of this cruelty.

---

[1] Honorius was condemned and excommunicated for this heresy by the sixth ecumenical Council, and the excommunication was confirmed by the seventh and eighth Councils. Every Pope till the eleventh century was required to pronounce an anathema on Honorius.

A tyranny so barbarous was effectual for a time in crushing out protest ; but only for a time. Under a later Pope, Adeodatus (677 A.D.), the controversy was renewed, and communion broken off with Constantinople. An emperor of a different stamp was now on the throne—Constantine Prognatus—whose sincere desire for peace led him (678 A.D.) to make proposals for a new Council. This, with the concurrence of Agatho, the Roman bishop, was finally convened at Constantinople in 680 A.D., and ranks as the *sixth* ecumenical, or first Trullan (from the chamber in the palace in which the meetings were held). The attendance was not large—never more than 200—but the proceedings were marked by more decorum and impartiality than those of previous councils in these controversies. The doctrinal outcome was a brief formula, based on a letter sent by Agatho to the Emperor, in which the essential clause is the affirmation of " two natural wills, and two natural operations (energies) in Christ, without division, change, separation, or confusion," though it is added that the human will is invariably subject to the divine. The formula was agreed to with only one or two dissentients. It will be seen that it does little more than take over the Chalcedonian determinations about the nature, and apply them specifically to the will ; and it is liable, of course, to the same criticism, that, while it wards off the Monothelite errors, it affords no help to a positive solution of the problem. Perhaps, as before, it is an advantage that it does not complicate its statement with any elements that can be called speculative. But the fact remains that the formula with which it leaves us—two wills and two operations subsisting side by side—cannot be regarded as either perfect or final.

Glancing at the discussion as a whole, I may

observe, first, that there is an ambiguity in the term
"will" which somewhat complicates the understanding
of the question.   When ordinarily we speak of will, we
mean by it strictly the faculty of volition—of self-
determination or choice.   But there is a larger use of
the word not uncommon in the usage of philosophy and
theology, in which it includes the whole of what are
sometimes termed "the active powers," *i.e.*, the instincts,
appetites, desires, affections, with their corresponding
aversions.[1]   All this in the old controversy was covered
by the term "will"; and the question of whether Christ
had a natural will was extended to include the possession by Him of all these natural impulses, desires,
aversions, etc.   It covered, *e.g.*, such a question as
whether Christ was capable of fear, or of the natural
shrinking from suffering and death.   It will be seen
from this how serious was the peril of denying, as the
Monothelites did, that Christ had a distinct human will,
and how the assertion of the one will tended to give
Christ's humanity an entirely docetic character.[2]
Against such a view the Dyothelites rightly protested.
Still this, as manifestly, does not clear away the
difficulty of assuming what we may call two will-
systems in the one personal consciousness, nor explain
how, if the power of self-determining choice is included
under will—is, indeed, of the core and essence of it—
there could be two self-determining centres in the one
personal life.

This brings me back to my former position that
the main source of the difficulty here arises, just as in

[1] Thus, *e.g.*, Dr. Reid divides the powers of the mind into understanding and will, and says—"Under the term will we comprehend our
active powers, and all that lead to action, or influence the mind to act—
such as appetites, passions, affections"—*Intellect. Powers*, I. ch. vii.
[2] Cf. Neander on Maximus, v. 252 (Bohn).

the earlier discussion on the natures, from the mistaken assumptions with which both parties in the controversy started. The human and divine are first arbitrarily separated, and an opposition is set up between them which makes true union afterwards impossible. It is assumed that a human will united with the divine—energised by it—in which God Himself truly wills and acts, becomes by that fact less a truly human will, instead of being, as is really the case, heightened and perfected by this participation in the divine. It is assumed that if the Son of God really took our nature upon Him, and entered into all the conditions of a true human life,—growth, development, volition, included,—His willing, *because* human, could not be also divine ; there must, it is supposed, be alongside of it in the consciousness of Christ *another* will, which has all the attributes of deity—omnipotence, omniscience, and the rest. Thus far there is an element of truth in the protest of Monothelitism. Christ's will, even as man, is a divine-human will—the will of the One Personal Logos who has appropriated humanity with all its laws and conditions, natural desires and aversions not excepted, and so is as truly human as it is divine—*theanthropic.*

We may gain a point of view for the better understanding of this subject if we recall that there is a sense in which there are two wills in every man—what we sometimes speak of as the higher and the lower will : a will which seeks to maintain its union with that law of reason and duty which we confess to be God's presence within us,[1] and a natural will which strives against the former, and even in the Sinless One experienced the shrinkings from pain and death which

[1] Cf. Paul's experience in Rom. vii.

are inseparable from our human state. How erroneous our view of human nature would be, were we to separate these two wills, or modes of will, putting one on the side of a divine nature, and the other on the side of a human nature, as if both did not belong to the truth and unity of our humanity! But this is in effect what the Monothelites did in the case of Christ. It is interesting to observe, however, that as the controversy went on, there came to be glimpses of the higher reconciling view which lays stress on the constitution of the soul as involving a God-like element—a subsistence from the first in and through the Logos—in which lies the potency of that perfect union of the human will with the divine (yet in harmony with the laws of natural sensibility) which is perfectly realised in Christ.[1]

There is, of course, a higher sense in which we may and must speak of *two wills* in Christ—a will of the divine and a will of the human nature—though it is not properly the sense of this controversy, and is only brought into it with danger of confusion. There is the transcendent side of the Person of Christ—His Logos-side, or subsistence in "the form of God"[2] as member of the Sacred Trinity—His pre-existent, eternal side, in which He wills and acts in an unchangeably divine manner under quite different conditions from those in which He wills and acts as man. There is, again, the human or incarnate side of Christ's personality, in which He wills under the conditions and within the limitations of humanity. These are not two wills in the one human consciousness; but rather

[1] These views are chiefly found in Maximus and his disciple Anastasius. Cf. Dorner, iii. 188 ff.
[2] Phil. ii. 6.

two *spheres* or *modes of existence* of the one divine Son, which faith must acknowledge, though it may be unable perfectly to comprehend their relationship.[1]   Even here, however, we shall err if we assume that these two spheres or sides of existence were held during Christ's earthly life rigorously apart — that there were not frequent inburstings, if I may so say, of the powers of the higher life into the lower.   The Gospel narratives, with their examples of supernatural knowledge and consciousness on the part of Christ—of such events as the transfiguration, the walking on the sea, the Resurrection — are proofs to the contrary. This interaction of higher and lower furnishes the key to many of the facts which formed the subjects of dispute in these controversies.

SUPPLEMENTARY

The views given in the foregoing lecture may be supplemented by reference to one or two later Christological developments.

1. There is the question of the *Impersonality* of Christ's human nature.   If the Nestorian view is rejected, it seems to follow that the human nature of Christ never subsisted in a personality of its own : that it was assumed by, and subsisted only in, the Person of the divine Logos or Son.   Still this term "impersonality" (ἀνυποστασία) is unfortunate, as suggesting a possible independent impersonal existence of the

---

[1] It will be seen that I cannot see my way to accept those theories of Kenosis which assume a " depotentiation " of the Logos to the extent of His parting with all His divine attributes, and even with His divine consciousness.   This view appears to me to demand what is inconceivable, that God should cease to be God ; that the Son should resign His functions as Creator and upholder of the world, and be temporarily blotted out of the life of the Trinity.   Cf. Lecture X.

humanity of Christ, which is not in the least intended. The term "en-personality" (ἐνυποστασία) is less objectionable, as bringing out the idea of sub-sistence "in" in the Person of the Logos. The doctrine of *enhypostasia* is found in Leontius of Byzantium (483-543 A.D.), but is most fully de-veloped by John of Damascus (about 750 A.D.).[1] Another favourite doctrine of John's is that of the "circumcession" (περιχώρησις), or interpenetration of the natures,[2] which is really an attempt to do justice to the element of truth in Monophysitism, though in John's hands it passes legitimate bounds, and tends to nullify the human.

2. *The Adoptionist Controversy* (782-799 A.D.). This controversy was of Spanish origin, and prob-ably arose from a desire to make the doctrine of the Trinity more acceptable to the Mohammedans. Its author was one *Felix of Urgellis.* The point in it is that Christ was held to be properly Son of God in respect of His divine nature ; as respects His humanity, He was Son of God only by *adoption.* This view was rejected by his opponents as Nestorian, and was condemned at the Synod of Frankfort in 794 A.D.—the same which condemned image-worship. Alcuin, the great scholar of the court of Charlemagne, had before this (792 A.D.) entered the lists with Felix at a Synod in Aachen, and in a disputation of six days, had succeeded in convincing him of his error. The heresy died out in Spain in the middle of the next century.

---

[1] Cf. Harnack, iv. 232, 264 (E.T.) ; Dorner, iii. 210 ff. (E.T.).
[2] Cf. Dorner, iv. p. 216.

VII

THE DOCTRINE OF ATONEMENT—ANSELM AND ABELARD
TO REFORMATION (ELEVENTH TO SIXTEENTH
CENTURIES)

"As the Lord wills not to destroy in us that which is His own, He still finds something in us which in kindness He can love. For though it is by our own fault that we are sinners, we are still His creatures; though we have brought death upon ourselves, He had created us for life. Thus, mere gratuitous love prompts Him to receive us into favour. . . . Accordingly God the Father, by His love, prevents and anticipates our reconciliation in Christ. Nay, it is because He first loves us that He afterwards reconciles us to Himself."—CALVIN.

"That the work of Christ consisted in what He achieved, that it culminates in His sacrificial death, that it signifies the overcoming and effacing of the guilt of sin, that salvation consists consequently in the forgiveness, the justification and adoption of man, are thoughts which in no church teacher are wholly absent. In some they stand out boldly. In the case of most they find their way into the exposition of the dogma of redemption."—HARNACK.

"It is certainly most remarkable, and most honourable to the Christian sagacity of this ancient Father of the Church (Anselm), that he was able, as a pioneer of doctrine concerning this profoundly difficult subject, to make out an account of it which shocks no moral sentiment, and violates no principle of natural reason, as almost all the doctors and dogmatising Fathers have been doing ever since."—BUSHNELL.

"God can only forgive sin by forgiving nothing to Himself, by Himself bearing what He forgives, and Himself performing what he commands, as Jesus did in His form of servant."—SARTORIUS.

LECTURE VII

The Doctrine of Atonement—Anselm and Abelard to
Reformation (Eleventh to Sixteenth Centuries).

WE come in this lecture to Soteriology in its objective
aspect ; in plainer terms, to the connection of man's
salvation with Christ's doing and suffering, and specially
with His death, regarded as an Atonement for sin.
Christianity being above all things a religion of
redemption, it might be supposed that the doctrine
of atonement would have been one of the first to
which the mind of the Church would be theologically
applied.   The fact, however, was not so ; and, in
accordance with the law of development already stated,
could not well have been.   The doctrine of atonement could not be profitably investigated till attention
had been given to those doctrines which form its presuppositions—the doctrines of God, of human nature,
of sin, of the Person of the Redeemer.   By the time
the controversies on these subjects had run their course
the Church was well advanced into the Middle Ages.
Europe had been merged in barbarism, and in the
confusions that ensued it seemed as if an arrest
were put on further intellectual progress.   But in the
schools of the age of Charlemagne the light of a new
learning was kindling ; and the corruptions of the
Church could not stifle the intellectual impulse which

a century or two later manifested itself in the vigorous life of the universities.

The soteriological epoch in the history of dogma is properly reached in the end of the eleventh century with Anselm of Canterbury,[1] first of the greater schoolmen, as we may name him. This accords with the place the doctrine holds in the logical scheme between Christology and the doctrine of the Application of Redemption, a new proof of the soundness of my general thesis. A glance at any Church history, or history of doctrine, will show that I state the matter correctly. Neander, *e.g.*, begins his section on the doctrine of atonement in the Anselmic period by remarking that "the arriving at a distinct conception of the way in which the salvation of mankind was wrought out by Christ was a matter on which little attention had thus far been bestowed in comparison with the investigations on the other subjects belonging to the system of faith," and adds that "the twelfth century constitutes an epoch in the history of this doctrine."[2] Ritschl similarly commences his history of the doctrine of atonement with Anselm.[3] We may affirm, therefore, that from Anselm to the Reformation is the classical period for the formation of this doctrine as it appears in our creeds, and the fundamental determinations then arrived at, subsequent thought, I believe, has failed to unsettle.

[1] Anselm died in 1109. His *Cur Deus Homo* was finished in 1098.

[2] viii. pp. 200, 201 (Bohn). Before this the subject is hardly touched on in his pages.

[3] Harnack in a left-handed way makes the same acknowledgment. The early Church, he says, had treated this doctrine as "a sacred mystery. . . . It was reserved for the Middle Ages and our modern time to cast off all modesty and reverence here" (iii. p. 306).

In recognising this, we must not, with some, fall into the opposite error of supposing that up to this time the Church had no doctrine of atonement, or at best only some mythical speculations on a ransom paid by Christ to Satan for man's deliverance. On no subject is it more necessary to distinguish between doctrine as held in the immediacy of faith, and the examination and discussion which result in giving that doctrine scientific shape. Anselm in his *Cur Deus Homo* does not profess to be stating new doctrine, but only to be giving, or aiming at giving, rational ground to a doctrine which the whole Church believed, but in regard to which, as he tells us, there had come to be much cavilling and questioning. That, even as regards theological elaboration, Anselm and his successors found much material prepared to their hand in the statements of early writers, will be evident, I think, from the brief sketch of the previous stages in the development of the doctrine to which I now proceed.

I. It would, indeed, have been strange if the *early Church* had shown no traces of a doctrine of atonement, seeing that the Epistles of the New Testament are so full of the subject. But the Church never was without the rudiments of such a doctrine. It may confidently be affirmed that there never was a time when the Church did not know itself redeemed by Christ, and did not attribute a propitiatory efficacy to His death, or regard it as the ground of God's gracious dealings with men in forgiveness and renewal. Exceptions there are ; but generally early Church writers show a lively sense of the reality and manysidedness of Christ's work, and exalt His Cross as the means by which men are saved from sin's curse and Satan's tyranny. All this, I grant, is loosely conceived and imperfectly expressed. There is free use of Scripture language without much real insight into its meaning; and there is necessarily the absence of what, in later times, we would call a developed "theory" of the atonement. At the same time there are seldom wanting in the greater writers profound thoughts, and glimpses into the heart of the matter which surprise us by their clearness; and occasionally we meet with tentative *sketches* of a theory which go far to anticipate future results. I can glance only at outstanding points.

The *Apostolic Fathers* are profuse in their allusions to redemption through the blood of Christ, though it cannot be said that they do much to aid us in the theological apprehension of this language. Thus Clement will have us " look steadfastly to the blood of Christ, and see how precious His blood is in the sight of God "—the blood " shed for our salvation." [1] Barnabas, who abounds in this class of references, declares, " For this cause the Lord was content to suffer for our souls, although He be the Lord of the whole earth "—" If, therefore, the Son of God . . . hath suffered that by His stripes we might live, let us believe that the Son of God could not have suffered but for us . . . He was Himself one day to offer up His body for our own sins." [2] Ignatius exhorts his readers " by the blood of Christ," and as those who " have peace through the flesh and blood and passion of Jesus Christ "—" who died for us, that so believing in His death, ye might escape death "—" who suffered all these things for us, that we might be saved." [3] Polycarp strikes a strong and clear evangelic note,

---

[1] *Ep.* 7.   [2] *Ep.* 5, 7, etc.
[3] *Eph.* 1 ; *Trall,* 1 ; *Smyrna,* 2, etc.

"Our Lord Jesus Christ, who suffered Himself to be brought even to the death for our sins"—"who His own self bare our sins in His own body on the tree." [1] The *Epistle to Diognetus*, most strikingly and beautifully of all: "He Himself took on Him the burden of our iniquities, He gave His own Son to be a ransom for us, the Holy One for transgressors, the Blameless One for the wicked, the Righteous One for the unrighteous, the Incorruptible One for the corruptible, the Immortal One for them that are mortal. For what other thing was capable of covering our sin than His righteousness? By what other one was it possible that we, the wicked and ungodly, could be justified than by the only Son of God? O sweet exchange! O unsearchable operation! O benefits surpassing all expectation! that the wickedness of many should be hid in a single Righteous One, and that the righteousness of One should justify many transgressors." [2]

The case is not different with the *Old Catholic Fathers*, who never question the redeeming virtue of the death of Christ, while their modes of explanation of its efficacy vary.[3] Irenæus, the earliest of these Fathers, furnishes us, in the doctrine of the *recapitulatio*, formerly adverted to,[4] with a singularly interesting point of view from which to regard the atonement. Under this idea he brings the thought that Christ recapitulates in Himself all the stages of human life, and all the experiences of these stages, including those which belong to our state as sinners.[5] He applies the idea

---

[1] *Phil.* 1, 8.

[2] *Ep.* 9. Even Hermas, the least evangelical of this group, knows that the Lord has "purged our sins" through His toils and pains (*Sim.* v. 6).

[3] Dorner observes, "Nevertheless one thing may be said: the idea of substitution is common to all the Fathers" (*Syst. of Doct.* iv. p. 8, E.T.).

[4] Cf. Lect. II. p. 70.   [5] Iren. ii. 22, 4; iii. 7.

first to a redeeming *obedience* of Christ on our behalf—our
redeeming Head passing through the whole curriculum
of our experience, and in every part of it rendering a
perfect obedience to God.   Thus He retracted the disobedience of the fall,[1] our salvation being achieved, as
Dorner expresses it, by a recapitulation of the history of
mankind *per oppositum.*[2]   It is only the other side of
this thought when he applies it next to a complete
victory over Satan on our behalf.   Satan held men in
bondage ; it was necessary that man's Redeemer should
enter into conflict with the adversary, and under the
full stress of his temptations, should carry off a glorious
victory.[3]   But this Father applies his idea also in certain
passages to a substitutionary satisfaction to justice.   There
is a passage in which Baur thinks he sees the germ of
the theory of a ransom paid to Satan ;[4] but I do not
think it can fairly bear that interpretation.   It can the
less do so that Irenæus in the context quite explicitly
speaks of Satan's dominion over man as one unjustly
obtained.   His idea seems rather to be that there is a
righteousness in the ordinance of God by which man,
through his apostacy, has become subject to Satan, to
corruption, and to death ; and that this righteous condition of things requires that the Redeemer should
submit to death for us.   " The mighty Word and very
Man," he says, " redeeming us by His own blood in
a manner consonant to reason, gave Himself for a
redemption for those who had been led into captivity.
. . . The Lord has thus redeemed us through His own
blood, giving His soul for our souls, His flesh for our
flesh, and has also poured out the Spirit of the Father

---

[1] iii. 18, 6 ; 21, 10 ; v. 21, etc.   [2] *Per. of Christ,* i. p. 319 (E.T.).
[3] iii. 21 ; v. 1, etc.
[4] In v. i. 1, he speaks of the Word of God redeeming us from the
apostacy.

for the union and communion of God and man." [1]   In
the fullest way He teaches that Christ by His passion has
reconciled us to God, and procured for us the forgiveness of our sins.[2]   We are debtors, he tells us, to none
but God, and Christ by His cross has obliterated that
debt.[3]   Origen in like fashion, to take only one other
instance among these Fathers, speaks freely of Christ's
death as a sacrifice by which He redeems us from our
sins.   There are rhetorical passages in which he connects this with the idea hinted at above, viz., that
Satan through our fall obtained certain rights over us
which Christ annuls by giving Himself as a sacrifice in
our stead.   He even speaks in one place of Satan being
deceived in this transaction, thinking he could hold the
sinless soul of Christ, but finding, when he got it, that
it was a torture to him.[4]   Too much, however, may
be made of these casual utterances, for undoubtedly
Origen's prevailing view is that the sacrifice was offered
to God.[5]

In the *Nicene* period a distinct landmark in the
history of this doctrine is reached in Athanasius, who,
in his remarkable tractate on *The Incarnation of the
Word*, written before the Arian controversy broke out,
almost anticipates Anselm in his answer to the question
why God became man.   The special merit of Athanasius is that he brings the incarnation into direct

[1] v. I.   [2] iii. 16, 9.
[3] v. 16, 3 ; 17, 3 etc.   [4] On Matt. xvi. 8.
[5] Harnack declares that Origen " propounded views as to the value of
salvation, and as to the significance of Christ's death on the cross, with a
variety and detail rivalled by no theologian before him."   He mentions as
chief points that he regarded Christ's death (1) as a victory over the
demons ; (2) as an expiation offered to God—all sins requiring expiation,
and innocent blood having greater or less value according to the value of
him who sheds it ; (3) as a vicarious sacrifice ; (4) as a ransom paid to
the devil (ii. p. 367).   Plainly in a logical mind like Origen's the last
position could not be seriously held with some of the others.

relation with redemption. To explain the reason of the incarnation, he goes back to the original constitution of man, and to his fall. Had man stood in his integrity, he would, he thinks, have overcome the natural tendency of his body to corruption, and been confirmed in holiness. Death, on the other hand, is attached to disobedience as its penalty. The race by sin has come under this condemnation, and can do nothing to relieve itself from death and corruption. Repentance alone would not suffice, for God, having ordained death as the penalty of sin, must abide true to Himself in inflicting the penalty if atonement is not made. " It is monstrous," he says, " that God, having spoken, should lie—so that, when He had imposed the law that man, if he transgressed the commandment, should die, after the transgression man should not die, but His word be broken. For God would not be true, if, having said he should die, man did not die." [1]   Still, he argues, it is not fitting that God should allow His creation to perish ; so the Logos, the very Creator of the world, in whose rational image man was made, took our nature upon Him that He might redeem us. This He did, as respects the penalty of sin, by enduring it in our stead ; positively, He brings into the race anew the principle of incorruption. Taking our body, he says, " He surrendered it to death instead of all, and offered it to the Father . . . in order that by all dying in Him the law with respect to the corruption of mankind might be abolished. . . . The Logos of God, being above all, by offering His own temple and bodily instrument as a substitute for the life of all (ἀντίψυχον), satisfied all that was required by His death." [2]   Similar views are often expressed in his discourses against the Arians. *E.g.,* " Formerly the world, as guilty, lay under

[1] *On Incarnation,* 6, 8, 9, etc.   [2] *Ibid.* 8, 9.

the condemnation of the law, but now the word of God has taken on Himself the judgment, and having suffered in the body for all, has bestowed salvation on all." [1]

It will be seen from these instances how little ground there is for the assertion that the only, or prevailing theory, of the atonement in the early Church was the mythological one of a ransom paid to Satan. That theory is indeed found, and had a place with others in post-Nicene times and in the Middle Ages. The germ of it, we have seen, is met with in Origen ; and Gregory of Nyssa, in the fourth century, gives it explicit statement. The devil is supposed by man's sin to have acquired certain rights over him, which God in equity cannot set aside. He will not conquer even Satan by violence, but in justice, and gives His only-begotten Son for the ransom of the world. Only, Satan is deceived in the transaction, for, accepting Christ in lieu of the world of sinners, he finds he cannot hold Him.[2] Even this grotesque view, as Dorner points out, is a distorted witness to the fact that atonement has a respect to justice. Always, however, there were those who would have nothing to do with this mythical theory, and even where it is found, it is generally alongside of other representations, which show that it is more or less a rhetorical conception. If Gregory of Nyssa has it—and it is chiefly through his influence it found its way into Mediæval theology [3] —his friend and namesake Gregory of Nazianzus as decisively rejects it. " To whom," he asks, " was that

---

[1] *Orat.* i. 60.   [2] Gregory, *On the Great Catechism*, 22-26.

[3] Gregory, however, has many profound thoughts, emphasising, *e.g.*, the idea that in Christ God united Himself with the whole of humanity, so that in this One all died, and His resurrection and exaltation is the resurrection and exaltation of all. He lays stress also on the element of obedience in Christ's sacrifice.

blood offered that was shed for us, and why was it
shed? I mean the precious and lordly blood of our
God and High Priest and Sacrifice. We were retained
under bondage of the evil one, sold under sin, and
receiving pleasure in exchange for wickedness. Now,
since a ransom belongs only to him who holds us in
bondage, I ask, to whom was this offered, and for what
cause? If to the evil one, shame on the outrage! Then
the robber receives a ransom, not only from God, but
which consists of God Himself, and has such an
illustrious payment for his tyranny, a payment for
whose sake it would have been right to have left us
alone altogether." [1]

It is naturally, however, in the Western Church,
where a more juristic habit of mind prevailed, that we
are specially to look for the development of the idea of
Christ's death as a satisfaction to justice. The cases
just cited show that this idea is by no means confined
to the West;[2] but it is in Western writers, as Hilary,
Ambrose, Augustine, that it is more frequently met
with,[3] though here also generally in combination with
other points of view. It is at the same time important
to notice that Augustine and the others never lose
sight of the fact that it is God's love which is the *cause*
of the reconciliation. It is not in their view an angry,
vengeful God whose wrath is appeased by the sacrifice
of His Son—though this is a representation often given
of their doctrine. " For it was not," says Augustine,
" from the time that we were reconciled unto Him by

[1] *Orat.* xlv. 22.
[2] Gieseler, *e.g.*, finds the basis of the satisfaction theory in Athanasius,
Cyril of Jerusalem, Greg. Naz. (?), Cyril, and Chrysostom (*Dogmengesch.*
p. 383).
[3] Cf. Harnack, iii. p. 312 (E.T.); Ritschl, *Justif. and Recon.* i. pp.
197, 198 (E.T.).

the blood of His Son that He began to love us ; but
He did so before the foundation of the world. . . . .
Let not the fact, then, of our having been reconciled to
God through the death of His Son be so listened to
or understood as if the Son reconciled us unto Him in
this respect that He now began to love those whom
He formerly hated, as enemy is reconciled to enemy, so
that therefore they became friends, and mutual love
takes the place of their mutual hatred, but we were
reconciled unto Him who already loved us, but with
whom we were at enmity because of our sins." [1]

Yet another witness, if such were needed, that
Christ's death was universally regarded in the early
Church as a propitiatory sacrifice—the ground of the
forgiveness of sins, and of all saving blessing—is to be
found in that observance which is the greatest historical
perversion of the doctrine of the cross, viz., the
sacrifice of the mass. The change from the original,
simple conception of the eucharist as a spiritual
sacrifice of prayer and thanksgiving, to the conception
of it as a " sin-offering," in which the priest, as sacrificer,
offers for the people's sins, is already well accomplished
by the time of Cyprian, in the middle of the third
century. But, however strenuously we may reject this
conception, it will not at least be doubted that the idea
which underlay it—which, indeed, made it possible—
was that of Christ's death as a propitiatory sacrifice for
sin. The early liturgies make this clear beyond dispute.
" The Lord Himself," says the Liturgy of Mark,
" delivered Himself up for our sins, and died in the

[1] On John xvii. 21-29 (*Tractates on John*, cx. 6). Calvin endorses
the passage, *Instit.* ii. 16. 3, 4. Such passages refute the statement of
Harnack (iii. p. 313) that the Latin view of the work of Christ was that
of " the propitiation of an angry God "—therefore betrayed " a low state
of moral and legal views " (p. 311).

flesh for all." The Liturgy of James speaks of the offering to God of " this dread and bloodless sacrifice." Many similar testimonies might be quoted.

II. There can be no reasonable question, therefore, as to the general faith of the Church in the truly atoning virtue of the death of Jesus Christ ; but as yet there had been no systematic attempt to bring the various aspects of Christ's saving work into unity, or to give them the necessary theological grounding. This was the task undertaken by Anselm, and it is the fact of his undertaking it, and accomplishing it with so striking a measure of success, which gives him his epoch-making importance. From the opening portion of his *Cur Deus Homo*, it is evident that the subject of the nature and necessity of redemption was in that age occupying many minds ; and, moreover, that it was from the Christological side—the side of the reason or necessity of the Incarnation—that it was commonly approached. The doctrine of the Person of Christ being settled, men had time to reflect on its soteriological bearings ; and the thing which above all staggered them—which was principally urged as an objection—was that so amazing a condescension as is implied in the Son of God taking upon Him the nature of the creature, and stooping to such shame and humiliation in His sufferings and death, should be necessary for the forgiveness of sins, and, generally, for man's salvation. That it *was* necessary was the assumption on both sides—but why? Could not God, in the exercise of His omnipotence, have redeemed us as easily as He had created the world? Could He not forgive sins out of His pure mercy without this infinite expenditure of means? Or, if mediation was necessary, why, should not an angel, or some inferior, yet glorious

Being, be chosen as Mediator instead of the only-begotten Son?[1]

It cannot be denied that these are questions which naturally arise, and press themselves upon the thoughtful mind, in connection with this great subject. For, once the reality of the incarnation is acknowledged, it is impossible not to concede that there must be some stupendous exigency or occasion calling for it; and once it is allowed, again, that the incarnation and the sufferings and death that followed from it are connected with the forgiveness of sins, it can scarcely be questioned that this connection has its ground in deep principles of the divine character and government; that there are reasons which make *imperative* this amazing interposition. This method of salvation, with its awful entail of suffering and shame on the Son of God, can be no mere *preferential* scheme of the divine wisdom—one which God has *chosen* to adopt while others less costly and painful were open to Him. Still less is it conceivable that it has been chosen, though sins could have been remitted, and the sinner restored, by an act of pure grace. Wherein then lies the necessity? Anselm's significance results from the fact that he was the first who, with a complete view of the problem, raised this question in its whole compass, and sought to give it a reasoned answer.

The general nature of Anselm's answer will be most easily shown by a brief review of the main points of his argument. Anselm rightly saw, at the outset, that if there existed a necessity for the incarnation, and for such sufferings as those to which the Son of God submitted, that man's salvation should be secured, this necessity must lie, where Scripture already places it, in

[1] *Cur Deus Homo*, i. 1, 3, 5, 6.

the nature of sin as wrong done to God, and in the
principles of the divine character which unchangeably
regulate God in His treatment of sin. What then were
these principles?   This was an inquiry which had
never hitherto been formally instituted.   Augustine
had probed deeply the evil of sin—had given the
Church a profound sense of its gravity—had shown
how it involved the individual and the race in condemnation ; but he had not investigated this other side
—what there is in the character of God which requires
Him to react against sin in the form of punishment,
and under what conditions the forgiveness of sin is
possible.   He had not, in short, investigated the
subject on its Godward side, or in its bearings on the
character and necessity of Christ's work.   Here Anselm
takes his step forward.   His book is in the form of a
dialogue, in which, by question and answer, he gradually
brings his interlocutor round to the acknowledgment of
his position.   He first disposes of the ransom to Satan
theory ;[1] which, condemned likewise by Abelard, has
thereafter but slight influence on the history of this
doctrine.

The way thus cleared, Anselm goes straight to the
idea of sin as that which robs God of His due honour,
and from this conception proceeds to develop his
own theory.   Obedience he regards as a debt which
man owes to God.   The nature of the obligation is
thus forcibly expressed—" The whole will of a rational
creature ought to be subject to the will of God."[2]
Paying this debt none sins ; who withholds this, does
sin.   Whoever renders not to God this due honour
takes from Him that which is His, and does Him dishonour.   And this is sin.   This first step leads logically
to a second.   Even were the creature able to pay back

[1] i. 7.   [2] i. 11.

to God (which he is not) that which he has taken away,
this would not satisfy for the wrong already done.
Besides the paying back, and rendering thereafter of
the due obedience, there would still be required satisfaction for the dishonour done by *dis*obedience.   Here
it is obvious that Anselm moves in faulty categories—
categories borrowed from the sphere of private rights—
and this hampers his treatment throughout.   But it
should also be recognised that the fault lies more in
the form than in the essence of his argument.   Anselm
certainly does not mean that God's relation to the
sinner is wholly analogous to that of a civil suitor
pursuing the person who has injured him for damages.
The further conduct of his argument is directed to
show that God's action is regulated, not by injured self-
love, but by the highest moral necessity.   Anselm is
absolutely right in his starting-point, that the whole
will of a rational creature ought to be subject to God.
Anything less than this, or contrary to this, is sin.   He
is right, too, in holding that there is more in sin than
the intrinsic wrong of the action ; that in addition the
creature is guilty *towards God* in the fact that he
violates his duty towards *Him*.   Anselm speaks of the
" honour " of God.   We speak rather of the supreme
obligation to "glorify " God, and of sin as the with-
holding from God of the " glory " due to Him — in
Pauline phrase, "glorifying Him not as God " [1]—but
the meaning is the same.

The question now arises whether it is possible for
God to forgive sin by an act of mercy alone — no
satisfaction being made to His injured honour.   It is
God's command, as the objector points out, that man
should forgive freely.   Why may not God forgive
freely also ?   Would it not be a higher thing for God

[1] Rom. i. 21.

freely to forgive an injury done to Himself than to require satisfaction for it? Anselm answers "No"; and precisely for the reason that God is not a private person, but is *God.* God's will is not His own in the sense that anything is permissible to Him, or becomes right or proper simply because He wills it. "It does not follow," he says, "that if God would lie, it would be right to lie, but rather that he were not God."[1] God therefore cannot will at pleasure that which is inconsistent with His honour, or treat violations of His honour as if they were not. As the Supreme One, whose judgments are ever according to truth, God cannot call sin aught but what it is, or deal with it otherwise than according to its actual desert. If it is not punished, or adequate satisfaction made for it, it is unjustly forgiven. He argues that this view is confirmed if we take a just estimate of the guilt involved in not rendering to God His due honour. Rightly considered, he says, there is nothing in the universe more intolerable than that the creature should take away from God His glory.[2] As he puts the matter later, were the alternative that we disobey God, or that the whole world should perish, and go to nothingness— nay, were worlds multiplied to infinity, and the same choice presented—our duty would still be to obey God in however slight a command He laid upon us.[3] Such, he says, is the exceeding gravity of sin. Hence also the necessity—the *rationale*—of its punishment. Either man of his own free-will yields due submission to God, or God subjects the transgressor unwillingly by punishment, and so declares Himself Lord; in other words, vindicates His honour upon him. "Therefore," he says, "should any man or bad angel be unwilling to be subject to the divine will and rule, yet he cannot

[1] i. 12.   [2] i. 13.   [3] i. 21.

escape from it ; for, trying to flee from under the will that commands, he rushes under the will that punishes." [1]

This being so, the question recurs with redoubled force—Who then can be saved ? If sin can be forgiven only on condition that a proportionate satisfaction is made for it, while in enormity its guilt is practically infinite, how is such satisfaction possible ? Man, as Anselm brings out, clearly cannot make this satisfaction from his own resources ; for all he could bring he already owes to God, and he has not the ability to bring what God requires. Neither repentance nor future obedience can suffice to obliterate the past.[2] From this point Anselm goes on to develop the conditions under which a true satisfaction is possible, and to show in what way these conditions are fulfilled in Jesus Christ. Briefly, the satisfaction must be such as will outweigh all the guilt of mankind, which yet is of a degree that it could not be compensated for by the whole created universe. It is such a satisfaction, therefore, as can be offered only by God. Yet it must be offered in human nature, else it would not be man that made amends : it would not be a satisfaction for man. Hence the necessity for the Redeemer being God *and* man—for the incarnation.[3] The deity of Christ gives infinite value to all He does ; His humanity is the medium in which the satisfaction is rendered. But what is the nature of this satisfaction ? Obedience is necessary, for it was needful that, as by the disobedience of man death had come upon the human race, so by the obedience of man should life be given back.[4] But obedience even in the case of Christ is not enough, for in this He does not go beyond what His

---

[1] i. 15.　　　　[2] i. 20, 23, 24.　　　　[3] ii. 6, 7.
[4] i. 3. There is here a glimpse of the representative idea.

duty as man requires of Him.[1]   Christ, as man, is
under obligation to obey the whole law of God ; but
Christ, as sinless, was not under obligation to suffer and
die.   God could not justly have laid this as a necessity
upon Him.[2]   It was His own voluntary act to encounter suffering and death in the faithful discharge of
His duty to His Father, and for righteousness' sake.[3]
But by this voluntary surrender of Himself to death in
fidelity to His Father's will, He rendered God a glory
which can only be measured by the magnitude of the
sacrifice it entailed.   For it were more meet that the
whole creation should perish than that anyone should
take the life of the Son of God.[4]   Yet this infinitely
precious life Christ sacrificed to His Father's honour.[5]
Here then is a deed done in human nature by One
who did not owe it which brings infinite glory to God ;
the merit of which more than counterbalances all the
demerit of man's sin ; which may, therefore, be accepted
by the Father as a satisfaction for the sin of the world
and a ground for the forgiveness of that sin.[6]

Such, in outline, is Anselm's theory, and, apart from
the over-scholastic form in which it is cast, it is easy
to perceive its chief merits and defects.   Its strength
lies above all in the basis it lays for a *need* of satisfaction for sin in the immutable character of God, which
renders it impossible that He should permit the violations of His honour to go unpunished.   On this basis
Anselm rears his demonstration that for the rendering
of this satisfaction a divine as well as human Redeemer
is necessary.   It is strong, further, in the *ethical* view
it takes throughout of Christ's sufferings—laying the
stress, not, as many theories do, on the *quantum* of the

---

[1] i. 9 ; ii. 11.   [2] ii. 10, 11.   [3] i. 4.   [4] ii. 14
      [5] ii. 18.   [6] ii. 19.

sufferings, but on their character as sufferings voluntarily endured for righteousness' sake, in fidelity to the Father.[1]   On the other hand it will be noticed that, in one important respect, the theory differs from earlier and later satisfaction theories (from that of Athanasius, for example), in that it has no place for the idea of endurance of the *penalty* of sin.   In other words, while starting with so strong an assertion of the punitive will of God, it yet at no point brings the satisfaction of Christ into direct relation with this punitive will. Christ's satisfaction consists purely in His sufferings unto death conceived as a meritorious tribute voluntarily offered by Him to the honour of the Father.   He gave up His life because this was required of Him as a witness to righteousness for His Father's sake. Obedience throughout life was required of Him as a duty.   His death was, in Catholic phrase, a work of supererogation—something which could not justly have been demanded of Him—the merit of which, therefore, could be applied to compensate for the demerits of others.   The scheme, in short, is drawn up, in form at least, on the assumptions of the Catholic doctrine of merits, and shares the defects of the latter.   It is clearly inadmissible to conceive of the atonement as a simple balancing of merits and demerits, with the effect of a cancelling of the one through the overplus of the other.   With this is connected another fault of the theory, arising in part from the too strong insistence on the idea of debt, viz., that its treatment of salvation is almost entirely objective.   The sinner's debt is paid by One who stands outside of him, and prominence is not given to the *nexus* of faith — that spiritual identification of sinner and Saviour — which alone

---

[1] This is the feature of it which attracted Bushnell, in the preface to his *Vicarious Sacrifice*.

makes the sinner a real partaker in that which Christ
has done for him.   Anselm, in speaking of that which
makes the sinner participant in Christ's merit, hardly
ever gets beyond the relation of *discipleship*—the mere
following of Christ's example.[1]   Yet it would not be
just to make too much of this ; for Anselm, too, knew
well what it was to trust the Saviour, nay, to trust
Him with a whole-hearted reliance on His death for
salvation.   The words in the direction for the visita-
tion of the sick usually attributed to him [2] have often
been quoted : " Dost thou believe that thou canst not
be saved but by the death of Christ ?   Go to, then,
and while thy soul abideth in thee, put all thy confidence in this death alone—place thy trust in no other
thing—connect thyself wholly with this death—cast
thyself wholly on this death—wrap thyself wholly in
this death.   And if God would judge thee, say, ' Lord !
I place the death of our Lord Jesus Christ between me
and Thy judgment, otherwise I will not contend, or
enter into judgment, with thee.'   And if He shall say
unto thee that thou art a sinner, say unto Him, ' I place
the death of our Lord Jesus Christ between me and my
sins.'   If He shall say unto thee that thou hast deserved
damnation, say, ' Lord ! I put the death of our Lord
Jesus Christ between Thee and all my sins, I offer His
merits for my own, which I should have but have not.'
If He say He is angry with thee, say, ' Lord ! I place
the death of our Lord Jesus Christ between me and
Thy anger.' "   Here is all the nexus God requires
between Christ's death and any soul of man !

It is remarkable that Anselm's speculations seem to
have produced little, if any, immediate effect.[3]   At least

---

[1] ii. 19.   [2] The authorship is, however, doubted.
[3] " He stands alone," Baur says, " and does not seem to have con-

their influence is not traceable on Abelard and Bernard, who come directly after.[1] If Abelard is really independent of Anselm, the fact is only another proof of how men's minds at this period were naturally converging on this problem. The significance of Abelard is that he represents the opposite pole of soteriological doctrine from Anselm. A brilliant dialectician, but, as events showed, sadly lacking in moral depth and stability, his view of atonement is defective precisely on the side on which Anselm's was strong. With Anselm he rejects the theory of satisfaction to Satan, but, together with this, rejects every form of the satisfaction doctrine. "How cruel and unjust it seems," he says, "that any one should require the blood of the innocent as a price, or in any way think it right that the innocent should be put to death. Much less has God accepted the death of His Son as the price of His reconciliation to the whole world."[2] Of course, the teachers who thought differently could and did reply with Augustine that they did not regard the atonement as the cause, but as the fruit and expression of God's love.[3] Abelard, however, places the effect of Christ's sufferings and death wholly in their moral results. The amazing love of God in giving up His Son to suffering and death for us enkindles in us a responsive love which is ready for any sacrifice, and this becomes the ground of the forgiveness of our sins. "Redemption," he declares, "is that greatest love enkindled in us by Christ's passion, a love which not only delivers us from the bondage of sin, but also acquires for us the true freedom of children,

---

vinced any of his successors of the necessity of the standpoint which he assumed."—*Versöhnungslehre*, sect. 189.

[1] Abelard (1079-1142); Bernard (1091-1153).

[2] On Rom. iii. 22-26.

[3] Thus Bernard, the Lombard, Aquinas. On Bernard, cf. Neander, viii. p. 211 (Bohn).

where love instead of fear becomes the ruling affection." [1]
The design of God, therefore, in the Son's incarnation
and passion is to produce this responsive love in us.[2]
Abelard does, indeed, occasionally cross this representation with thoughts more in accordance with the ordinary
Church doctrine, as where in one place he says that
what is wanting in our merits Christ supplies from His
own ; and even, on Gal. iii. 13, speaks of the propitiation
of divine justice by Christ, who on the Cross became a
curse for us.[3]   But these expressions must either be
treated as inconsequences—accommodations to current
views—or be interpreted in harmony with the general
strain of his teaching.[4]   In Abelard, then, we have the
typical representative of what is called the *moral* view
of the atonement, as in Anselm we have the representative of the *satisfaction* theory.   To one or other
of these generic forms all theories of atonement may
be in principle reduced.   But the fact to which attention has to be drawn is, that Abelard's doctrine was at
once resisted by his great opponent Bernard, as alike
in itself inadequate, and out of harmony with what had
been always the faith of the Church.   In reducing
Christ's sufferings and death to an example of love,
Bernard holds that Abelard robs them of that profoundly redemptive significance with which the Church,
following Scripture, had always invested them.   Bernard
has not Anselm's speculative ability.   He frames no
theory of his own ; defends, indeed, in a modified way
the old idea of a redemption from Satan, whose dominion

---

[1] On Rom. iii. 22-26.

[2] This, of course, is in itself a thoroughly true thought.   The question
is as to its adequacy as a theory of atonement.

[3] Cf. Ritschl, *Justif. and Reconcil.* i. pp. 37-38 (E.T.) ; Dorner,
Syst. of Doct. iv. p. 19 (E.T.).

[4] Harnack also makes it a complaint against Abelard that he does not
teach that Christ bore the *penalty* of sin, though it is not easy to understand his own meaning in this connection (vi. p. 80).

over us, if unjustly acquired, is justly permitted, and beyond that treats the atonement as an unfathomable mystery of God's wisdom and grace. "Why," he says, "did He accomplish that by His blood which He might have accomplished by a word? Ask Himself. It is vouchsafed to me to know the *fact*, not the wherefore."[1] He points out, as all these teachers do, that it is not the mere shedding of the blood of Christ, but the *will* of Him who offered it, that was acceptable to God. But the special contribution of Bernard—one which marks a real advance in the history of this doctrine, though the germ is much older—is the idea of the organic relation of Christ and His people as explaining how the satisfaction of one should avail for the many. The atonement is not a case of bare external substitution— a view which always creates offence—but the vicarious suffering of the Head for the members. His own memorable words are, "The Head satisfied for the members, Christ for His own bowels" (*satisfecit caput pro membris, Christus pro visceribus suis*).[2] On 2 Cor. v. 14 he explains himself thus, "Clearly the satisfaction of one is imputed, as if that one bore the sins of all, nor is there any longer found one who sinned, and one who satisfied, because the one Christ is Head and body."[3] This undeniably supplies an element lacking in Anselm.

I pass by other schoolmen to come at once to the greatest of all, Thomas Aquinas,[4] with whom the development of the doctrine in this age may be said to culminate.[5] What one remarks chiefly in Aquinas is

---

[1] Cf. Neander, viii. p. 210 (Bohn).

[2] *Tractate against Abelard*, vi. 15.

[3] Cf. Ritschl, i. p. 54 (E.T.); Hagenbach, *Hist. of Doct.* ii. p. 284 (E.T.). [4] 1227-1274.

[5] The chief link in the transition to Aquinas is Peter the Lombard in his *Sentences*. Peter makes deliverance from the devil depend on deliver-

the *comprehensiveness* of his survey — his desire to embrace in his view all sides and all elements in the atonement which inquiry had brought to light.[1] His theory, from this eclectic tendency, has not the close logical cohesion of that of Anselm ; in some respects it falls behind it, while in others it shows an advance. Aquinas falls distinctly behind Anselm in his failure to ground the atonement in a necessity of the divine nature. In harmony with the prevalent scholastic tendency to exalt the *will* of God, he held not only that it was possible that another way of salvation might have been found — a view in which he but followed Augustine, Bernard, the Lombard, and others [2] — but that in His sovereignty God might have dispensed with satisfaction altogether. This concession, as Anselm had already demonstrated, weakens the whole foundation of the doctrine of satisfaction, and introduces an element of arbitrariness which readily passes over into the *acceptilation* theory of Duns Scotus,[3] the theory, viz., that the atonement has only the value which God's will chooses to put upon it.[4] On the other hand, Aquinas advances beyond Anselm in his adoption of Bernard's principle of Christ satisfying as the Head of the Church,—" As a natural body," he says, " is a unity, so is the Church, the mystical body of Christ, reckoned along with Christ her Head as one person," [5]—and also

---

ance from sin ; repudiates the position that Christ appeased the wrath of the Father, who was thereby induced to love ; teaches that Christ bore the *penalty* of our sins, and leaves it open to affirm that another mode of redemption was *possible* to God, though this was the best. Cf. Ritschl, i. p. 42.　　　　　　　　　[1] Cf. his *Summa*, iii. Quests. 46-49.

[2] Cf. Neander, viii. p. 210 (Bohn) ; Ritschl, i. p. 43 ; Harnack, vi. p. 191.

[3] Died in 1308.　　　　　　　[4] Cf. Ritschl, i. pp. 68-69.

[5] Cf. Ritschl, i. pp. 54, 56 ; Hagenbach, ii. p. 287. In strictness this would yield the view of a limited atonement. We guard against this by recognising that Christ is not only the Head of the Church, but in a true sense also the Head of humanity—the new Head of the race.

in apparently recognising that Christ's satisfaction embraced as one of its aspects the endurance of the penal consequences of transgression. " Christ," he holds, " must take upon Himself that punishment which is the termination of all others, and which virtually contains all others in itself—that is, death." [1]   This thought of penal endurance, indeed, is not, as we have seen, a new one.   It is as old, in fact, as the doctrine of Atonement itself ; is found in Athanasius, in Augustine,[2] in many others ; and though it had no place in the theory of Anselm, which went on the other line of a meritorious endurance of undeserved sufferings, it underwent a considerable revival after Anselm's day—is found, *e.g.*, in the Lombard, and in Pope Innocent III.,[3] from whom it probably passed to Aquinas.   In all these writers, however, it still holds a loose and insecure place—is not grounded, as Anselm's theory had been, in clearly-defined principles.   Aquinas, like the others, does full justice to Christ's love and will of obedience, not less than to the dignity of His Person, as that which gave value to His sacrifice ; and is as emphatic as his predecessors in declaring that it was not the atonement of Christ which was the cause of God's love to men, but the amazing love of God which is displayed in providing the atonement.[4]

III. The scholastic period did much for the advancement of the doctrine of atonement, but it is in connection with the great religious upheaval of the *Reformation* that we find the doctrine assuming the more complete form in which it entered the great Protestant creeds.   The Reformation was not, indeed, im-

---

[1] Cf. Neander, viii. pp. 213-214 ; Ritschl, i. pp. 4, 49, 197.
[2] Cf. Ritschl, i. p. 197.   [3] Cf. Neander, viii. p. 213.
[4] Cf. Ritschl, i. pp. 43, 44, 45.   On Anselm's proof of the consistency see *Cur Deus Homo*, ii. 5.

mediately concerned with the doctrine of atonement. The absorbing question which occupied men's minds in that crisis was rather the question of the sinner's justification before God.[1]   What men sought above all was the grounding of the certainty of their peace with God through His free and gracious pardon of their sins, and acceptance of their persons.   But this intensely personal interest could not but react with transforming influence on the doctrine of Christ's work, as that which laid the foundation of the sinner's peace.   The clearer light which had been shed on the way of salvation by the doctrine of justification helped to set the atonement also in its right place in the Christian system.   For the consciousness of justification, as the Reformers understood it, is more than the mere assurance that God has forgiven our sins, and received us into His fellowship.   It is the assurance that this forgiveness and acceptance of God takes place *upon a righteous basis*—that I am truly set right by God in presence of His own law, so that there is now no more condemnation, or possibility of it, no charge which the law itself can bring against me, of which it can be said, " This claim has not been satisfied." [2] Only thus can we have a peace fundamentally secured.   Dorner excellently puts this point in the following passage :—" Justification is the disburdening of the personality from guilt at the tribunal of God's primitive justice, and therefore from punishment ; but this in such a way that the believer has the consciousness that divine justice itself has been satisfied by Christ ; that no exception has been made at the cost of justice ; that his is not simply the experience of divine long-suffering, including neither definitive forgiveness, nor satisfaction made to justice.   On the

[1] See next Lecture.   [2] Cf. Rom. viii. I, 33, 34.

contrary, the believer knows that, despite His own unrighteousness, harmony with the law and with justice has been restored by Christ. In this knowledge is rooted his peace of conscience, his elevation above those doubts which conscience would always suggest, in case forgiveness came to the sinner in the way, so to speak, of a partial act of exception, through a breach with justice, and violation of the eternal law. But by this means, since it is only faith in Christ which knows itself justified, Christ's acts and sufferings enter into direct relation with the penal law, and with our guilt which has to be blotted out, Christ being thus the Atoner, to whom the consciousness of justification attaches itself."[1] These at least were the convictions which inspired and sustained the consciousness of justification in the Reformation struggle ; and the corresponding test applied to a doctrine of atonement was its adequacy to support these convictions. This, may I not add, must be the test of a satisfactory doctrine of atonement still, viz., its power to sustain the consciousness of peace with God under the heaviest strain which can be put upon it from the sense of guilt, and of the condemnation which guilt entails.

There was another cause which co-operated with this revived sense of the need of forgiveness to aid the reconstruction of the doctrine of atonement at the Reformation. I mentioned above how the notion of a sovereign omnipotence in God led even Aquinas to entertain the view that an expiatory satisfaction for sin might, had God so chosen, have been dispensed with. But the extremes into which this doctrine was driven by Duns Scotus and his school, with whom everything—morality included—was made to depend

[1] *Syst. of Doct.* iv. pp. 22, 23 (E.T.).

on the arbitrary *will* of God, produced a reaction, and
led to the long conflicts between Thomists and Scotists
turning on this very point—whether moral distinctions
had their ground in the mere will of God, or in His
nature, which was above His will.   Is a thing right
because God wills it, or does God will it because it is
right ?   Once the question was put in this way, it was
easy to see where the genuine religious interest lay, and
the Reformers all take their stand, as Anselm had *implicitly* done before them, on the immutable character
of the divine righteousness, and on the idea of the
moral law as grounded, not in the mere will of God,
but in His essential nature.   The commanding will of
God, in other words, is the expression of His essential
holiness, and moral law, as the embodiment of the re-
quirements of that holiness, is as unchangeable as itself.

In contrast with the scholastic views, accordingly,
the ground of the Reformation doctrine of atonement
is, as Ritschl correctly says in his extremely suggestive
chapter on that subject, the conception of sin as " a
violation of the order of public law that is upheld by
God's authority, a violation of the law that is correlate
with the eternal being of God Himself." [1]   The Reformers one and all—and the fact is the more noteworthy when it is remembered that Luther and
Zwingli represent independent developments—in the
same writer's words, " estimated the atoning work of
Christ by reference to that justice of God which finds
its expression in the eternal law." [2]   This is a distinct
advance on the Mediæval doctrine.   It lifts the
subject out of that sphere of private rights, the
associations of which still clung about Anselm's formulations.   It secures a basis for the atonement,

[1] *Justif. and Recon.* i. p. 197 (E.T.).
[2] *Ibid.* p. 209 ; cf. pp. 197, 198, 200, etc.

which excludes the earlier scholastic ideas of the atonement as simply the " most suitable " expedient of the divine wisdom ; and no less already excludes in principle the governmental, Socinian, and purely moral-influence theories of later date. It accords with this that in Reformation doctrine full stress is laid on the necessity of satisfaction to the law of God in its *penal*, not less than in its *preceptive* aspects.[1] This, no doubt, was also the design of Anselm—to show how Christ could so satisfy justice as to furnish a righteous ground for the remission of sin's penalty ; but he failed, as we saw, to bring the sufferings of Christ into any direct connection with that punitive will of God, of which death and the other outward evils to which our race is subject are the expression. The Reformers saw deeper, and did not shrink from saying, in harmony with Scripture, that Christ, as our Lord and Representative, bore our condemnation—entered into the full meaning of the judgment of God against our sins, and under experience of its uttermost *temporal*, and even as far as a sinless being might, of its *spiritual* woes, the pain and shame of our human sin, the assaults and temptations of Satan, the hiding of His Father's countenance—did honour to the righteousness implied in this connection of sin with suffering and death. Thus He endured the sharpness of death, and, having abolished its curse, opened the Kingdom of Heaven to all believers. The Reformers were at one in this view of the expiatory character of the death of Christ, as rendering satisfaction to the majesty of the law of God, violated by sin ;[2] and in all the great Protestant creeds, accordingly, is enshrined in some

---

[1] *Justif. and Recon.* pp. 197, 198. Ritschl finds an anticipation in John Gerson (p. 198).

[2] Cf., *e.g.*, Luther on Gal. iii. 13.

form of words the testimony—" He satisfied the divine justice."

While the Reformers held the view of Christ's sufferings and death as a satisfaction rendered to divine justice, it is proper now to notice that this by no means exhausted their conception of the redeeming work of Christ.   Luther in particular is rich in the aspects in which he delights to extol the Cross of Christ, viewing it, as he always does, in connection with the life that preceded it, and the resurrection that followed.   He revels in the thought of how Christ by His passion and death conquers sin, the law, the devil, death, and hell ; and he and his fellow-Reformers carefully guard themselves against the idea that God's original attitude to men was one of wrath, and that the Cross has changed this attitude into love.[1]   With them, as with Augustine, and the greater schoolmen, love is the spring of the whole redeeming counsel, and the grace of God in salvation is safeguarded by the fact that it is God Himself who provides the means of reconciliation.   Nor, again, at the risk of repetition I venture to point out, is there one of the Reformers who views the worth, or satisfactory virtue, of Christ's sufferings as depending solely on the pain that was endured ; but emphasis is laid invariably on the voluntariness of the sacrifice, on the love of Christ, and on His will of obedience, as the qualities which gave value to His sufferings.[2]   It is the *doing* of Christ along with, and even more than, His suffering, which appears, as Ritschl has pointed out, " as having laid the foundation of the reconciliation He effected between God and man."[3]   What came to be spoken of afterwards as the

---

[1] Cf. Ritschl, i. pp. 201, 202, etc.
[2] *Ibid.* pp. 210, 213, etc.   Cf. Calvin, *Instit.* ii. 16. 5.
[3] *Ibid.* p. 209.

"active obedience" appears from the first, along with the "passive," as an element in the satisfaction of Christ; and though a distinction which tends to over-refinement soon begins to be drawn between the "passive obedience" as that which atones for guilt, and the "active obedience" as that which grounds for the believer his title to eternal life, the fact that both are described as "obedience" shows that the will is conceived of as present in each.[1]

It is, nevertheless, not to be disputed that, while the Reformation doctrine of atonement is not exhausted by, it involves what is sometimes called the "forensic" element; and this, it is frequently declared, modern thought must reject. If, however, by "forensic" is meant the treatment of man as subject of *moral law*— such law as conscience reveals, and God's character as Moral Ruler and Judge of the world involves—it is yet to be shown that this is not part of a true and scriptural conception of the relations of God and man; or that any doctrine which wholly omits it is not thereby condemned as inadequate for the needs of man as sinner. God's love, and even Fatherhood, do not divest Him of those fundamental attributes which constitute Him the Upholder and Vindicator of moral law in the universe; and if redemption reveals an infinite and all-compassionating love for the world, it does not detract from this love that it manifests itself toward sinners in "reigning through righteousness" unto life,[2] not in annulling righteousness.

---

[1] The true thought involved in this distinction is that the work of Christ does not merely atone for the past, but grounds also a new and blessed relation to the believer in which the inheritance of everlasting life is included. The distinction is not emphasised by Calvin, who views justification predominatingly as the blotting out of guilt and non-imputation of sin, while recognising, of course, that all positive blessing is the gratuitous gift of God in Jesus Christ. Cf. *Instit.* iii. 11. 21, 22; 18. 2, 5, etc.

[2] Rom. v. 21.   Cf. further in last Lecture.

VIII

The Doctrine of the Application of Redemption;
Justification by Faith; Regeneration, etc.—
Protestantism and Roman Catholicism
(Sixteenth Century)

"So far from being able to answer for my sins, I cannot answer even for my righteousness."—BERNARD.

"At the beginning of our preaching, the doctrine of faith had a most happy course, and down fell the Pope's pardons, purgatory, vows, masses, and such like abominations, which drew with them the ruin of all Popery. . . . And if all had continued, as they began, to teach and diligently urge the article of justification—that is to say, that we are justified neither by the righteousness of the law nor by our own righteousness, but only by faith in Jesus Christ—doubtless this one article, by little and little, had overthrown the whole Papacy."—LUTHER.

"That doctrine (of justification) is now to be more fully discussed, and discussed in such wise that we may not forget that it is the principal hinge on which religion must be supported : on which account we should bring to it the greater attention and care."—CALVIN.

LECTURE VIII

The Doctrine of the Application of Redemption; Justification by Faith; Regeneration, etc.—Protestantism and Roman Catholicism (Sixteenth Century).

IF I have succeeded in carrying conviction with me thus far in the explication I have given of the course of the development of dogma, there should be little difficulty in gaining assent to the next step I have to take—that, viz., which identifies the period of the Reformation with the group of doctrines connected with the *Application* of Redemption, or as it is sometimes termed, Subjective Soteriology. It will hardly be disputed by any that it was this group of doctrines, and specially the great doctrine of justification by faith —*articulus stantis aut cadentis ecclesiæ,* as Luther called it—which supremely occupied the minds of men in the momentous religious crisis of the sixteenth century. Every doctrine, I have urged, has its "hour"—the period when it emerges into individual prominence, and becomes the subject of exhaustive discussion; and the crisis of the Reformation unmistakably brought this hour for the doctrine now named. Positively, the way was prepared for it by the previous developments of the doctrines of sin and atonement; negatively, it was prepared by the crushing burden of legalism in the Romish Church, which in earnest minds developed a despair of salvation by work-righteousness similar to

that wrought in Paul by his experience of the Jewish
law, and drove them back, as it did him, on the free
grace of the Gospel as an absolute necessity, only to
discover that the grace they sought had been con-
fronting them all the while on the Gospel page, though
their eyes were holden that they could not see it.

Thus again is evinced in the most striking manner
the harmony of the logical and the historical schemes.[1]
It was not by accident that at various centres—for it
should never be forgotten that the Reformation had not
one, but several independent centres [2]—the minds of
men awoke, as it were simultaneously, to the clear
apprehension of this great doctrine of justification, so
long obscured in the official teaching of the Church ;
or that, amidst minor differences, so remarkable a
harmony should have prevailed among the Reformers
and the Churches which they founded regarding it.
Then, although, as we shall discover, in its essence
nothing new, it broke on men's minds with the force of
a revelation ; wrought, too, on the old corrupt Church
with the force of a revolution.   That this doctrine was
the real citadel round which the battle of the Reformation was fought, and had in it the power to revolutionise
the whole theological as well as ecclesiastical scheme
of the Papacy, is evident from nothing so much as its
treatment by the Church of Rome itself.   When the
Papal Council met at Trent, it was understood by
everyone that the doctrine of justification was the chief
matter to be debated.   The subject was confessedly a
perplexing one ; as one of the presiding legates naïvely
put it, it was a new one to the Fathers, and had never
been strictly considered by any previous Council of the

---

[1] Cf. Ritschl, *Justif. and Recon.* i. pp. 94, 123, 124 (E.T.).
[2] In France, Switzerland, Germany.   See below, p. 256.

Church.[1]   But interest specially attaches to the terms
in which this important doctrine was submitted to the
Council.   It was described as the matter on which all
the errors of Luther were founded.   Then the statement went on—" That said author, having commenced
with attacking *indulgences*, seeing that he could not
accomplish his object without destroying those works of
penance, the default of which indulgences supply,
had not found a better means than the unheard-of
doctrine of *justification by faith alone*. . . . That, as a
consequence, he had denied the efficacy of the sacraments, the authority of priests, purgatory, the sacrifice
of the mass, and all other remedies instituted for the
pardon of sin—and that by opposing argument *it was
necessary* for the establishing of the body of Catholic
doctrine to destroy this heresy of *justification by faith
alone*, and to condemn the blasphemies of the enemy of
good works." [2]   This, of course, is not quite the history
of the Lutheran movement ; but the statement is undoubtedly correct in the point most essential, viz., in its
perception of the fact that the admission of this
doctrine means logically the overthrow of Rome's
whole doctrinal and sacramental system.

It is precisely here, however, that, in the light of
my contention in these lectures, a difficulty may be
felt to arise.   I have endeavoured to show that one of
the tests of a genuine doctrinal development is its continuity with the past, its organic connection with what

---

[1] Sarpi, Bk. ii. 75.   Cf. Cunningham, *Historical Theology*, i. p. 481 ;
Buchanan, *Justification*, p. 139.

[2] Sarpi, Bk. ii. 73.   It should be stated that there were many shades
of opinion in the Council itself on the subject, some of them approaching
very nearly the Protestant doctrine.   The original draft of the article on
justification was so Protestant that it was indignantly repudiated by the
majority of the members.

has gone before. But it has just been admitted that
the Protestant doctrine of justification by faith presented itself as a *revolt* against the past, a rupture with
the doctrinal development on this head so far as it
had yet proceeded, a condemnation of that development ; and, as a consequence, the throwing off of a
mountain load of errors and practices that had resulted
from it, to the grievous injury of men's consciences.
This was, in fact, the very charge brought by the Roman
Church against the doctrine, by which it sought
to discredit it, that it was novel, unauthorised, and
schismatic.   It is, of course, open to the Protestant to
reply that he goes back to a yet more primitive source
—the Apostolic doctrine in Scripture—and this is true.
But it does not quite turn the point of the objection as
respects the law of the progress of dogma.   A more
pertinent answer would be that no law of history can
exclude the possibility of false and perverted developments in doctrine and institutions, such as we know,
in fact, to have often taken place in the history of
the Church.   As for ages men believed in astrology,
and till the days of Galileo and Copernicus accepted
unchallenged the Ptolemaic theory of the heavens,
without the progress of astronomical science being
discredited thereby ; so there is nothing to preclude
the supposition that, misled by the admission of a
false principle, theology may enter on a wrong line of
development, and rear up a structure of wood and hay
and stubble on the Christian foundation, which, when
the hour of judgment arrives, it must bear the pain of
seeing consumed.   We have, however, happily, a far
more complete answer to offer.   Widely as the Church
may have gone astray, theoretically and practically, in
its apprehension of this doctrine, it is not the case
that the Reformation was in any real sense a rupture

with the past.   On the contrary, it stood in direct continuity with what was deepest, most vital, most characteristic in the piety of the past, and was its legitimate
outcome and vindication.   This, as we shall see, was
the position assumed by the Reformers themselves.
In preaching this doctrine, not one of them would have
allowed that he had broken with the religious tradition of the past.   Each claimed to be standing, even
doctrinally, in line with the best and purest part of
that tradition.   Nor could there, in truth, be a breach,
in the proper sense, with previous authoritative formulations of this doctrine ; for the point of my contention
is (as the Fathers at Trent also admitted), that not
till now had the doctrine emerged into independent
importance, or been accurately considered.   It was
only now its "epoch" had arrived ; only now the
conditions were present which admitted of its satisfactory investigation and formulation.   I shall best
illustrate these statements by looking, as before, at
the earlier development of the doctrine on its sides
both of error and of truth ; then at the contrast between
the Protestant and Roman Catholic (Tridentine)
doctrines at the Reformation ; after which a glance
may be taken at the subsequent sixteenth century
discussions.

I. There is no question, then, from the Protestant,
and I believe also from the Scriptural standpoint, but
that the Church, from a very early period, went seriously
astray in its doctrinal and practical apprehension of
the divine method of the sinner's salvation.   Many
beautiful utterances, I know, can be cited to show that
the thought of acceptance through God's grace, on the
ground of Christ's merit alone, was never absent
from the consciousness of the Church—nay, was its

deepest note all through.[1]   But these cannot overbear
the fact that ideas early crept in, and came to have
controlling influence, which were in principle antagonistic
to that consciousness.   Partly, no doubt, this was due
to the inevitable blunting of Pauline ideas in their
passing over to the Gentile world, imperfectly prepared,
through lack of a training under the law, to receive
them ; partly, also, is attributable to the fact already
noticed, that, in order of time, the doctrines of sin,
grace, and atonement, which are the presuppositions of
this doctrine of justification, had not yet been theologically investigated.   But the main source of error
must unquestionably be sought in the early introduction
into the Church of, and the place given to, the *sacramentarian* principle, which, wherever it enters, is bound
to exercise a disturbing influence on doctrine.   The
chief stages in the development of this principle in its
bearing on our subject are logically, and to a large
extent also historically, the following.   First came the
connection of regeneration and forgiveness of sins with
baptism — the doctrine of *baptismal regeneration*.   In
train of this, as its natural consequence, came the use
of the term " justification " to cover the entire change
supposed to be effected in baptism — both the divine
forgiveness and the divine renewal ; in other words,
the taking of justification to mean, not, as in Pauline
usage,[2] the *absolving* of a sinner from guilt, and *declaring*
him to be righteous in God's sight, on the ground of
what Christ has done for him, but peculiarly the *making*
of the sinner righteous by the infusing into him a
new nature, then, on the ground of this *justitia infusa*

---

[1] An interesting *catena* of these may be seen in Buchanan's *Doctrine
of Justification* (Cunningham Lectures), iii. 93 ff.   See also Sanday and
Headlam's note on the history of the Pauline doctrine in their *Romans*,
pp. 147 ff.
[2] See below, p. 259.

declaring him righteous.[1]   We have next the still more serious restriction of this benefit to the cleansing away of sins committed *before* baptism, so that post-baptismal sins, as not covered by the initial justification, had to be expiated in some other way, by good works and satisfactions of the sinner's own.   On the ground thus laid was built in due course the whole elaborate system of penance in the Romish Church to which reference falls to be made later—its scheme of confession, of priestly absolution, of meritorious satisfactions, of purgatorial suffering for sins not completely satisfied for on earth, of masses and indulgences as a means of relief from these pains of the life beyond. A main support of this sacerdotal system was its doctrine of merits—such ideas, *e.g.*, as that good works must be added to the initial justification to give a title to eternal life ; that good works have an inherent merit —a merit of " condignity," as the schoolmen phrased it—giving a claim in strict justice to eternal reward ; that it is possible to go beyond duty in works of supererogation, the merit of which, as not needed for one's self, can be applied in indulgences to make up for the deficiencies of others, to relieve them from purgatory, etc.   So buried is the true doctrine of God's grace beneath this superstructure of error that hardly a vestige of it seems left, and the difficulty I proposed above returns, How can a doctrine like that of the Reformers, which is the repudiation, root and branch, of this whole system of superstition, be supposed to be, in any sense whatever, in continuity with it ?

It is not enough, in answer to this question, to show,

---

[1] In Catholic doctrine remission tends to be treated only as a negative condition of justification—the true justification being the making righteous by infusion of grace.   The *justitia infusa* is, in scholastic language, the formal cause of our justification—that on account of which God declares us righteous.   See below, p. 265.

what no doubt is historically true, that there never was wanting, within the Catholic Church itself, a minority, sometimes breaking off into protesting sects, which saw more clearly than others the unavailingness of this official apparatus of salvation, and sought, with more or less success, to go back to Scriptural foundations. All honour to this chain of evangelical witnesses, extending down the whole course of the Church's history, who laboured to keep the lamp of truth alive when those who should have tended it were unfaithful! The reproach of heresy attached to them in their own day is now their glory. But the continuity of doctrine we desire to establish must carry us much farther than this. We gain a key in part to the solution of our problem when we observe, in the first place, how, even in the official teaching of the Church, there was never a denial of the fact that the ultimate ground of all forgiveness, grace, merit, acceptance, was the Cross and propitiatory work of the Lord Jesus Christ. Whatever might come after, the first reception of the sinner into favour by the forgiveness of sins and bestowal of righteousness was an act purely of grace. No doubt in the scholastic age even this was vitiated by the introduction of the idea of a "merit of congruity" attached to the acts of repentance, faith, hope, love, etc., by which the sinner was supposed to fit himself for the reception of grace in baptism.[1] But this may be discounted in view of the more serious element in the piety of the Church,—we meet with nothing of it, *e.g.*, in Bernard, in à Kempis, or Tauler, or the *Theologia Germanica*,—and also of the fact that even the "prevenient" grace which renders such acts possible is traced to the merit of Jesus Christ. Even as regards the so-called "merits" of the believer, and still more his

---

[1] See below, p. 263.

expiations and satisfactions, there was always the recognition in the deeper spirits that it was the grace of God which was the source of these merits, and that they would have no meritorious character at all but for the covering of their imperfections by the merits of the Redeemer. It was formerly shown that this was the view of Augustine,[1] whose thought ruled so powerfully in Middle Age theology ; it was also the doctrine of Anselm, of Bernard, of Aquinas, in short, of spiritual minds everywhere.

See now how this bears on the subject before us. What we have to fix attention on here is less the official theology of the Church, than what Ritschl aptly calls " the religious self-estimate "[2] of the godly men whose intellect still worked in the forms of that theology. That " religious self-estimate " had always one decisive mark—the consciousness, namely, of having received everything from grace, and of continued dependence on grace. It would be easy to multiply quotations from the great writers of the Church from Augustine downwards to illustrate this temper, but it is scarcely necessary. Bernard is a typical example. The whole strain of Bernard's sermons is, as Ritschl says, to lead his hearers " to disregard their own contribution to their merits, and to take into account only the operation of God's grace in them ; or, generally, to direct their attention from these particular works to God as the Founder of every hope of salvation. Paradoxically he says that the humility which renounces all claim to merit, and trusts in God alone, is the only true merit."[3] How entirely the fourteenth and fifteenth century mystics rejected all righteousness of works and fell back

[1] Lecture V. p. 151.
[2] i. pp. 94, 111, 115, 133, 137, etc. (E.T.).
[3] Ritschl, i. p. 98 ; cf. Calvin, *Instit.* iii. 12. 3. Formally Bernard maintains the ordinary Catholic standpoint.

on God's free grace need not be insisted on.[1]   There
were, in fact, two poles or tendencies between which the
Catholic doctrine and Catholic consciousness were continually oscillating.   If the external, legalistic, self-
saving side of the doctrine was fastened on,—as it would
be by the worldly, the corrupt, the self-righteous,—the
grace of the Gospel disappeared in a vast ecclesiastical
mechanism of salvation by works.   If, on the other
hand, with the feeling of the insufficiency of their own
works, men went back, as the saintly souls were always
doing, to the fountain-head of all mercy in the grace of
God in Jesus Christ, and sought their ultimate comfort
and satisfaction there, then, whatever the type of their
theology, they were really affirming the Protestant
doctrine of justification by faith.   One striking example
will suffice to illustrate what I mean.   The Roman
Church in the age of the Reformation had no more
redoubtable or uncompromising champion than Bellarmine.   In him we have the strongest opponent of the
Reformation doctrine of justification, and the unqualified
defender of the counter-dogma of the meriting of
eternal life by good works.   But what is Bellarmine's
own last word in the discussion?   It really amounts,
as Dr. William Cunningham has said, to a virtual
repudiation of the whole five books he had written in
defence of the Catholic contention.[2]   Bellarmine's
words are [3]—" On account of the uncertainty of one's

---

[1] Luther writes of Tauler to Spalatin—" If it will gratify you to become
acquainted with a solid theology in the German tongue, perfectly resembling
that of the ancients, procure for yourself John Tauler's Sermons, for
neither in Latin nor in our own language have I seen a theology more
sound, or more in accordance with the Gospel " (in Ullmann's *Reformers
before the Reformation*, ii. p. 212).   Melanchthon shared this view.   Cf.
Ritschl, who points out the differences (i. pp. 104 ff.).

[2] *Historical Theology*, ii. 109.

[3] *De Instit.* v. 7.   Cf. Martensen's *Dogmatics*, p. 394 (E.T.), for the
dying words of Pope Pius VII.   " What ! " he exclaimed, " *Most Holy
Father !*   I am a poor sinner."

own righteousness, and the danger of empty boasting, *it is safest to place one's whole trust in the mercy of God alone*, and in His goodness." Similarly Luther in his Galatians testifies of some of the religious orders of his day : "Wherefore they, finding in themselves no good works to set against the wrath and judgment of God, did fly to the death and passion of Christ, and were saved in their simplicity." [1]

We can now perhaps understand how it was that the Reformers, in their proclamation of the doctrine of justification by faith, could uniformly claim to stand in unbroken connection with the Church of God in the past. As to the fact that they did so there can be no dispute. Apart from express utterances, the evidences are patent to any one who observes how freely they appeal in their works to the great Church writers, as Augustine and Bernard ; [2] how they identify themselves with the Church consciousness of the past, as represented in its devoutest utterances ; how they claim to be of one faith with the godly of their own generation. Ritschl is right in repudiating, on behalf of Luther, the idea that "in the thought of justification by faith he propounded something that up to his time had been utterly unheard of." [3] "In common with the congregation of Christ's people," says Luther, "I hold the one common doctrine of Christ, who alone is our Master." [4] Yet it is just as evident that there existed a contradiction between this "religious self-estimate" of saintly men and the formal theology of the Church ; and the consciousness of this became only the more

---

[1] On Gal. ii. 16.

[2] This is specially noticeable in Calvin. Cf. *Instit.* iii. 12. 16, etc.

[3] i. p. 164. It is one of the merits of Ritschl's *History* that he brings out this fact so prominently.

[4] *Ibid.* Cf. Luther's words quoted below, p. 259.

acute, the more earnestly men yearned for deliverance
from the yoke of bondage which the Church, in its cere-
monies and penitential exercises, imposed upon them.
It is further plain that once this contradiction came
into clear consciousness, it could only be resolved in
one way. The true continuity did not lie in upholding
the defective and erroneous forms of doctrine against
which the living consciousness of the Church was a
protest. It obviously lay in allying itself with that
"religious self-estimate" which had regulated true piety
all through, and in bringing the doctrinal forms of the
Church into harmony with *it*. This, accordingly, is
what we see men striving to do in the prelusive and
imperfect movements which preceded the Reformation
proper—those, *e.g.*, of Wyckliffe, Huss, and the Mystics
—which we mark coming to expression in individuals
like Staupitz, Luther's master, who yet never left the
communion of the Roman Church—which at length
found full-tongued utterance in the declarations of the
Reformation. It was in its essence no new commandment which the Reformers taught, but an old
commandment which the Church had from the beginning ; and the true breach of continuity would have
been to adhere, as the Tridentine Fathers did, to the
letter of Catholic dogma against the consciousness of
salvation by grace alone, with which that dogma stood
in contradiction.

There is, however, yet another line of preparation
for the Reformation doctrine, on which, before I pass
from this point, a word ought to be said. To none of
the Fathers, as we have seen, did the Reformers more
entirely serve themselves heir than to Augustine. It
was, however, a weakness in Augustine, as we also
saw, that, while investigating so exhaustively the doc-

trines of sin and grace, he left the doctrine of justification by faith very much where he found it. He failed,
that is, to distinguish between justification as an act
of grace, founding the sinner's new relation to God in
pardon and acceptance, and the accompanying or con-
sequent regeneration or sanctification of the believer—
the *making* of him righteous by infusion of grace.
This was connected with the fact that the entire side
of God's dealings with the sinner which had relation to
law was at that stage imperfectly understood ; and
that, in particular, the nature and scope of Christ's
atoning work had not received careful attention. I
showed in last lecture how the Reformation doctrine of
justification reacted to bring about a clearer apprehension of the doctrine of atonement. But it is equally
to be recognised that the more thorough examination
of the doctrine of Christ's work initiated by Anselm
could not be without its profound effect on the Catholic
mode of conceiving of justification. The clearer it
became that Christ had made a satisfaction of infinite
value to God for the sins of the world, the more palpable
must the incongruity appear of adding to this the puny
satisfactions of men as any part of the ground of
salvation. The reasonings of Anselm, in truth, destroyed the logical basis of every doctrine of human
satisfaction ; and each stage in the perfecting of the
doctrine of the atonement brought with it a call for a
new adjustment to the doctrine of justification. Hitherto
such an adjustment had scarcely been attempted. In
the *Summa* of Aquinas the doctrine of justification is
actually treated prior to Christ's work, and out of all
direct connection with it. In Roman theology to the
present hour justification is hardly exalted to the
dignity of a special article, but is merged in the doctrine
of baptism, of which, in strictness, it forms a part. Yet

nothing is more evident than that the doctrines of atonement and justification stand in essential relation, and
that the view taken of Christ's work must in the end
determine the shape of the doctrine of justification.
Here, then, was another task which the Reformers had
to perform—one, too, obviously of the nature of development. The adjustment of doctrines, in short, was
reciprocal. The better apprehension of the doctrine of
atonement now attained laid the foundation for clearer
views of the free forgiveness and unmerited acceptance
of the sinner ; on the other hand, the consciousness of
justification needed for its support the rock-like foundation of a work of atonement resting on an eternal
ground of righteousness—not a mere governmental
expedient, but such a work as would secure the conscience against all sense of arbitrariness in the pardon
bestowed.

II. That in the beginning of the sixteenth century
the doctrine of justification by faith alone was " in the
air "—was in the thoughts and almost trembling on the
lips of men—is sufficiently evidenced by the fact
already alluded to, that well-nigh simultaneously it
began to be preached at various centres by men to
whom God had revealed it independently. Le Fèvre
in France, Zwingli in Switzerland, and Luther in
Germany, were each led in their several ways to the
acknowledgment of this truth, and into conflict with
the doctrines and practices opposed to it. The story
may or may not be correct, that it was as he was pain-
fully mounting the steps of the *Scala Santa* at Rome
that Luther heard as it were a voice from heaven—
" The just shall live by faith " ;[1] but the spirit of the
story at least represents the fact. It was not flesh and

---

[1] Cf. Hagenbach, *Hist. of Reform.* i. p. 88 (E.T.).

blood that revealed this doctrine to the Reformers, but their Father who was in heaven. It is equally important to notice that, as it came to them in response to practical needs, so it was not a doctrinal or speculative, but a vital, practical interest which gave it supreme value in their eyes, and led them to make it the centre of all their preaching. They were not theorists spinning doctrinal cobwebs from their brains, but men intensely in earnest in finding out the true way in which a sinner could be at peace with God. And the great truth that came to them—born of a clear view of what Christ had accomplished for them on His Cross—was this, that the sinner, penitent for his sins, has the right of free access to God, without intervention of priest, church, sacrament, or anything else to stand between him and his Maker; and that God freely forgives and accepts everyone laying hold on His promise in the Gospel, without works, satisfactions, or merits of his own, but solely on the ground of Christ's atoning death and perfect righteousness, to which faith cleaves as the only ground of its confidence. This is the essential meaning of justification by faith— that it is not by works of righteousnesss that we have done, but according to His mercy that God saves us;[1] that even my faith is not a ground of merit before God, but is only the hand by which I lay hold on the mercy freely offered; that whenever I turn to God with a sincerely believing heart, He answers me there and then, without any period of probation, or torturing delays, with His "Thy sins which are many are forgiven thee,"[2] receiving me to His fellowship, and making me, still for His Son's sake, an heir of eternal life; and further, that this absolution, acquittal, acceptance, or however we please to phrase it, is full, free,

---

[1] Titus iii. 5. [2] Luke vii. 47.

unconditional, an act done once for all, and neither
requiring, nor admitting of, repetition. Doubtless, as
all the Reformers recognised—and this is the element
of truth in the Catholic doctrine—such an act of
justification cannot take place without an accompanying
act of moral renovation. The sinner, through the same
act of faith in which he knows himself forgiven and
accepted, dies to sin, that he may thenceforth live to
God and to Christ, instead of, as heretofore, to self;
becomes through his union with Christ and reception
of the Spirit, a "new creation,"[1] with new thoughts,
aims, desires, and spiritual affections.[2] But this change
is in no wise or degree the *ground* of his acceptance,
but is a concomitant or result of it—the *end* for which
he is justified. The new nature comes into being with
the new standing; but it is not because we are holy—
even because of the "germinal" holiness of faith[3]—that
we are forgiven and received; but God accepts us, as
laying hold on His free gift of righteousness in Christ,
that *He* may make us holy, as part of the salvation He
destines for us. In the noble words of Luther himself,
expounding his own doctrine—"I, Dr. Martin Luther,

[1] 2 Cor. v. 17.   Calvin devotes himself, before even expounding
justification, to show that faith is not, as he puts it "otiose" to good
works (iii. 11. 1).

[2] This is not a qualification of the Reformation doctrine, but part of it.
Luther, *e.g.*, says : "Now after that a man is once justified, and possesseth
Christ by faith, and knoweth that He is his righteousness and life,
doubtless he will not be idle, but as a good tree, he will bring forth good
fruits.   For the believing man hath the Holy Ghost, and where the Holy
Ghost dwelleth, He will not suffer a man to be idle," etc.—On Gal. ii.
18.

[3] This favourite refinement of the doctrine is really a departure from
the Reformation standpoint.   The righteousness which makes a man just
before God is not held germinally in faith, but is a righteousness which is
a gift of God, received "through" faith.   Sanday and Headlam at least
lean to the above view when they make the divine judgment apparently
an anticipation of a righteousness afterwards to be realised in the believer
(*Romans*, pp. 25, 30, 38, etc.).   Ritschl very firmly rejects this "germ"
theory.

the unworthy evangelist of the Lord Jesus Christ, thus think and thus affirm :—that this article, viz., that faith alone, without works, justifies before God, can never be overthrown, for . . . . Christ alone, the Son of God, died for our sins ; but if He alone takes away our sins, then men, with all their works, are to be excluded from all concurrence in procuring the pardon of sin and justification. Nor can I embrace Christ otherwise than by faith alone ; He cannot be apprehended by works. But if faith, before works follow, apprehends the Redeemer, it is undoubtedly true that faith alone, before works, and without works, appropriates the benefit of redemption, which is no other than justification, or deliverance from sin. This is our doctrine ; so the Holy Spirit teaches and the whole Christian Church. In this, by the grace of God, will we stand fast. Amen." [1]

Now that this, which is the Protestant doctrine, is also the Pauline doctrine—the doctrine of the Epistles to the Romans and the Galatians—might, in these days of scientific exegesis, almost be taken for granted. There is at least hardly an exegete of the first rank who will dispute that in Paul's usage the word δικαιοῦν, "to justify," is employed uniformly in the sense of absolving, acquitting, *declaring* righteous before the law, and can never bear the sense of *making* righteous,[2]—is used, in short, in the "forensic" sense, as the opposite

---

[1] In Buchanan's *Justification*, p. 129.

[2] See the emphatic notes by Sanday and Headlam in *Romans*, pp. 30, 31, 36. Even Dr. J. H. Newman, in his *Lectures on Justification*, allows that this is the proper force of "justify," but takes it in a *creative* sense, as equivalent to "Be righteous." It is "an announcement or fiat of Almighty God, which breaks upon the gloom of our natural state as the creative word upon chaos"; in declaring the soul righteous, it *makes* it righteous (Lect. III. 10). No proof can be adduced for this as part of the meaning of "justify."

of "to condemn,"—and that the ground of this absolving sentence is not "works of righteousness," or incipient holiness,[1] in the person justified, but "the redemption that is in Christ Jesus, whom God set forth to be a propitiation, through faith, by His blood."[2] It was before remarked that the Reformers were far from regarding justification as a simple amnesty, or passing by, or forgiveness of sin, without regard to what is due to the condemnatory testimony of His law against sin. Justification was not in their view, any more than in the Apostle's, the simple setting aside of the claim of the law upon the sinner, but was the declaration that that claim had been satisfied, and that the law had no more any charge to bring against him.[3] It is justification on an immutably righteous basis ; only that the righteousness which grounds this new relation is not in the sinner himself, but in the Saviour with whom faith unites him. How vitally Luther apprehended this truth, and how warmly he expressed it, can best be shown by culling a few of his own energetic sentences. "But we," he says, "by the grace of Christ holding the article of justification, do assuredly know that we are justified and reputed righteous before God by faith only in Christ. . . . For like as neither the law nor any work thereof is offered unto us, but Christ alone, so nothing is required of us but faith alone, whereby we apprehend Christ, and believe that our sins and our

---

[1] Hence my difficulty in admitting that the righteousness which accrues to the sinner, and is imputed to him, on the ground of Christ's work, can be the *anticipated* (actual) righteousness of the believer, as Sanday and Headlam seem to think. This would be a transition εἰs ἄλλο γένοs.

[2] Rom. iii. 25. Cf. above, p. 234.

[3] Hence again my hesitation in saying with Sanday and Headlam that justification "is simply forgiveness, free forgiveness" (p. 36). Forgiveness might be simple amnesty, but justification, as Paul and the Reformers understood it, is something more. And this the theory of the authors themselves implies.

death are condemned and abolished in the sin and
death of Christ. . . . Let us rest upon the principal
point of this present matter ; which is, that Jesus Christ,
the Son of God, died upon the cross, did bear in His
body my sins, the law, death, the devil, and hell. . . .
If then thou take good hold of that which Paul here
teacheth, thou wilt answer, I grant I have sinned.
Then God will punish thee. Nay, he will not do so.
Why, doth not the law of God so say ? I have nothing
to do with that law. Why so ? Because I have
another law which striketh this law dumb, that is to
say, liberty. What liberty is that ? The liberty of
Christ, for by Christ I am utterly freed from the law.
. . . If therefore in the matter of justification thou
separate the Person of Christ from thy person, then
thou art in the law, thou livest in the law and not in
Christ, and so thou art condemned of the law, and dead
before God. . . . Faith, therefore, must be purely
taught, viz., that thou art so entirely and nearly joined
unto Christ, that He and thou art made as it were one
person ; so that thou may'st boldly say, I am now one
with Christ, that is to say, Christ's righteousness,
victory, and life are mine. And again Christ may say,
I am that sinner, that is, His sins and His death are
mine, because He is united and joined unto me, and I
unto Him. For by faith we are so joined together that
we are become one flesh and one bone, we are the
members of the body of Christ, flesh of His flesh, and
bone of His bone." [1]

The Roman Catholic doctrine of justification was
for the first time authoritatively defined in the Reformation age by the Tridentine Fathers in antithetic
relation to the Protestant. It may be serviceable,

[1] On Gal. ii. 18-20.

therefore, briefly to consider it, both as helping to
throw the Protestant doctrine into greater distinctness,
and in view of the numerous influences at work tending
to a revival of Catholic ideas.   The deliverances of the
Council of Trent bear on them the marks of the compromise in which they originated, but in their broad
contrast with Protestant doctrine they measure
practically the whole distance between the two
Churches.   Some of the points have already been
provisionally touched on.[1]

A first contrast relates to the place assigned in
justification to *faith*.   Justification, in the Protestant
doctrine, is by faith.   In the language of the schools,
faith is the " instrumental cause " of our salvation.   It
is that by which we apprehend and appropriate to ourselves the divine benefit exhibited to us in the Person
and propitiatory work of Christ.   For faith, as the
instrumental cause of justification, the Church of Rome
substitutes *baptism*.[2]   It is in baptism, duly administered,
that we are washed from our sins and spiritually renewed
—in Rome's sense " justified."   Faith, in this view, sinks
to the level of a predisposing cause.   It is through faith,
regarded as assent to what God, or rather the Church,
teaches, that we are *moved* to seek justification by baptism.[3]   And even this place as predisposing cause is
not peculiar to faith, but is shared, along with faith, by
a number of other virtues directly to be mentioned.

A second contrast relates to what we may call the
approach to justification.   Protestantism teaches that
justification is granted to those who turn to God with
penitent and believing hearts.   Penitence and faith are
inseparable elements of the one spiritual state ; for the

---

[1] I base on the *Decrees* and *Canons* of the Council of Trent, taken in
conjunction with the *Catechism*, which enters into some points more fully.
[2] *Decree on Justif.* 7.   [3] *Ibid.* 6, 8.

faith which apprehends Christ can only spring from a genuinely contrite heart, and, conversely, the germ of faith in God's mercy is already present in penitence, else it would not be evangelical penitence at all. But merit, in the Reformation view, is not implied in either ; both rather are the explicit renunciation of merit. This requirement of penitence and faith in justification Rome elaborates into a long-drawn-out doctrine of *pre-paration* for justification. God, it is taught, bestows " prevenient " grace, in order that, in the language of the Council, " those who by sins are alienated from God may be disposed through His quickening and assisting grace *to convert themselves to their own justi-fication* by freely assenting to, and co-operating with, the said grace." [1] More particularly the preparation consists in the acquirement of the seven virtues of faith, fear, hope, love, penitence, the purpose of receiving the sacrament (baptism), and the purpose of leading a new and obedient life.[2] After all, when this is accomplished, the individual is only in the forecourt—is prepared, or *disposed*, for justification : a most unscriptural notion. A question of some nicety here is—Is any meritorious character ascribed to these preparatory exercises ? The words of the Council seem explicit enough— " We are said to be justified freely, because that none of those things which precede justification— whether faith or works—merit the grace itself of justification." [3] This, however, is precisely one of the ambiguities in the language of the Council which cover differences of opinion. It was, as formerly hinted, one of the subtleties of the schoolmen to distinguish *two* kinds of merit—one the strict merit of condignity (*meritum ex condigno*), which gives a claim in justice ;

---

[1] *Decree on Justif.* 5.   [2] *Ibid.* 6 : cf. Bellarmine, i. 12.
[3] *Ibid.* 8.

the other, the lesser merit of congruity (*meritum ex congruo*), which gives a claim only in equity. Now it was a doctrine held by leading divines in the Council that, though works done before justification did not merit that grace by the merit of condignity, they *did* merit it by the merit of congruity, *i.e.*, they made it right in equity that God should bestow the blessing. That the language of the Decree is not meant to exclude this lower grade of merit is evident both from the recorded debates, and from the teaching of Bellarmine and most Roman theologians. Bellarmine expressly states that, when preparatory works are affirmed not to merit justification, this merely means that they do not merit it *ex condigno*, and he maintains that they do merit it *ex congruo*. He explicitly asserts that the above-named virtues are the meritorious causes of justification, and most Roman theologians, as I say, follow in his steps.[1]

This preparation assumed, we come next to the *act of justification* itself. Justification, as I have already said, is connected by Rome with baptism. What then happens in baptism? In the first place, it is declared that the person baptized is perfectly and inwardly cleansed from all original and actual sin : further, that he has infused into him a new and supernatural righteousness, constituting him holy and a friend of God.[2] This is his justification, in antithesis to the Protestant doctrine, which, I have shown, explains it of God's act in declaring the sinner righteous on the ground of Christ's completed work. Lest, however, we should be stumbled (as we well may) at finding how much sin can still appear in a soul declared to be purged from all traces of it, the Council goes on to explain that " concupi-

---

[1] *De Justif.* i. 21. Cf. Cunningham, *Hist. Theol.* ii. pp. 26, 27.
[2] *Decree on Orig. Sin*, 5 ; *On Justif.* 7.

scence "—another name for inordinate desire—is left
for the exercise of the Christian's virtues ; and the
difficulty of its presence is got over by the declaration that concupiscence is not truly and properly of
the nature of sin, though admittedly the Apostle Paul
calls it such.[1] Not only, moreover, does the Romish
doctrine perpetuate the error of confusing justification
with regeneration and sanctification [2] (which *might* be
only a mistake of nomenclature), but it takes the more
perilous step of speaking of this infused righteousness
as, in scholastic phrase, the " formal cause " of our justification,[3] *i.e.*, the proximate ground on which God pro-
nounces us righteous, restores us to favour, and gives
us the title to eternal life. The Cross of Christ,
indeed, is still declared to be the *ultimate* meritorious
cause ;[4] but it will readily be seen that there is an immense difference between saying that Christ's propitiatory sacrifice is the sole ground of my acceptance, and
saying that Christ's sacrifice and merit have purchased
for me grace by which I am now able to merit my
salvation for myself, which is the Tridentine point of
view.[5]

It is but the logical carrying out of the same
scheme when justification, begun in the manner described, is next regarded as *completed by the believer's
own good works*. Good works are now viewed as
having the full value of merit of condignity, and as
creating a proper title to eternal life. " We must
believe," says the Council, " that nothing is wanting to
the justified to prevent them being accounted to have,
by those very works which they have done in God,
fully satisfied the divine law, according to the state of
this life, and to have truly merited eternal life, to be

---

[1] *Ibid.* and *Catech.* pt. ii. ch. 2, quest. 42.   Cf. Rom. vii. 14, 17.
[2] *On Justif.* 7.   [3] *Ibid.*   [4] *Ibid.*   [5] *Ibid.* 3, 7.

obtained in its due time." [1]   Justification, we discover,
admits of degrees and increase, and a title has to be
earned by the addition of good works before salvation
is fully attained.[2]

All this is grave enough, but its effects in distorting
the doctrine of justification are cast into the shade by
the place given in the Roman system to *penance*.[3]
We saw in an earlier part of the lecture that the forgiveness obtained in baptism is held to apply only to
sins committed *before* baptism, and that *post*-baptismal
sins are left to be expiated in some other way.   The
Tridentine dogma holds to the assertion that this
justification, commenced in baptism, and perpetuated
and increased by good works, avails only for the
removal of pre-baptismal sin.   The moment the soul
lapses into sin *after* baptism—at least into *mortal* sin
—the whole work has to be begun anew, this time on
a totally different basis.[4]   This, the most remarkable
development of all in Romish doctrine, does not seem
to me to have received nearly the amount of attention it
deserves.   Even supposing we could accept everything
this Church has hitherto taught us of the way of
justification, it would still avail us little, seeing that,
with scarcely an exception, all fall from this first state
of grace, and need to be restored on quite a different
footing.   What I mean is, that there are practically not
any who have not forfeited the grace of their original
baptism by mortal sin, as the Roman Church defines
that class of sins, and do not need to be justified
afresh by the methods laid down in the sacrament of
penance.   It is not the *first* justification accordingly,
but this *second* justification, on which, in the practical

---

[1] *On Justif.* 16.   [2] *Ibid.* 10, 16.
[3] *Ibid.* 14 ; *Decree on Penance* (cf. ch. 1).   [4] *Ibid.* 15.

working of the system, the stress mainly lies. And here it is, that, having made our bow to the scriptural doctrine, we take our final leave of it, and launch out unrestrained on other waters. I can only indicate the drift of the new departure.

Sins committed after baptism are, we are told, of two kinds—*venial*, which weaken grace in the soul, and *mortal*, which destroy grace.[1] The mortal sins are pride, covetousness, unchastity, anger, gluttony, envy, sloth ; and who is there, it may be asked, who does not, at some period in his life, fall into one or other of these? Suppose then we have fallen from grace by committing a mortal sin, what is the remedy? Baptism avails no more, but God in his mercy has provided a new sacrament—a " second plank," as it is called—viz., penance.[2] It is in this article of penance, as I say, if anywhere, that we are to seek the real doctrine of justification in Romanism as a working system. And here grace retreats finally into the background, and works come to the front. Assume grace to be lost, what is to be done? The penitent is exhorted to contrition (contrition without grace?), and is even assured that, if his contrition were perfect, it alone would suffice to procure forgiveness.[3] But contrition seldom or never is perfect ; God, therefore, has provided an easier method in *confession*, for which a lesser degree of penitence, called attrition, will suffice.[4] Confession made, the priest, in virtue of the divine authority delegated to him, gives *absolution*, at the same time prescribing certain works of penance as satisfaction.[5] It might appear as if, by this absolving act, the

---

[1] *Decree on Penance*, 5. [2] *On Justif.* 14 ; *On Penance*, 1.
[3] *On Penance*, 4 ; *Catech.* pt. ii. ch. 2, quests. 34-36.
[4] *Ibid.* 5. Attrition is said to be "commonly conceived either from the consideration of the turpitude of sin, or from the fear of hell and its punishment " (ch. 4). [5] *Ibid.* 6, 8, 9.

penitent were again justified; but it is not so. He is
freed only as respects the *eternal penalty* of his sin.
Even after the guilt and eternal punishment have been
remitted, there remains a *temporal penalty*, and this
must be discharged by the sinner's own efforts and
endurances in good works and penances.[1] Supposing
the whole of this obligation is not discharged—and
practically it never is in this life—the balance is carried
over to purgatory, and has to be wrought off there.[2]
This, be it remembered, after the soul has received
absolution, and died in a state of grace, or justification!
There are still remedies—masses, indulgences, merits
of the saints—which can be applied to relieve from
purgatory; but into this region, thorny with questions
on which doctors themselves differ, I do not enter.
Yet this is the system—error piled on error, as I believe
it to be—which Rome substitutes for the scriptural
doctrine of justification; which is, as I have said, her
working doctrine! And after it all, if that church is
to be believed, no man can ever know that he *is*
justified, or will be saved.[3] It is a dark, doubtful,
fearful way by which Rome leads her votaries, with
purgatory in the immediate foreground, and heaven as
a distant perhaps beyond! Against this travesty of
the grace of God, the Reformers did surely an incalculable service in sounding forth, for the comfort of
their own and succeeding generations, the grand
emancipating truth, " Being justified by faith, we have
peace with God, through our Lord Jesus Christ." [4]

III. The chief points in the doctrine of justification
at the Reformation, viz. :—(1) that justification is of
God's free grace, and not of works; (2) that it is

---

[1] *On Justif.* 14 ; *On Penance*, 8.   [2] Cf. *Decree on Purgatory*.
[3] *On Justif.* 9.   [4] Rom. v. 1.

through faith alone; (3) that it includes the forgiveness of
sins and the pronouncing of the sinner righteous before
God ; (4) that it is to be distinguished from the internal
change we designate regeneration and sanctification,
and does not proceed on the ground of this change ;
(5) that it is nevertheless not a mere amnesty, but has
its ground in the perfect righteousness of Christ, and
the atonement made by Him for sin ; and (6) that it
is instantaneous and complete, an act of God never to
be repeated,—these cardinal points in the doctrine, on
which all the Reformers were at one, were then fixed,
I believe, beyond the power of future recall. Yet the
strong religious assertion of these truths, and even the
clear demarcation of them from the counter Romish
errors, were far from completing the theological development on the subject. The theological task, indeed, only
properly commenced when, the immediate impulse
having spent itself, men were led to inquire more carefully into the meaning of the terms they used, and into
the relations of the ideas represented by them. It is
difficult in such a process to avoid falling back into the
faults of an over-eager scholasticism, and the post-
Reformation Church by no means escaped that danger.
Still, we cannot help seeing that the controversies which
sprang up so thickly in the days immediately succeeding
the Reformation had their place and meaning in the
history of dogma, and, while marred by human infirmity, and the violence of party passion, were such as
were bound to arise in the thorough investigation of the
problems to which the newly-won evangelical consciousness gave birth. It was not merely the ever-present
antagonism of the Roman Church which forced the
Reformers into controversy. The Reformation itself
had set loose a multitude of forces—mystical, rationalistic, revolutionary—from which sprang new and

vigorous forms of opposition. Equally keen were the disputes between the Lutheran and Reformed sections of Protestantism, though these did not much affect the article of justification. There were again the sharp conflicts which arose within the bosom of the Lutheran Church itself, with the errors and one-sidednesses they involved. These may be said to have run their course by 1577, when the *Formula of Concord,* which was drawn up to settle them, was adopted. A glance also may be taken before I close at the Socinian opposition.

One thing which greatly helped the Reformed Church in these controversies, in comparison with the Lutheran, was its possession of the consummate constructive genius of Calvin, who gave its doctrines a compactness and consistency never attained in the rival communion. It had further the advantage of shaking itself entirely clear, as the Lutheran Church did not, from the doctrine of baptismal regeneration. There must always be a difficulty in combining consistently a doctrine of justification by faith with a doctrine which regards every baptized person as regenerate. For if regenerate, then surely also justified and saved. With Luther, accordingly, faith, in the case of the baptized, tends to be regarded more as the coming to consciousness of a blessing already possessed, than as the entrance into a new state of forgiveness and acceptance. There is an important aspect of truth in this view also, which needs to have justice done to it. The Church is before the individual; and regeneration, in the case of those brought up under gracious influences, may antecede the clear knowledge of the state of privilege into which faith in Christ introduces us. But it is erroneous to bind this up with a sacramental theory. The Reformed Church, hampered with no such theory, while far from depreciating the sacraments, was able to work out its system with greater precision and coherence.

It was the aim of the Reformers to preserve the balance between the objective and subjective sides of salvation, and errors arose on one side or the other according as this balance was disturbed. In *Anabaptist* and *mystical* circles the tendency was to the rejection of the forms of an imputation theology, and reversion to the notion of justification by *imparted* righteousness. A peculiar type of mysticism is represented by Osiander, to whom Calvin devotes so much attention.[1] Osiander did not exactly deny objective redemption, though this is put into the background with him ; but, with much else of a dubious order, he explained justification as the infusion into the soul of an essential divine righteousness—the righteousness of God's own being. Christ's humanity thus becomes at best the medium by which He conveys to us, and makes us participate in, His essential nature as Deity. In defending their doctrine against this class of objectors, the Reformers had to show that the imputation they contended for was no legal fiction, but the ascription to the sinner of that standing before God and His law—that immunity from condemnation, and claim to favour—to which his connection with Christ really entitled him. If he was not condemned, but was pardoned, and received to fellowship, it was because no charge could any longer, in light of his relation to Christ, be rightfully brought against him.[2] And they safeguarded their doctrine from antinomian abuse by making vital union with Christ the condition of justification—a union in which " we have adopted that One in whom obedience and suffering took place for us, and even thus do we receive

[1] Cf. *Instit.* iii. 11.   [2] Cf. Ritschl, i. pp. 273 ff.

with Christ also the effects of His life and suffering " ;[1] in which, not less, Christ unites Himself with us, and dwells in us, as the source of every spiritual blessing. To those who accused their doctrine of opening the way to sin, they pointed out that acceptance of Christ in faith is acceptance of the *whole* Christ—of Christ in *all His offices*, and for *all the ends* of His work—for sanctification as well as for justification,[2]—and that, holiness being the end of pardon, for anyone to think of accepting Christ for forgiveness, while refusing to own Him as Lord, is only thereby to show that he has not yet attained a glimpse of what true faith means.[3]

It is unnecessary to enter into the complicated details of the *Lutheran Controversies*, though, as has been said, they were not mere products of a spirit of strife, but discussions which it was inevitable should arise in the attempt at a more exact settlement of the doctrine on its different sides. Justification had, on the one hand, an aspect of relation to Christ's work ; on the other, an aspect of relation to regeneration, and to the new life and good works of the believer. Hence questions which we are apt to think frivolous, but which had, nevertheless, a good deal of substance in them, as to the relation of justification to Christ's active and passive obedience ; as to whether the notion of justification is exhausted in the forgiveness of sins (Piscator), or does not also include the idea of the conferring of a positive title to the blessing of eternal life ; as to the relation of the believer to the law, of faith to repentance, of good works to ultimate salvation, etc. One point only may be here touched on for its intrinsic

---

[1] Dorner, *Prot. Theol.* i. p. 353 (E.T.). Cf. Calvin, *Instit.* iii. 1 ; ii. 16. 16, 19.

[2] *Instit.* iii. 2. 7 ; 16, etc.   [3] Cf. Rom. vi.

interest, viz., the question so much canvassed in the age
of the Reformation, and often discussed since, as to the
relative priority of regeneration or justification, or, as it
is sometimes called, the question of the *ordo salutis*.[1]
It may be said to arise from such language as I have
just used as to the necessity of spiritual union with
Christ for justification.   Broadly, the difficulty is this :
if vital union with Christ precedes justification, and
faith, by which this union is effected, is the act of a
quickened soul, we seem committed to the paradox that
a sinner is regenerated, or becomes a child of God,
before he is justified, *i.e.*, while yet under condemnation.
If, on the other hand, we put justification first, we seem
driven to admit either that there is justification before
faith, or that faith is an act of an unregenerated soul.
Distinction in order of time, it may be granted, there is
none ; but in order of thought, it is held, one state must
condition the other, and a dilemma seems to arise on
either alternative.   Theologians have wavered on this
subject in the most remarkable manner.   Ordinarily,
perhaps, regeneration is placed first, and regarded as
the cause of faith ; many, on the other hand, contest
this view, and place justification first.   This involves
the grave difficulty that consistency seems to require
them to put justification even before faith ; but they do
not shrink from this consequence.   *In foro dei*, they
hold, justification has already taken place—is an eternal
act ; faith only puts the believer subjectively in possession of a blessing actually his.[2]   I do not think that
this is sound Reformation theology, or is the light in
which the Scripture presents the matter.   Even in the

[1] Ritschl presses the question very strongly in his criticism of the
Reformation theology. Cf. his *Justif. and Recon.* i. 188, 268, 271,
276, 279, etc. ; Dorner, *Prot. Theol.* ii. 157-163 (E.T.).

[2] Thus, *e.g.*, Dorner, Ritschl, A. A. Hodge, etc. Cf. article by the
last-named in *Princeton Review for* 1878.

divine mind justification cannot be thought of save as the object of it is viewed as in a true sense in union with Christ; but that union as surely implies an antecedent operation of the Spirit to bring it about. If it were argued that behind man's regeneration stands Christ's completed work, and God's *purpose* to justify, there would be less difficulty, for undoubtedly justification is the end of all God's gracious operations in bringing souls to faith. But the truer view would seem to be that regeneration, in the full sense, can as little be said to precede justification, as justification to precede it; for it is the same supreme act which unites us to Christ for our justification in which regeneration also is spiritually completed.[1] What does precede faith, and beget it, is the exhibition of God's gracious disposition and His promise of salvation in Christ. We err, it seems to me, in endeavouring to separate the factors in a process all the elements of which are *reciprocally* conditioning. As well might we ask whether, in the apprehension of truth, the act of intellect precedes the possession of the truth, or *vice versa*. For clearly, unless in some sense the truth were already within the mind's ken, it could not be grasped by it. The psychological process in which God reveals His Son in a soul is too subtle and swift-glancing for our categories of before and after.

The assault on the Reformation doctrine from the side of *Socinianism* went certainly to the root of the matter; yet, from its obvious want of religious depth and earnestness, it failed to make much impression on the general consciousness of the Church. The Socinian objection may be summed up in the proposition, often repeated since, and attractive by its plausibility—satis-

---

[1] Regeneration also is used sometimes in a wider, sometimes in a narrower sense. Calvin uses it in a wide sense.

faction and remission exclude each other. If sins have
been satisfied for by Christ, they cannot be freely
remitted; their remission is of debt. If they are freely
remitted, there is no place left for satisfaction.[1] Yet
Christian faith, which knows the magnitude and free-
ness of the blessing it has received, and at the same
time gratefully traces all it has to the mediation of
Christ, knows beforehand that the would-be dilemma
involves a fallacy, and, in feeling, if not in intellect,
already overleaps the contradiction. Nor, if we avoid
pressing unduly the analogy of a debt, which in moral
relations is only applicable within limits, does the
difficulty seem a serious one. This is, indeed, the
divine paradox of salvation, that it is both of these
things at once—an act of infinite grace, wholly unsought
and unmerited by the sinner; yet, on the other hand, a
blessing bestowed in harmony with the claims of
righteousness, and on the ground of a perfect atonement for sin. The grace is shown, not in dispensing
with atonement, but in providing it. The forgiveness,
as respects the sinner, is free; as for the Forgiver,
He takes the burden of what is needed for the satisfaction of the claims of righteousness upon Himself, and
to the grace of forgiveness adds the further grace
of seeing that the conditions of its bestowal are
righteously fulfilled. Under no aspect is the transaction a purely external or legal one. Spiritual and
ethical elements are involved at every point. Saviour
and sinner do not stand apart from each other. There
is a relation of kinship and sympathy on the one
hand; the spiritual bond of faith on the other. It is
the old idea of Bernard: the Head satisfies for the
members, yet the members no less recognise the grace
that flows to them from the Head.

[1] Cf. Calvin, *Instit.* ii. 17.

IX

POST-REFORMATION THEOLOGY : LUTHERANISM AND CALVIN-
ISM—NEW INFLUENCES ACTING ON THEOLOGY AND
THEIR RESULTS IN RATIONALISM (SEVENTEENTH
AND EIGHTEENTH CENTURIES)

"We must have the living faith of Luther, as well as his orthodoxy."—
Spener.

"Grapes do not grow on bramble bushes. Illustrious natures do not form themselves upon narrow and cruel theories. . . . Calvinism has borne ever an inflexible front to illusion and mendacity, and has preferred rather to be ground to powder like flint than bend before violence or melt under enervating temptation."—Froude.

"To omit Calvin from the forces of Western evolution is to read history with one eye shut. To say that Hobbes and Cromwell stand for the positive results of the intellectual revolution in Protestant countries, and that Calvin does not, is to ignore what the Calvinistic Churches were, and what they have done for moral and social causes in the old world and the new. Hobbes and Cromwell were giants in their several ways, but if we consider their power of binding men together by stable association and organisation, their present influence over the moral convictions and conduct of vast masses of men for generation after generation, the marks they have set on social and political institutions wherever the Protestant faith prevails, from the country of John Knox to the country of Jonathan Edwards, we cannot but see that compared with Calvin, not in capacity of intellect, but in power of giving formal shape to a world, Hobbes and Cromwell are hardly more than names writ in water."
—J. Morley.

"The Christian religion does not need to beg for pity or mercy : it need not fall on its knees and cry out imploringly for life : the day will reveal whether it has gold and silver or straw and stubble to oppose to these devastating flames."—Semler.

LECTURE IX

Post-Reformation Theology; Lutheranism and Calvinism—New
   Influences acting on Theology and their Results in Rationalism (Seventeenth and Eighteenth Centuries).

WITH Professor Harnack the history of dogma closes
at the Reformation.   Protestant theology, from a
different motive, has gone practically on the same
hypothesis.   It plants itself upon the creeds of the
sixteenth and seventeenth centuries, and regards any
deviation from these, or tampering with them, as a
species of defection.   There is thus far justification for
Harnack's view, that, with the exception of the dogma
of Papal Infallibility, promulgated by the Vatican
Council in 1870, of which he takes account, there has
been no attempt since the Reformation period to
formulate a new doctrine in documents having general
authority.[1]   The Protestant creeds of Post-Reformation
date—the Canons of the Synod of Dort, and the Westminster Confession, for example, only bring up the rear
of the Reformation movement, and do little more than
reproduce or crystallise its results.   Yet everyone who
knows the history of theology is well aware that the
development of doctrine did not stop with the sixteenth
century.   It has passed through momentous phases
since, and is still in progress under the action of ideas

[1] Pius IX. promulgated in 1864 the dogma of the Immaculate Conception of the Virgin, but it is not embodied in any creed.

and influences that continue profoundly to modify it.
One branch of theology, indeed, I have not yet touched
on at all, viz., Eschatology.   For, though the doctrine of
the Last Things has necessarily always had a place in
Church thought and speculation——had even in the
Mediæval Church an extraordinary mythological development [1]——it can hardly be said to have had an
" epoch " or period in which it was exhaustively discussed as other doctrines have been.   I have thrown
out the suggestion [2] that, if any age can be named as
an " epoch " for this doctrine, it is our own age, with its
generally widened outlook on the universe, its larger
conceptions of the divine love, its better knowledge of
heathenism, its *fin de siècle* feeling——all which have
combined to press on it with peculiar intensity the
questions of the future destiny of the individual and
the race.   In any case the subject is one which can
only be profitably discussed as the outcome of an
intelligent apprehension of all the other doctrines of
the Christian system.   I leave it, therefore, till the last
lecture.   Meanwhile I proceed to look at the general
causes which have tended to modify doctrine since the
age of the Reformation, and at some of their principal
effects.

I. I have already hinted that the Reformation age
was marked by its productivity in *Creeds*.   We do well
not lightly to estimate the gain that accrues to us from
these creations of the sixteenth century spirit.   We
shall greatly err if, following a prevalent tendency, we
permit ourselves to think of them only as archæological
curiosities.   These creeds were no dry-as-dust produc-

---

[1] Cf. Lect. X.   The classical representation of Mediæval eschatology
is in Dante's immortal epic.
[2] Cf. Lect. I. p. 29.

tions, but came molten and glowing from the fires of a living faith, and enshrine truth which no Church can part with without serious detriment to its own life. They are the classical products of a distinctively *creed-making* age, by which I mean an age that possesses a faith which it is able to state intelligibly, and for which it is ready, if need be, to suffer—which, therefore, cannot but express itself in forms that have enduring worth. Such ages do not come at men's bidding, and till they do come, the process of creed-making, or creed-tinkering, will not have much success. It is a significant fact that the creeds of the Reformation age remain, as I have said, in practically unchanged form, to this hour the doctrinal bases of the great Protestant Churches. What modifications have been made on them are unimportant, and the efforts to displace them by newer symbols have not had much success. The Lutheran Church, *e.g.*, notwithstanding the rationalism that has abounded within its borders, still stands broad-based on its Augsburg Confession ; the Anglican Church on its Thirty-Nine Articles ; our Presbyterian Churches on the Westminster and similar Confessions.[1] These creeds have stood as witnesses, even in times of greatest declension, to the great doctrines on which the Churches were established ; have served as bulwarks against assault and disintegration ; have formed a rallying-ground for faith in times of its revival ; and have always, perhaps, represented with substantial accuracy the living faith of the spiritual part of their membership.

There is another point of view, however, in which

[1] I do not forget the great Wesleyan, Baptist, and Independent Churches, but so far as these have creeds they are in substance evangelical.

those creeds more nearly concern us.   It follows from
the line of thought I have endeavoured to pursue in
these lectures, that only now had the Church obtained
a position in which it was possible for it to exhibit in
the form of a creed the whole round of Christian
doctrine.   So long, *e.g.*, as the Church was occupied
only with Theological questions—that is, with the doctrines of God and the Trinity—it could but give expression to the results attained in that department ; so
long as it was concerned only with Christological problems, it could but formulate Christological results : not
till a practically complete survey had been taken of the
entire round of Christian doctrines did it become possible
to produce creeds embodying the whole Christian system.
This now is the peculiarity of the creeds of the Reformation.   The Reformation creeds *do* give, and give
practically for the first time, a survey of Christian
doctrine in all its great articles.   Framed as they were
with special reference to justification by faith and its
connected doctrines, they could not do otherwise.   For
these doctrines look back upon and presuppose the
statement of all the doctrines that precede.   For the
same reason the Roman Church, in drawing up its
antithetic symbol at Trent, found it necessary for the
first time to frame a creed covering the whole ground
of doctrine.

We shall do injustice to the Reformers—let me say
further—if we fail to notice another great fact about
these creeds, viz., their explicit reference to Scripture.
It is not uncommon to hear it said, that, while the
parts of the Reformation creeds which sprang from the
evangelical consciousness of the age—the doctrine of
justification and its related doctrines—are fresh and
vital, it is different with the remaining parts, which are

taken over unchanged from the Catholic tradition. It
is made a reproach to the framers of these creeds, *e.g.*,
that they simply stood in the paths of the earlier
decisions on the Trinity and the Person of Christ, and
did not attempt a reconstruction of these doctrines in
the light of the new evangelical principle.[1] I cannot
agree that this reproach is well founded.[2] It is the
case, no doubt, that the Reformers adhere to the older
Church definitions on the Trinity and Person of the
Redeemer, but the reason is obvious. In the first place,
they required these doctrines as the foundation of their
own evangelical faith. A Saviour truly God and truly
man—and not less a divine Spirit proceeding from the
Father and the Son—were an absolute necessity as
the basis of their doctrines of redemption, of justification, of regeneration. But, in the next place, they did
not take these doctrines simply from tradition, but
accepted them from a clear perception that they were
Scriptural and true. No men were less likely to accept
doctrines on the ground of simple tradition. They
swept away piles of error which formed part of the
existing Church system, some of it of hoar antiquity,
because they found no support for it in Scripture. If
they clung to these ecumenical doctrines of the Son
and Spirit, it was because they as clearly perceived that
the Scripture taught them. And as this was the basis
on which their creeds were constructed, so it is in fair-
ness the test by which they should now be tried. We
may, if we please, challenge the sufficiency of Scripture
as a basis of doctrine, but we should at least remember
that Scripture is the ground on which *these* exhibitions
of doctrine profess to rest, and should do them the

---

[1] Thus Ritschl, Harnack, etc.

[2] I do not mean that there may not be call in some respects for such
reconstruction. See next Lecture.

justice of testing them, in the first instance, by their own claim.

II. I come now to speak positively of the theological developments which have taken place on the basis of these Reformation creeds, and within the Churches represented by them.   It will be obvious that the theological task in this period differs in one important respect from that of the earlier stages.   Then, as we have seen, many of the doctrines had not been developed at all, or were only in process of development ; now, each of them — eschatology excepted — had passed through an epoch-making phase, and the results were embodied in accepted creeds.   That work, already done, had not to be done *de novo*.   There might in the future be declension from attainments already made, relapses into bygone errors, or revivals of the latter in new forms, or there might be positive advance ; but whatever shape the development assumed, it could not but be conditioned by the fact that the Church had now the whole range of doctrine before it, and could view the development from the commencement to its close.   This naturally had an effect on the idea of system.   In the construction of its doctrines, one by one, in history, the Church was not guided by the idea of system.   The system lay in the nature of the case, not in any perception of the Church as to whither the process tended.   The earlier doctrines were not framed with any knowledge of the controversies that were to arise later.   There was no call or attempt, therefore, to fit the one accurately into the other, as the idea of a perfect system required.   There was, of course, throughout a *feeling* of the unity of the faith, which exercised a certain regulating influence, but it could not supply the place of consciously directed

effort.   Now, however, that a provisional goal had
been reached, there were room and need for a revision
and adjustment of the doctrinal system in its completeness.   Part could now be fitted more accurately into
part, weaknesses detected, modifications made, while
the new questions that emerged in the light of the
construction of the whole, or with the further advance
of knowledge and thought, made it possible to carry
the development further.   I do not, of course, mean
that systematic theology had no existence prior to the
Reformation.   It had its beginnings as far back as
Origen, although as a special discipline it dates really
from the time of the schoolmen.   These built up
huge, but very imperfect, systems on the basis of the
Sentences of Peter the Lombard, or similar works.
But at the Reformation it entered on a distinctively
new phase, corresponding with the greater completeness that had been attained in the apprehension of
doctrine.   Then, on the ground both of the Lutheran
and the Reformed Churches,—but unequally, for the
Lutherans of the sixteenth century did not excel in
the systematic gift, and hardly got farther than *Loci*,
or topical treatment of doctrines, while the Reformation
Church had a systematic genius of the first order in
Calvin,—vast systems of dogmatics arose, and started
a multitude of questions which occupied men's minds
with all the keenness of the old scholastic disputes.

But, besides these causes of development in the
Church itself, there were other and yet more powerful influences which came into play from without, the
full effect of which was only felt later.   I refer to the
great intellectual awakening which the Reformation
brought with it ; or rather, which began in the revival
of learning of the preceding century, and now received

a mighty impulse from the mental liberation implied in the Reformation doctrine of the right of private judgment. Everything helped to intensify this impulse. The past had been laid bare in the recovery of the literary treasures of Greece and Rome ; the conception of the world was widened by the discovery of a new continent, and by the circumnavigation of the globe ; a yet vaster expansion was given to men's ideas of space by the promulgation of the Copernican theory of the universe. The printing-press had furnished knowledge with wings ; the era of physical science, with Lord Bacon as its prophet, was dawning ; philosophy was on the eve of commencing the mighty cycle only completed in our own (nineteenth) century ; society was emerging from the feudal stage into that of the modern monarchy. Everywhere there was upheaval, a shaking of old institutions and conceptions, a setting free of forces, some destructive, others wholesome and creative. To this new spirit of the time, in all its forms of working, the theology of the Reformation had to adjust itself. I think we hardly realise the magnitude of its task in comparison with what we take to be the greater difficulties of our own age. It was impossible for such a process to be gone through without the encountering of many hazards, many temptations to deflection on right and left. As little was it possible for it to be gone through without enormous gain and quickening in every direction. Let me try to trace in outline the path it actually followed.

A glance has already been taken at the internal disputes which agitated the *Lutheran* Church up till the compilation of the Formula of Concord in 1577. In a twofold respect, apart from distinctions in worship and government, the Lutheran Church signalised its difference from the Reformed—first, in falling back, under the guidance of Melanchthon, on a less rigorous, but, as is generally admitted,[1] a logically inconsequent view of predestination ; and, second, in its insistence on a real, corporeal presence of Christ in the eucharist, and on a doctrine of the *ubiquity* of Christ's humanity connected therewith. It is to the latter of these divergencies that the peculiarities of later Lutheranism specially attach themselves. The Christology of the Lutherans, in fact, is not an independent development, but is conditioned throughout by the doctrine of the Lord's Supper. If a real presence of Christ's flesh and blood " in, with, and under " the elements of the Supper (consubstantiation) is maintained, it seems evident that a ubiquity—an omnipresence, or at least multipresence —of Christ's body must be affirmed. A doctrinal basis has then to be sought for this in the idea of a *communicatio idiomatum*, or perfect participation of the humanity of Christ in all the attributes of deity, including omnipresence. Disputes inevitably arise as to the nature of this ubiquity, and then we have controversies like those between Brentz and Chemnitz—the former upholding an *absolute* omnipresence of Christ's glorified humanity, the latter contending for a *relative* ubiquity, *i.e.*, a ubiquity dependent on Christ's will, though evidently this implies an absolute omnipresence *in potency*.[2] A kindred controversy is that in the seventeenth century between the Giessen and Tübingen theologians regarding the manner of Christ's possession, or rather use,[3] of this attribute on earth. The Reformed

---

[1] Cf. Dorner, *Hist. of Prot. Theol.* i. 401 ; Schaff, *Creeds of Christendom*, pp. 314, 330.

[2] Cf. Schaff, as above, pp. 290 ff. ; Bruce, *Humiliation of Christ*, pp. 111 ff.

[3] Whether surrendered (κένωσις), or only *secretly* exercised (κρύψις) Cf. also Dorner, *Hist. of Doct.* iii. 229-38.

Church was saved from these extravagancies of speculation by its more sober view of the Supper, though it
leans, perhaps, to the opposite error of too severe a
separation of the divine and human natures.[1]   Even
as between the two sections of the Church, however, it
is surprising to see how largely the controversy resolved
itself in the end into a matter of words.   Pressed to
explain, the Lutheran had to acknowledge that he
did not mean that Christ was everywhere present in a
crass, material fashion ; but only that He was present
dynamically, in some invisible, incomprehensible manner,
in power or energy—in the *virtue*, not in the substance of His body.   It then was not easy to see
how this doctrine differed essentially from that of the
Calvinist, who granted also that Christ was present in
and with His people in the power of His risen life as
Lord of all.

The settlement of doctrine on the basis of the
Formula of Concord was followed in Germany by a
century of almost undisturbed Lutheran orthodoxy—a
principal controversy being that of the Giessen and
Tübingen divines on the Lord's humiliation above
referred to.   This is the period known as that of the
Lutheran Scholasticism, when theology, though cultivated
by men of marked learning and ability,[2] tended increasingly to become arid and formal,—when orthodoxy
of the letter became the chief concern, and piety of the
heart was put into the background in comparison.

---

[1] The saving point in the Lutheran doctrine is the richer view of the
communion of the natures.   In it lies the thought of the humanity as
receptive of the divinity.   In these disputes Melanchthon agreed with the
Reformers.

[2] As, *e.g.*, Gerhard, Quenstedt, Calovius, Musæus, Carpzovius.   In both
the Lutheran and Reformed scholasticism we have an alliance with
Aristotelianism.

Yet here again we must be careful not to exaggerate. The ornaments of the Universities were, many of
them, men of genuine godliness; alongside the rigid
Lutheranism there were milder and more Catholic
tendencies—in the Calixtine school,[1] for example;
mysticism could give birth to a genius like the Görlitz
shoemaker, Jacob Böhme; while, that a warm and
living piety subsisted in the hearts of the people in
those dreary days—even in the most unspiritual part of
them, viz., during the Thirty Years' war,[2] when religion
seemed trampled under foot amidst the ruthless
passions and unspeakable devastations of the time—is
evidenced by the exceptionally rich outburst of Church
Song which is so strangely a feature of the period.
Many of the most popular of the German hymns well
up from this unpromising fountain-head. Gradually
this undercurrent of earnest religious feeling reacted on
a dogmatic which had ceased to minister to life, and,
ere the close of the century, had brought in the era of
Pietism, which, with the devout Spener and the Bible-
loving and philanthropic Francke as leaders, and the
new University of Halle as a working centre, gained,
after many struggles, a temporary ascendency. But
Pietism failed in the long run by reason of that which
was originally its source of strength—its *subjectivity*.
Laying, as was proper, the chief accent on personal
religion, on works of love, and on the actual keeping of
Christ's commandments, it exalted Biblical study, but,
on the other side, depreciated human learning, and
looked askance at doctrinal theology, which had become
distasteful to it through its barren subtleties, and substitution of orthodoxy for life. This one-sidedness of

[1] Calixtus represented a liberal and irenical, if latitudinarian, tendency,
with a wide range of scholarship. He was keenly opposed by the stricter
Lutherans.
[2] 1618-1648.

the movement, once the first warm impulse had spent itself, brought with it its own penalty. Decadence set in after the death of the leaders, and what had begun as a true work of God became marked by narrowness, poverty, and jejuneness of spirit. For the healthy objectivity of the piety of the Reformers, it substituted a morbid brooding on subjective states ; while, in a scientific respect, it could offer no satisfaction to minds aroused to ask the *meaning* of the Christian doctrines, and their relations to the wide fields of knowledge opening up around them. It cannot be thought surprising, therefore, that, from these causes and others to be afterwards referred to, both Pietism and the older orthodoxy, which had itself largely become a species of intellectualism, should, about the middle of the eighteenth century, fall a prey to the rationalism which at that time was overspreading Europe.[1]

From this glance at Lutheranism, I return to look at the stronger *Calvinistic* development. Calvin's *Institutes* were published in 1634, and the Reformer's connection with the city of Geneva, which speedily raised him to the position of theological dictator to the Reformed Churches in Europe, commenced in 1636. The extraordinary grasp, breadth, and logical cohesion of Calvin's thinking gave his system a hold upon the minds and consciences of men, which, in union with the more flexible type of his Church organisation, enabled it to spread and take root under diverse national conditions, as Lutheranism was unable to do. It is hardly necessary, in a summary sketch of this kind, that I should enter on the defence of Calvinism from the shallow and often very ignorant criticisms that are sometimes passed upon it. Enough to say that it is the

---

[1] See below, p. 306.

profoundest thinkers and ablest historical students who do it, and its influence, the greatest justice.[1] I may be permitted to quote words I have myself ventured to use elsewhere:—" Calvin's system is the reflection of his mind—severe, grand, logical, daring in the heights to which it ascends, yet humble in its constant reversion to Scripture as its basis. Mounting to the throne of God, Calvin reads everything in the light of the eternal divine decree. Man in his state of sin has lost his spiritual freedom, and the power to do anything truly good, though Calvin freely admits the existence of natural virtue, and attributes it to a working of divine grace even in the unregenerate.[2] God's providence is all-governing and all-embracing, taking up into itself every act of man, and every event, natural and spiritual. Everything that happens is thus the bringing to light of part of an eternal counsel. Whoever is brought into the kingdom of God is brought there by a free act of grace, and even the passing by of the unsaved, however mysterious, must be traced to an origin in the eternal divine will. The will of God thus contains in itself the ultimate reasons of all that is. It is not an arbitrary, but a holy and good will, though the reasons for what actually takes place in the government of the world are to us inscrutable. . . . His Church polity extended to many countries. His system, passing like iron into the blood of the nations which received it, raised up in the French Huguenots, the English Puritans, the Scotch, the Dutch, the New Englanders, brave, free, God-fearing peoples. Abasing man before God, but exalting him again in the consciousness of a new-born liberty in Christ, teaching him his slavery through sin, yet restoring to him his freedom through grace, leading him to regard all things in the light of

[1] See Schaff, *Swiss Reformation*, ii. pp. 220 ff.   [2] *Instit.* ii. 2 12-17.

eternity, it contributed to form a grave, but very noble and elevated type of character, reared a race not afraid to lift up the head before kings." [1]

The head and front of the offending of Calvin's system is undeniably its doctrine of *predestination.* In the lecture on Augustine I tried to show how some of the objections to that doctrine might be met and the doctrine relieved of its appearance of arbitrariness, by a more organic view of the divine purpose. It ought to be noticed, further, that, however fundamental this doctrine may be in Calvin, it is brought in, not at the head of his system,—not, therefore, in the all-dominating place it holds, *e.g.,* in the Westminster Confession—but towards the close of his third book as a corollary from his exposition of the work of the Holy Spirit in regeneration and sanctification.

This is true, yet in a theological respect, there is undoubtedly a side here of Calvin's system which urgently calls for rectification and supplement. Nor, from the more favourable position we now occupy, do I think it is difficult to place the finger on what must be regarded as its especial defect. That defect does not lie simply in the doctrine of predestination. It lies rather in the idea of God behind that doctrine. I have spoken of the correction to be made by a more organic view of God's purpose in history ; but that organic view already implies an altered standpoint in thinking of God Himself. Calvin exalts the sovereignty of God, and this is right. But he errs in placing his root-idea of God in sovereign will rather than in love. Love is subordinated to sovereignty, instead of sovereignty to love. God's will, certainly, is not with

[1] Lecture on Calvin in volume on *The Reformers*, pp. 292-94. Cf. Froude on " Calvinism," in *Short Studies.*

Calvin an arbitrary will.   In the passage in which he speaks most strongly on the subject, he expressly repudiates the idea that God's will is *exlex*.[1]   It is a holy, wise, and good will—along a definite line, apart from natural bounty and mercy which are toward all, even a loving will ;[2] but love, in this more special sense, takes the direction which sovereignty gives it—it does not regulate the sovereignty.   The conception is, that God wills, as the highest of all ends, His own glory ; that is, the manifestation of His whole character, wrath as well as love ; and the plan of the world is directed with infinite wisdom to the attainment of this end.   Its supreme aim is, indeed, the salvation of those chosen to eternal life ; but alongside of this is the dark shadow cast by the fate of the others in whom God is pleased to reveal His wrath.   These may be the objects of the goodness and long-suffering of God in other respects, and their ruin is never viewed save in connection with their sin.   But sovereign grace has not chosen them for salvation ; they are not the objects of God's love in the more special sense.[3]   Now this, I think I may safely say, is not a conception in which the Christian mind can permanently rest.   Our deeper penetration with Christ's doctrine of God as love, as well as the express

---

[1] *Institutes*, iii. 23. 2.   "We, however, give no countenance to the fiction of absolute power, which, as it is heathenish, so it ought justly to be held in detestation by us.   We do not imagine God to be lawless . . . the will of God is not only free from all vice, but is the supreme standard of perfection, the law of all laws."

[2] Cf. Bk. i. 5.   Yet Calvin interprets " world " in John iii. 16, without restriction.   Cf. also Bk. ii. 16. 1-3.

[3] I speak of the broad impression which Calvin's system makes upon us.   If we take into account the position in Bk ii. ch. 16. 1-3, we find qualifying matter even as regard God's natural relation to men.   It might be shown that Calvin's view does not necessarily *negate* that suggested above, though it certainly does not do justice to it.   It should be observed also that every system acknowledges a special love of God to some, on whatever ground it is based.

testimony of Scripture respecting God's character and love to the world, forbid it. No distrust we may feel of our own reason, or even the reflection that Calvin is only viewing *sub specie æternitatis* what actually happens in time, will reconcile us to it. We are sure that if God is sovereign, yet not sovereignty but love must be enthroned as the central principle of His character ; that as Martensen has said, " All the divine attributes are combined in love as in their centre and vital principle. Wisdom is its intelligence ; might its productivity ; the entire natural creation, and the entire revelation of righteousness in history, are means by which it attains its teleological aims." [1] With this connects itself the organic or teleological conception of history of which I have already spoken. Love lies behind the divine plan ; but even love can only work out its designs in gradual stages, in harmony with righteousness, and with regard to the laws of human nature and freedom. Sin therefore cannot be simply abolished by an act of power. It must be allowed to develop itself—to manifest its whole nature—that it may at length be the more effectually overcome. Divine sovereign wisdom is exhibited in the determination of the lines along which, the persons in whom, the bounds within which, this development is allowed to take place ; and sovereign grace is displayed in the counteracting of that evil and the carrying forward of the ends of God's Kingdom, through nations and individuals prepared for that service, and in due season called to their task. I do not, therefore, abate one whit from the sovereignty of God in the election, calling, and salvation of such as are saved ; [2] but I do feel strongly that

[1] *Dogmatics*, p. 99 (E.T.).

[2] Sovereignty is here opposed to conditioning or control from without ; not to determination by righteousness, love, and wisdom within God Himself.

this election of God must not be disjoined from the context in which it is set in God's historical purpose, which, grounded in His love, embraces the widest possible ultimate blessing for the whole world. I hold as strongly as Augustine or Calvin that only as God chooses men will they ever choose him ; only as grace does its saving work in them will they ever be brought to repentance, faith, and eternal life ;[1] but if God's method is thus necessarily one of election, it is in order that in each soul saved He may set up a new centre —a point of vantage, shall I say, chosen with infinite wisdom—from which He may work with greater effect for the accomplishment of wider ends.

It was inevitable that the rigorous and exclusive aspect of Calvin's system now indicated should provoke a reaction, and the danger was that this reaction, falling in a time of weaker spiritual grasp and less profound experience, should tend to the loosening of the foundations even of what was strong and true in Calvinism. This, accordingly, is what we now see accomplishing itself in the *Arminian* protest in Holland. In Lutheranism the rigour of the predestination doctrine had been softened, at the expense of logical consistency, under the milder humanistic influence of Melanchthon. In the hands of Calvin's disciples, on the other hand, it tended to become more severe, exclusive, and unyielding than Calvin himself had made it. With Calvin, as I have stated, predestination is a corollary from the experience of salvation, and so is treated in the *Institutes*. With his successor Beza, and, after him, with Gomar of Leyden, predestination is placed

---

[1] The necessity for election in the Augustinian and Calvinistic sense results from the fact that only as divine grace renews men will they be brought to true faith or repentance. The good will is itself in this view a fruit of grace. Cf. Lecture on Augustine.

at the head of the theological system, and is so treated
that everything else—creation, providence, and grace—
is viewed as a means to the fulfilment of this initial
purpose.   Two schools of opinion are now to be
distinguished among Calvinists—the milder, or *infra-
lapsarian*, which, starting with man as, in the divine
view, already fallen, regarded election as interposing to
save a portion of the fallen race ; and the sterner, or
supralapsarian, which, mounting to a point antecedent
to creation itself, viewed creation, the fall, sin, and all
events in providence, equally with redemption, as so
many links in the execution of the original decree of
the predestination of some to life, and the ordaining
of others to wrath.   A doctrine of this kind, which bids
us think of beings not yet conceived of as even created
(therefore only *possibles*)—not to say as sinful—set apart
for eternal blessedness or misery, and of the fall and
redemption as simply means for effecting that purpose,
is one which no plea of logical consistency will ever get
the human mind to accept, and which is bound to provoke revolt against the whole system with which it is
associated.[1]   From the first there had been in Holland,
where the Church had adopted Calvinism with comparatively mild doctrinal symbols, those who maintained
a protest against the sterner aspects of this system, and
specially its tenet of predestination (*e.g.*, Koornheert of
Haarlem, and Koolhaus of Leyden), and these had
many sympathisers and followers among the laity.   The
individual in whom the opposition came to a head was
James Arminius[2] of Amsterdam (1588), a pupil of

----

[1] It is right to say that it was the milder view which was the more
general, though the names of Beza and Gomar gave the other considerable
authority.   We shall see that at the Synod of Dort it was the milder, not
the sterner, view which prevailed.

[2] His Dutch name was Harmensen.   He was born in 1560 and died
in 1609.

Beza's. Selected to confute Koornheert on the doctrine of election, this able man was led to change his own view, and began, though cautiously, to declare for the conditionality of predestination and the universality of grace. His transference to Leyden as professor in 1603 gave wider scope to his activity, and, his opinions being spread abroad by his pupils, the Church was soon in a ferment, which conferences and debates of the leaders did nothing to lessen. After the death of Arminius in 1609 the party went further, and under Episcopius presented to the States of Holland (1610) their famous *Remonstrance*, in which they appeared as a body with a definitely avowed position. In its first or negative part, the statement sets forth in five propositions the Calvinistic doctrines which are rejected ; in its second part it gives the " five points " of its own doctrine. As compared with later Arminianism, the *Remonstrance* is temperately worded, affirming, *e.g.*, the necessity of the operation of the Spirit for regeneration, and for the production of everything spiritually good in man,[1] and declining to pronounce, as Arminius also did, on the question of perseverance.[2] As against Calvinistic limitation, it declared for the universality of the atonement—" that Jesus Christ," as it expressed it, " made an atonement for the sins of mankind in general, and of every individual in particular "[3]—and by implication for the universality of grace. Its more direct antithesis to Calvinism is seen in its basing of predestination on the foresight of faith,[4] and in its declaration of the resisti-

---

[1] Art. 3. The Calvinists refused to consider this article by itself, and took it in connection with the succeeding one on the resistibility of grace (see below).

[2] By the time of the Synod of Dort the Remonstrants had rejected this doctrine.

[3] Art. 2. The limitation of atonement is not taught by Calvin.

[4] Art. 1.

bility of grace.[1]   This last phrase is an unhappy one ;
for every one allows that in some sense grace is resistible,
the only question being as to the nature of the power
which, in the case of the regenerate, efficaciously overcomes that resistance.

It will be evident that this is in no sense a new controversy, but is in principle a revival of the old dispute
between Augustine and, if not the Pelagian, at least the
semi-Pelagian, section of his opponents.   It is, therefore,
not surprising that when at length, after many delays, a
general synod was convened—the celebrated Synod of
Dort (1618-1619)[2]—it should with practical unanimity
condemn the Arminian scheme, and frame its Canons in
the opposite Calvinistic interest.   If it condemned this
scheme, however, it is proper to observe that it did so
in the interest of the more *moderate* Calvinistic view,
and not in that of the Gomarists ; further, that while
connecting the death of Christ efficaciously with the
salvation of the elect through the divine decree, it
affirmed as strongly as the Remonstrants the infinite
sufficiency of the death of Christ to expiate the sins of
the whole world.   He died *sufficienter* for all men, but
efficienter for the elect only.[3]   Seeing that the Arminian
view itself does not get beyond "sufficiency"—the
atonement securing the salvation of none, but only
placing all in a "salvable" state—Dr. Schaff seems
justified in saying that "after such admissions the

---

[1] Art. 5.

[2] It does not enter into my plan to review the proceedings of the Synod
in detail.   It consisted of 84 delegates (58 Dutch and the rest foreigners),
who with 18 secular commissioners made up the assembly.   The Remonstrants, to the number of about 15 (of whom only 3 had been sent as
deputies), had not the standing of members, and early withdrew under
protest.   Schaff declares that it was "undoubtedly an imposing assembly,
and for learning and piety as respectable as any ever held since the days
of the apostles" (*Creeds of Christ.* p. 514).   The Remonstrants, of course,
judged very differently.

[3] Canon 2.

difference of the two theories (on the atonement) is of little practical moment." [1]

If, as I take it, the Synod of Dort was right in upholding against Arminianism the principle of efficacious grace, in which lies the nerve of the Augustinian and Calvinistic view, it is equally evident that it left the real antinomies of the Calvinistic system unresolved ; and, in the unqualified assertion of a divine sovereignty unharmonised with love to the world, prepared the way for renewed controversies. The " hypothetical universalism " of the Saumer school (Amyraldism)—*i.e.*, the doctrine of a general decree of salvation conditional on faith, with a particular exercise of efficacious grace in the case of the elect to produce faith—only, with the best of motives, introduced a new illogicality. On the other hand, while Arminianism had its relative justification in the above-named defects of the Calvinistic scheme, its subsequent history showed but too plainly the insecurity and weakness of its own theological foundations. The lustre of its great names—Episcopius, Grotius, Curcellæus, Limborch—and its elaboration in imposing tomes of the dogmatic material, cannot hide its flattening down of all the great doctrines, and its growing tendencies in an Arianising, Pelagian, and Socinian direction. This is specially marked in Curcellæus,[2] but in Limborch as well we have the undue minimising of the effects of sin on human nature, the

---

[1] *Creeds of Christendom*, p. 521.

[2] This author, *e.g.*, in speaking of the Trinity, says, " In what way these three are one, whether in will, power, or works alone, or indeed also in essence, it is not necessary to define." He reasons that the Arian view is free from the objections commonly brought against it, and even the opinions of the Socinians, he thinks, differ little from those of the orthodox. The divine Spirit that dwells in Christ is nothing else than the divine nature that Christians commonly attribute to Him (*Instit.* ii. chs. 19-21). God was able by His mere nod to remit our sins (v. 19), etc.

exaltation of man's natural powers, the weakening of grace in salvation, with, in consequence, a precarious and ill-grounded view of atonement, and a reduction of justification to a divine acceptance, for Christ's sake, of man's repentance, faith, and imperfect obedience. Arminianism thus tended to a type of doctrine but little different from Socinianism, for which it prepared the way in both Holland and England.[1] Wesleyanism, in the latter country, is sometimes classed with Arminianism ; but it essentially differs from it in the central place it gives to the work of the Spirit of God in regeneration.[2]

One doctrinal product, however, Arminianism had, which cannot be passed over without special mention. I refer to the new attempt at a construction of the doctrine of atonement by Grotius on the lines of what is known as the *Governmental* theory.[3] We saw before that the Reformers sought a basis for this doctrine in that eternal law which is one with the nature of God ; but Grotius, in harmony with the genius of Arminianism, shifts it from this ground, and seeks a new justification of it as a governmental expedient.   So far, he holds, as any wrong to God, or infraction of moral law, is concerned, sin might be passed over ; but the public good, regard to which is made the supreme principle of the divine government, requires that the penalties attached to sin should not be lightly remitted.   As, however, the sinner could not himself endure these without destruction, the divine mercy (or, as Grotius names it, God's rectoral

---

[1] Cf. Dorner, *History of Prot. Theol.* i. p. 427.   On the other hand, Crell in the eighteenth century adopted some elements from Arminianism.

[2] Dorner also truly says, "Methodism was on the whole far more removed, as far as saving doctrines were concerned, from Arminianism, than from the old Reformed System " (*Hist. of P. T.* ii. p. 92).

[3] In his work on *The Satisfaction of Christ.*

wisdom) devised that Christ should be put forth as a *penal example* in his stead. To the objection based on the innocent suffering for the guilty, Grotius, besides quoting Bible instances of such suffering, replies not without cogency by insisting on the peculiar relation of Christ to believers as Head to members. The weakness of this theory plainly lies in its reduction of the atonement from something rendered necessary by the essential relation of God to the sinner, to the level of a rectoral device, having no ground in essential justice, but intended only to produce an *impression* on the mind of the beholder. Penalty, in this case, is not conceived of as something inherently due to sin—inherently *deserved*—but as an arbitrary infliction which has for its sole end to deter others from wrong-doing. Christ's sufferings, in reality, have reference, not to sins *past*, to expiate them, but to sins *future*, to deter from them.[1] This, however, is totally to change the character of penalty; vitally also to change the meaning of Christ's death as an atonement for sin. The first element in just punishment is that, apart from all considerations of the impression it makes on others, it is *deserved*—that it is the sinner's desert, or due, for his transgressions— and only when this is recognised, and conscience sanctions the penalty as *in itself* righteous, can it produce the moral impression desired. When, therefore, Christ unites Himself with our race in its condemnation, and stoops to death, it is of the essence of His atonement that He should recognise that it is a just judgment to which He is submitting *with* us, and, as our sinless Head, in His substitutionary love, is bearing *for* us. The Grotian theory must thus be pronounced a distinct retrocession from the Reformation standpoint.

[1] Cf. Ritschl, *Justif. and Recon.* i. p. 313 (E.T.).

As in Lutheranism, so in the Reformed Church, the
seventeenth century is pre-eminently an age of *scholasticism.* While England fell away to Arminianism, Holland,
after the Synod of Dort, became increasingly the centre
of light to Churches formed on the Calvinistic model,
and gave an impulse to the study and elaboration of
theology which extended itself to France, Switzerland,
Scotland, and many other countries. Voetius, professor
at Utrecht from 1634 to 1676, bore a foremost part in
these labours, as also in opposition to the influences
of the new Cartesian philosophy, already beginning to
tell on theology.[1]   As, however, we saw in Lutheranism
that the rigidity of the orthodox dogmatics evoked a
reaction in Pietism, with its subjective and Biblical
tendency ; so, in Holland, a reaction in the Biblical
interest is witnessed in the school of Coccejus,[2] who
helped so largely to give to theology that stamp of
" federalism " it has till recently retained.   The claim
sometimes made for Coccejus of being the founder of the
Covenant Theology can only be admitted in part.   It is
certain that the leading ideas of that theology are found
in writers much earlier than he.[3]   The Westminster
Confession, e.g., which is based on the contrast of a
covenant of works and a covenant of grace, appeared
in 1647, a year before the publication of the work of
Coccejus on the subject.   In this work, however,
Coccejus undoubtedly gave the idea an extension and

---

[1] The names of Amesius, F. Turretine (of Geneva), and the elder
Spanheim, may be mentioned as other representatives.

[2] Professor in Franecker from 1636 to 1650 ; in Leyden till his death
in 1669. In other respects, *e.g.,* in strictness of life the Pietists had much
more affinity with the Voetians.

[3] It is found, *e.g.,* in Scotch (Rollock), German (Olevianus), and earlier
Dutch (Amesius) theology.   As early as 1570 Olevianus (one of the com-
pilers of the Heidelberg Catechism) had published a work treating on the
eternal covenant of grace between God and believers. (Cf. Dorner, *Hist.
of Prot. Theol.* ii. 36.)

systematic development which raised it to a place of importance in theology it had not formerly possessed. It not only is made by him the leading idea of his system ; he has not merely the general division into a covenant of works and a covenant of grace ; but in his treatment the whole development of sacred history is governed by this thought. The covenant of grace— which covers the whole period after the fall—has its three economies—the Patriarchal, the Mosaic, and the Christian ; and the history of the kingdom of God in the Christian Church is laid out in seven periods, corresponding to the epistles, trumpets, and seals of the Apocalypse. A better known exhibition of the federal type of theology is that of Witsius, in his book on the Covenants. No doubt there is a Scriptural idea at the heart of the conception, and it had the conspicuous merit of introducing the idea of historical progress into the study of the Biblical revelation. It brought the divine purpose into connection with time, and gave it something of that flexibility and movement — that *dynamical* character—which we have described as the corrective to the *static* conceptions of the eternal decree. At the same time it failed to seize the true idea of development, and by an artificial system of typology, and allegorising interpretation, sought to read back practically the whole of the New Testament into the Old. But its most obvious defect was that, in using the idea of the Covenant as an exhaustive category, and attempting to force into it the whole material of theology, it created an artificial scheme which could only repel minds desirous of simple and natural notions. It is impossible, *e.g.*, to justify by Scriptural proof the detailed elaboration of the idea of a covenant of works in Eden, with its parties, conditions, promises, threatenings, sacraments, etc. Thus also the Reformed

theology—the more that it had assumed this stiff and
artificial shape—failed to satisfy the advancing intellect
of the age, which, under the influence of new philosophical conditions, had already acquired a rationalistic
bent.

III. It is to this new movement in philosophy we
must now attend if we wish to understand the strange
change which passed over the face of theology about
the middle of the eighteenth century.   The real
origin of the movement goes a long way back.   The
awakening of the intellect in scholasticism at the height
of the Middle Ages was associated, at least ostensibly,
with profound reverence for the authority of the Church.
At the Reformation this bond was finally broken.   The
revival of learning had already stimulated independent
thought, and had led men back to the study of the old
philosophies. The Reformation completed this emancipa-
tion by shattering the idea of Church authority, and
establishing the principle of private judgment.   Even
thinkers within the Catholic Church—as Descartes
—felt the new impulse, and began a course of independent speculation.   It was in effect the founding of
a new era when Descartes[1] enunciated as the principle
of philosophy the maxim of universal doubt.   Everything is to be doubted till, in the process of thought,
we come to something which it is no longer possible
rationally to doubt.   From this basis of unchallengeable
certainty—which Descartes finds in the consciousness
of one's own existence (*cogito ergo sum*)—the work of
reconstruction is to begin, and only such materials are
to be built into the new edifice as reason can vouch for
as demonstrably true.   The test of truth is the clearness with which notions are perceived to be true.   God

[1] 1596-1650.

Himself is to be believed in because His existence is seen to be involved in the idea of a perfect Being bound up with our consciousness. Descartes had settled in Amsterdam in 1629, and his views early found acceptance in Holland, and considerably affected theology, especially among adherents of the Coccejan school. Philosophy, however, was not always idealistic as with him, nor was it always found in friendly alliance with religion. Spinoza's massive Pantheism, indeed, only became influential later;[1] but from the time of the revival of learning there had been never wanting a virulent and aggressive scepticism — now breaking out in libertinism,[2] now assuming the darker colours of materialistic atheism. Against these opponents thinkers like Cudworth in England [3] and Leibnitz [4] in Germany set themselves, by elaborate argument and impressive learning, to establish a rational basis for belief in God and in the moral government of the world; while Christian Wolff[5] and his school went farther in professing to furnish rational demonstrations of the special doctrines of Christianity. In view of this rational defence of religion, infidelity executed a complete change of front. Philosophers and divines had demonstrated that there was such a thing as rational religion. The opponents, as a writer on the subject has said, " now adopted that system of natural religion which had been reasoned out for them as their own, declared its proofs to have been always so clear and convincing that nothing but the artifices of priest-craft could have obscured them, and contended that revelation should at once be set aside as a superfluous

---

[1] Spinoza was born at Amsterdam in 1637, and died at the Hague in 1677. He did, however, exercise a powerful influence at the time through his *Tractatus*.

[2] Cf. Calvin's conflicts at Geneva.

[3] 1678.   [4] 1646-1716.   [5] 1679-1754.

encumbrance on its perfection." [1]   Thus arose English Deism, with its watchword of return to natural religion, though in its lineage from Herbert of Cherbury,[2] an advocate of the doctrine of innate ideas in the previous century, it can be shown to have older and native roots.[3] Deism was opposed in England by the eighteenth century apologists, who relied mainly on external evidences like miracles and prophecy ; while the influence of the movement spread by translations and other media into France[4] and Germany,[5] which were rapidly enough developing rationalistic movements of their own.

The result of these various influences can readily be predicted.   The exaltation of reason in the Wolffian school in Germany ; the chilling spread of Socinian ideas in Holland and elsewhere ; the decay of religious earnestness in Pietism ; the helplessness of an orthodoxy which had become formal, and had already parted with half of its contents : all could have but one issue—the downfall of positive dogma, and the substitution for it of that superficial philosophy which came into vogue in the second half of the eighteenth century, the chief characteristics of which were the overweening confidence of the understanding in its own powers, and the

---

[1] Bp. Fitzgerald in *Aids to Faith*, p. 45.

[2] 1581-1648.   His principal works were published in 1624 and 1645. Lord Herbert was a correspondent of Descartes, and his Deism was a precipitation of tendencies already widely prevalent. Cf. on Bodin (1588), a forerunner of "theological naturalism," in Ritschl, i. 324 (E.T.).

[3] Locke's influence should also be mentioned.   Locke, of course, did not grant "innate ideas," but he believed that the understanding could reach clear ideas on the fundamental truths of religion, and furnished even an *a priori* demonstration of the existence of God.   Deism in England and France followed his empirical tendency rather than the bent of Herbert.

[4] Cf. Morley's *Voltaire*, ch. ii.   Unbelief in France was a direct revolt against the Church of the period.

[5] Cf. Ritschl, i. 325, 326.

imagination that it possessed within itself an ample stock of clear notions on the fundamental matters in religion and morals, rendering superfluous the light of revelation. In Germany, the effect was seen in the triumph of that popular type of philosophy known as the "Illumination" (*Aufklärung*); in France, the sentimental naturalism of Rousseau and the sceptical attacks of Voltaire and the Encyclopædists swept everything before them. Positive theology was carried away in the current, the supernaturalism of a section of its defenders forming but a flimsy bulwark, seeing that little attempt was made to defend anything beyond the supposed rational content of belief. The only cries that had favour were those of return to nature, the sufficiency of reason, the perfectibility of man. Nothing could gain a hearing but what approved itself clear and useful according to the standards of the hour.

The prospect seemed indeed cheerless ; yet in the midst of it all the thoughtful eye could discern the " promise and potency " of better things. Reason could not long keep up this delusion of self-sufficiency. There was bound to come a time of awakening, when the hollowness and superficiality of the wisdom on which it prided itself would be discovered. The craving for return to the real, for contact with nature in the true sense of the word, was sure to assert itself. And prophecies, if nothing more, of that better coming day were not wholly wanting. The fine culture and genial humanism of a Lessing and a Herder revealed tendencies which were bound at no distant date to blossom into new creations of truth and beauty. In the spiritual atmosphere everything was not death. Wesleyanism held a great future in its hand in England ; and the foundations of an evangelical

dissent had been laid in Scotland.   But even in
Germany, beneath the hard secularity of the surface of
society, a genuine piety was still cherished in numerous
private circles : in characters like Lavater, in teachers
like Bengel, exercising a quiet but holy influence on
devoted disciples, in poets like Klopstock, in communities
like the Moravians, nobly represented by Zinzendorf,
a warm stream of godliness could still be felt flowing
through the land.   It is not, however, till near the very
end of the century that we see decisive evidences of
change, or that distinct transition is made to the era
of the great modern theological movement whose
pulses we yet feel.   Then, in the downfall of the prevailing dogmatic rationalism under the blows of the
philosophy of Kant ; in the growing strength of the
scientific spirit, with its recall of men to nature ; in the
breath of a healthy humanism, represented by Goethe
and Schiller ; in the shocks of the great Revolution,
fraught with so much disillusionment, but prophetic of
so much that was new ; above all, in the general
longing which now began to manifest itself for reconciliation with positive Christianity, and for profounder
acquaintance with its meaning—in these and similar
tokens we mark the beginning of what may justly be
regarded as a resurrection-era of the human spirit.

X

MODERN RE-STATEMENT OF THE PROBLEMS OF THEOLOGY
—THE DOCTRINE OF THE LAST THINGS
(NINETEENTH CENTURY)

"And yet we think it proper to place among the things wanting a discourse upon the degrees of unity in the city of God, as a wholesome and useful undertaking."—BACON.

"Will it never come? that age of light and purity of heart. Never? let me not entertain the doubt. Surely there will some day be revealed that eternal Gospel promised in the New Testament."— LESSING.

"We must revert to the elementary, fundamental, and eternally unshaken points, if we desire that the new generation should again be fed with the bread of life."—VINET.

" He (Pitt) ruled during the convulsion of a new birth at the greatest epoch in history since the coming of Christ."—ROSEBERY.

" Taking up its position, not without, but within the Christian consciousness, Christian theology has certainly the task of recognising and pointing out the development of the general religious spirit in its connection with the Christian truth as personally apprehended."—FRANK.

LECTURE X

Modern Restatement of the Problems of Theology—The
Doctrine of the Last Things (Nineteenth Century).

I COME, as the last stage in the long and difficult
journey we have been pursuing, to speak of the remarkable renaissance the theological spirit has experienced
in the nineteenth century—of its causes, of the shapes
it has assumed, of its results in permanent enrichment
of the theological system. There is no mistaking the
fact, however dimly at first we may apprehend the
reasons, that the spirit of man was in process of a new
awakening at the close of the eighteenth century. The
influences we enumerate as causes are themselves in large
part results—the visible manifestations of a change
which had been gradually accomplishing itself through
several decades. In last lecture I glanced at some of
these marks of a transition period. Enlarging the
outlook, I must now ask you to take a more particular
survey of the causes which have principally affected
nineteenth century theology, and given it its character
of advance upon the past.

I. Europe, at the beginning of the century, was
politically in the throes of convulsions that upheaved it
from its depths. The French Revolution, alike in the
hopes it inspired, the illusions it dispelled, and the
new democratic ideals it projected into, and made the

permanent possession of, society, was the cause of changes to a degree which we perhaps still imperfectly estimate. The terrible Napoleonic wars following the Revolution, with their sequel in the wars of liberation in Germany in 1813-14, aroused in the minds of the people of that country a patriotic enthusiasm and sense of unity, attended by a revival of earnest religious feeling, which prepared a soil for new developments. For a time, in its recoil from the insipidity and narrow utilitarianism of the illumination period, and its accompanying better appreciation of the achievements of the past, the awakening spirit took on a character of Romanticism ; but this was soon chastened through alliance with the philosophic and scientific temper which increasingly gained the ascendency.

At the head of the great *philosophical* movement, which has had so powerful an effect on theology in the nineteenth century, we must, without dispute, place the name of Immanuel Kant. Kant's immediate service was to destroy the superficial dogmatising of the older schools, and to drive the human spirit back on itself in search of a new principle of knowledge.[1] If, however, the pretensions of theoretic reason were abated, it was only that a firmer basis might be laid for morality and virtue in the testimony of the *practical* reason to God, freedom, and immortality. It would be hard to enumerate all the results that have been gathered in philosophy and theology, as in human thought

[1] It will be observed how every great era in philosophy is originated with a return of the spirit to its own depths—in the "know thyself" of Socrates, the *Cogito ergo sum* of Descartes, the *Critique of Reason* by Kant. Even Locke initiated by an *Essay on the Human Understanding* his empirical movement, which Hume completes by his *Treatise on Human Nature*.

generally, from the fruitful germs implanted by this epoch-making system.   Agnosticism and rationalism can each claim Kant as their parent.   But his nobler service to theology undeniably lay in his exaltation of the place of the practical reason, and in his conception, based on *its* postulates, of the world as a teleological moral system, with God as its author, and the Kingdom of God as its end.[1]   Kant himself, nevertheless, was purest rationalist in his treatment of the notions of *revealed* religion; and it may be affirmed that rationalism changed its form, but not its essential nature, in the boldly speculative systems of his successors—Fichte, Schelling, and Hegel.   Philosophy which, in Kant's hands, had been severely critical and ethical, now, under the idealistic impulse which like-wise was derived from him, ran, with these thinkers, a course of unexampled brilliance.   In Schelling it was romantic, mystical, theosophic; in Hegel it was dialectical, absolutist, all-comprehensive; but in both systems its vaulting ambition overleaped itself, and the recoil was speedy and disastrous from the overstrained heights of Hegelian idealism into sheerest materialism, and blank, avowed atheism.   A check to this reactionary movement was partly found in developments within the school itself,—in the historical constructions of Baur, and the speculative theism of the younger Fichte and others; but a corrective had specially been prepared in the positive spiritual influence (gained from the Moravians) of Schleiermacher, to whom, with justice, is generally ascribed the rejuvenation of theology in Germany in the beginning of the century.

Schleiermacher is in a certain respect the antipodes of Hegel in religion — Hegel resolving all religious conceptions in their essence into notions of the reason;

[1] See below.

Schleiermacher placing the essence of religion wholly in *feeling*, and subordinating knowledge to that as a secondary product.   The crossing and interblending of these divergent currents in various directions,—renewed attempts at their separation and again at reconciliation, —furnish the key to most of the phenomena of subsequent German theology.   The "mediating" school which sprang from Schleiermacher sought to combine with his theology of feeling more positive relations with historical Christianity and at the same time with the thought and culture of the age, and in some of its representatives (*e.g.*, Rothe, Dorner) displayed strong speculative tendencies.   The Lutheran Confessional party, on the other hand,—unfortunately stiffened in its adherence to the Symbols by the forced union of the Lutheran and Reformed Churches in 1817,—while sharing the common life-impulse, associated with this a tenacious regard (often more apparent than real) for the forms of traditional orthodoxy.   In distinction from both, the liberal or rationalising party[1] proclaimed the supremacy of reason, and in its more pronounced adherents would have no theology but that which unreservedly accepted the "modern" principle of the rejection of the supernatural in nature and history — in the form, at least, of the distinctively miraculous.   The later and now highly influential school of Ritschl represents a reaction against all these forms alike—against speculative rationalism, Lutheran orthodoxy, and the "mediating" blending of theology with philosophy and science, and aims, like Schleiermacher, at again bringing about a complete severance of religious faith, and of the "knowledge," or system of notions resulting from this, from theoretic thinking. Its positive religious conceptions it would derive, like

---

[1] The *Protestanten-Verein.*

Kant, from the practical necessities of the human spirit, confirmed, however, by historical revelation in Christ. Theology in Britain and America has been strongly influenced in the course of the century by all these currents from Germany;[1] and, though it has had its own spiritual thinkers of rare quality and force,[2] it probably derives from this source its chief modern peculiarities. The religious influences which have done so much, on the other hand, to keep theology in Britain believing and pure, it owes to its own evangelical revival, and to the energetic Church life connected therewith.[3]

Together with these influences derived from philosophy, it is necessary to take into account the not less remarkable effects produced by the growth and spread of the *scientific* temper. It would almost seem as if to the nineteenth century had been assigned as its peculiar service in the history of humanity the conquest of material nature, in the discovery of the laws which regulate it in its different departments, and in the application of these in innumerable ways to the various uses of mankind. If the fifteenth and sixteenth centuries, with their revival of learning, invention of printing, new theory of the heavens, and scientific and philosophical awakening, brought a trial to the human spirit, how shall we adequately estimate the effects on

---

[1] Through Coleridge, Carlyle, Maurice, etc., in Britain; through Emerson, and other transcendentalists, in America; later, through direct relations with the schools, and abundant translations of German philosophical, theological, and critical works.

[2] *E.g.*, Maurice, Erskine of Linlathen, J. M'Leod Campbell; in America, Bushnell, etc. But a German influence is discernible even here.

[3] We can hardly attribute to the Tractarian movement in England a creative effect on theology, though latterly it has shown tendencies in this direction (*Lux Mundi*, Canon Gore, etc.).

thought and belief of the astounding revelations of the
past hundred years, and of the novel and daring theories
propounded as the result of the all but magical strides
made by the inductive sciences in the same period?
Indirectly, through the introduction of new factors, as
steam and electricity, undreamt of in former ages, and
the enormous enlargement of the means of intercommuni-
cation, science has inaugurated an industrial era, and
given rise to new social conditions, the pressing problems
and keenly-felt evils of which create a ferment from
whose influence theology cannot, even if it would,
withdraw itself.   Theology cannot, *e.g.*, hold itself aloof
from the reconstructive theories and revolutionary ideals
of socialism.   But beyond this, the scientific spirit,
learning confidence by success, and perfecting its in-
struments by continual thought and use, is no longer
content to confine itself to material nature.   It pushes
itself into every department of human inquiry—extends
its methods, *e.g.*, to psychology, to ethics, to religion—
insists on the application of its principles to history, to
comparative religions, to the criticism of the Bible, to
the institutions of the Church, to the growth of dogma,
—in short, will let nothing pass that cannot vindicate
itself under the most rigorous scrutiny, where it does
not claim to reconstruct and transform by the help of
its own ruling ideas : those, for instance, of the reign
of law and of continuous evolution.   The influence of
the conception of evolution, in particular, in its appli-
cations to organic nature, to society, to the history of
religions, and to the claims to revelation in the Israel-
itish and Christian religions, can be described as nothing
less than revolutionary.

It is frankly to be recognised that it is the whole
compass of theology which is affected by these new

influences. One immediate result of the changed
stand-point, and of the vast increase of knowledge
it has brought with it, has been to compel a restatement of the problems of theology along the whole line,
—to break up mere traditional acceptance of dogmas,
and drive theology back upon its sources,— to force
it to revise, re-vindicate, and, if needful, recast its
positions, even where conserving, as I have striven to
show that a true theology must, the gains of the past.
Every one is conscious, in greater or less degree, of
this altered temper and stand-point of the age. To
realise it we have only to take up an apologetic or
dogmatic or exegetical book of the seventeenth, or
even the eighteenth century, and make the effort to
work ourselves back into its thought. We are speedily
conscious that, though our doctrinal basis, perhaps,
may not be substantially different from the author's, it
is not thus we would state, or illustrate, or define our
beliefs,—that the whole doctrinal perspective and mode
of conception is altered,—that we are breathing a
different atmosphere,—that a vast range of problems
has arisen for us which were not within the purview of
the earlier writer.[1] A world of new conceptions has
emerged ; a new sense of historical proportion has
been developed ; we read the Scriptures in a more
natural and textual way, with due regard to the distinctions of its parts, and to the progressiveness of the
revelation (for this, in part, we have surely to thank
the much decried criticism) ; we are touched insensibly
by the ideas which our minds have imbibed from the
study of the sciences and our wider knowledge of the
world. Every part of the Christian system is thus

[1] The fact that we do not feel this about the Scriptures, or do not feel
it in the same degree, is a striking testimony to their universal character
and permanent power.

touched—doctrines of revelation, of man, of sin, of Christ, of redemption, of the future.

It is, perhaps, not surprising that, feeling this change, many should begin to think, as I said in the first lecture, that the right thing to do is to throw away the old theology altogether, and derive directly from the sources a new Gospel in harmony with reigning ideas. The trouble is that the "reigning ideas" often harmonise as little with the Gospel of the sources as with the later dogmatic developments ; and the question with regard to them not unfrequently comes to be, just as of old, the acceptance of Christianity in principle or the rejection of it. We are not in reality, however, reduced to this alternative. I have not the least fear that, amidst all this revolution of thought, the doctrinal system which we have seen rearing itself up through the ages is about to be overthrown, or that any of its gains will be lost. Confident in the security of our basis, we can face calmly the extension of natural knowledge, and the materials brought to light by a multitude of investigators in the field of the science of religions, and criticism of the books, text, and antiquities of the Bible. My conviction is that the result has not been overthrow, but incalculable enrichment,—a deepening in the apprehension of individual doctrines, and a stronger, clearer grasp of the whole from a stand-point nearer the centre of the divine revelation,—a more organic view of the system, with a better perception of the closeness of its relation to the general scheme of the divine purpose, and the laws and methods of God's habitual working in the universe. Without dwelling further on generals, I shall endeavour to illustrate this statement by some particulars.

II. It is obvious, for one thing, that the conditions of thought at the close of the nineteenth century call for an *apologetic* different in many ways from what formerly sufficed.   It is not simply that the old external way of proceeding from miracle and prophecy to the truth of revelation is out of date.   Miracle and prophecy are themselves the subject of keen discussion, and require to be made credible by vindicating for them a place as constituent elements in a larger supernatural scheme.   Neither does it quite meet the case to say that, while the old apologetic dealt mainly with external proofs, the new apologetic stakes everything on Christ.   Christ, indeed, is central in any adequate exhibition of the grounds of our belief in divine revelation ; but even Christ, it may be said with reverence, cannot be understood as He needs to be, if His person is divorced from its context in the purpose of God through the ages.   We get nearer the heart of the situation if we observe how, during the century, thought has been controlled by the idea of the unity of the system of things of which we form a part. Philosophy, science, theology, in all their nobler efforts, have been at one here.   No conviction, probably, is more deeply engrained into the modern mind than that of the unity of the physical and moral worlds.   Kant gave the age one of its most fruitful thoughts when he affirmed that nature is not a self-sufficing system, but has a moral end.   The effect on theology is that Christianity comes itself to be regarded as part of a larger whole.   God's purpose for His world is one and all - comprehensive ; and to understand Christianity rightly is to understand its place in that purpose, as exhibiting its goal, and giving the key to its meaning. The new apologetic must adapt itself to this altered stand-point if it is to be really influential.   It will seek

to grasp Christianity in its widest possible relations,—
as a religion, in its connection with the general philosophy of religion ; as historical, in its place and context
as one of the great historical religions ; as a religion of
the Kingdom of God, in its relations with social strivings
and the general world-end of Providence,—and it will
feel that its safety lies in its doing so.   It will recognise
that the day of hard antitheses is passing.   Instead of
crudely opposing natural and supernatural, it will prefer
to look at their side of relation and friendship—to mark
how much of the supernatural there is in what we call
natural, and how the specifically supernatural is not
violently divorced from the natural, but is based on it,
analogous to it, and in continuity with it.   Instead of
treating Christianity as a religion apart from, and
opposed to all others, it will desire to find points of
connection, and to interpret Christianity in the light
of the satisfaction it yields to the universal human
need.   Instead of abruptly severing revelation from
God's working through the ordinary processes of mind,
it will conceive of God as in His essence self-revealing ;
and will make His continuous operation in nature and
in the human spirit the ground, not of denying special
revelation, but of showing how the gates of intercourse
between God and the spirit of man are ever open,
and how natural and indispensable it is that such
revelation should be given—God entering in word and
act into history—if man is to attain the true goal of
his existence.

It is this sense of the unity in the system of things
which will lead a true apologetic to reject the support
sought by some for religion in the divorce of faith from
reason, or, as with the Ritschlians, of " religious " from
" theoretic " knowledge.   Those who adopt this stand-

point would confine apologetic to showing the harmony of the Gospel revelation with the practical postulates of the moral and religious nature. But this, while an important part of the apologetic task — one worked with marked ability and success since the time of Kant — involves an unwarrantable restriction, and introduces a dualism into the house of knowledge which, if conceded, would tend to faith's undoing by the surrender of the conviction of the rationality of the universe, and of the fundamental Christian positions. It was a true intuition, as I have already granted, which led Kant to give the primacy to the practical reason, and to base the proof of God's moral purpose and world-end on that which alone can sustain it—the consciousness of moral law. But it is a mistake to seek to strengthen this position by theoretic Agnosticism. Hegel was right when he affirmed that it is only as thinking spirit that man has the capacity of religion at all ; and if the counter - theories of the universe—Materialistic, Pantheistic, Monistic—are to be confuted, it must be, not by handing over the whole region of the rational, or what is called " theoretic thought," to the opponent, but by meeting the theorists, as the old apologists did, on their own ground, and showing that the Christian theistic view is that most in harmony with right reason, as well as best established by the facts of religion. Philosophical Agnosticism, which cleaves to one side of Kant's philosophy and rejects the other, not only does an injustice to that thinker, but takes up an untenable position. It is strictly a counsel of despair in view of the difficulty which history is supposed to exhibit in attaining to a sure knowledge of God. That difficulty is exaggerated ; for surely, if we possess the power of distinguishing between the accidental and the abiding in religion, we

must acknowledge that there are no convictions to which
the human mind is more uniformly led,—towards which,
amidst all aberrations, it more constantly gravitates,—
to which, in its loftiest moments, it clings with a more
assured faith,—than those of the existence of a supreme
spiritual Power, and of a Providence ordering the world
for wise ends.   It is in any case of vital moment to a
Christian apologist to hold fast to the truth that the
very existence of religion is involved in the idea that
God is a self-revealing Spirit, who cares for man,
and can enter into relations with him.   Without this
conviction religion would cease to exist.   Agnosticism,
therefore, is not simply the negation of the particular
ideas men have entertained of their gods, but is
the negation of religion itself—the dissipating of
this most universal fact of human experience into
illusion !

   An important result of this changed stand-point is
that it has become clearer that Christian apologetic
can never be satisfactorily separated from the positive
exhibition of the Christian system.   It is felt to be hopeless to attempt to prove by external witness the bare
fact that a revelation has been given, and only after that
sit down to inquire what the content of the revelation is.
If we are to defend Christianity, we must define what
we are to defend.   On the other hand, when Christianity is set forth in its completeness as a system,—still
more when set forth in those larger relations I have
adverted to,—it will be found that the work of defence
is already in large part accomplished.   Christianity, in
short, is its own best apology.   The unfolding of it as
in its essence embracing a view of God, the world, and
man, and bringing a provision for man's spiritual needs,
in which both mind and heart can rest with fullest

satisfaction, is the surest certification of its divine original.

We are thus brought back to the Christian system, and, first of all, to the doctrine of *God*, which is ever determinative of the real character of a theology. And here, I think, the changes that may be noted as wrought by the modern spirit are chiefly two—both important, and of the nature of advance. One connects itself with what I have already said of the attempt to draw closer the relations of the natural and supernatural through a more vital apprehension of the doctrine of the divine *immanence*—to see God *in* the processes of nature, thought, and history, while yet infinitely transcending them—and in this way to find a point of view from which a providential guidance of the world, historical revelation, the higher plane of divine activity we call miracle, and even the stupendous fact of the incarnation, will be rendered more apprehensible, and be shown to involve no violent rupture with the natural system, but to be in continuity with it, and in some sense the completion of it. The temptation in this line of thought—in itself most profound and Scriptural [1]—is, of course, to obliterate the distinction of natural and supernatural altogether ; to merge the divine life wholly in the world-process, and substitute " natural supernaturalism " for faith in a God who has historically revealed Himself in words and deeds for man's salvation. Against these Pantheistic tendencies a sound theology may be trusted to protest ; [2] but it will not,

---

[1] Acts xvii. 28.

[2] On the Pantheistic view I have written in another connection : " Any view which, under the name of exalting the divine immanence, identifies God with the process of nature—makes the world as necessary to God as God is to the world—is fundamentally irreconcilable with a Scriptural theology. A God in process is of necessity an incomplete God—can never

therefore, feel called on to disown the side of truth for
which Pantheism is witness. " Natural supernaturalism "
can never be a substitute for faith in the God of revelation; but it has its utility in warding off a Deistic
separation of God and the world, and in reminding us
that the divine and human, nature and grace, evolution
and creation, providence and law, miracle and causa-
tion, revelation and psychological conditions, are not the
harsh antitheses they have often been conceived to be.

The other change in the modern way of conceiving
God I have referred to connects itself with the doctrine
of the divine *love*, and especially of the divine *Fatherhood*, as the highest expression for what Christ has
taught us to believe concerning God in His relations
to men and disposition towards them. I have spoken
in a previous lecture [1] of the difficulties inherent in the
undue exaltation by Calvinism of the idea of the divine
sovereignty at the expense of the idea of the divine
love, through its not seeking, as in Christ's teaching,
the interpretation of sovereignty through love. It is one
of the greatest advances of modern theology that it has
so largely succeeded in restoring *love* to its rightful place
in the centre of the divine character, and so strongly
insists on the whole purpose of God—in creation, in
Providence, in redemption—being read in the light of

be a true personal God. His being is merged in that of the universe;
sin, even, is an element of His life. I hold it to be indubitable that God,
in order truly to be God, must possess Himself in the eternal fulness and
completeness of His own personal life ; must possess Himself for Himself,
and be raised entirely above the transiency, the incompleteness, and the
contingency of the world-process. We are then enabled to think of the
world and history, not as the necessary unfolding of a logical process, but
as the revelation of a free and holy purpose ; and inconsistency is no
longer felt in the idea of an action of God along supernatural lines—above
the plane of mere nature, as wisdom and love may dictate—for the benefit
of His creature man."

[1] Lecture IX.

this supreme principle. Therewith is connected the other change I formerly referred to—the substitution of a more teleological way of viewing history for that which made the governing idea the election of the individual. It accords with this that instead of the older rubric of the *Covenants*—a covenant of works and a covenant of grace—into which everything in theology was fitted, there is now a widespread reversion to Christ's own idea of the *Kingdom of God*, as that which best expresses the end of the divine purpose, and of the general government of the world. Here again theology has found a fitting aid in the idea of the world-aim, excogitated (not without suggestion from Christianity) by Kant and others.

It is, however, in the prominence which has been given in recent times to the great truth of the divine *Fatherhood* that most, perhaps, will be disposed to see the peculiar character of modern theology. A common way of stating this altered stand-point—one which is distinctive of much that styles itself the " new theology " — is that God is now regarded as universal Father, whereas formerly this relation of Fatherhood was limited to believers.[1] This is taken to be the essence of the Gospel of Christ, that God is the Father of all men ; and the relationship of Fatherhood and sonship is held to exhaust the relation subsisting between God and mankind. In this representation there is, as I take it, both truth and error. It is profoundly true that the very core and essence of Christ's revelation is His discovery of God as Father. The best exegetical and theological thought of the age will,[2] nevertheless, bear me out that the matter requires to be much more care-

---

[1] In *this* relation the Fatherhood of God is not ignored in the strictest systems.

[2] The views of Dr. Sanday in Hastings' *Dictionary*, or of writers like Lipsius, Biedermann, Ritschl, may be compared.

fully stated than in the above generalisation. It is
to be noticed that in Christ's doctrine the Fatherhood
of God is defined, in the first instance, by relation to
Himself, not by relation to the world, or even to believers. Fatherhood is something eternal and essential
in the being of God, and its object is the *Son, the* Son,
the *only-begotten* Son, who therefore distinguishes His
relation to the Father from that of every other as primal
and incommunicable. It is in relation to the only-
begotten Son that we find, so to speak, the spring of
Fatherhood in the heart of God. In the next place,
Christ extends this relation of sonship to all the
members of His kingdom. The kingdom is the sphere
of God's fatherly love and rule, and those within it are
summoned to cherish the filial spirit, and to call on
God and trust Him as Father. But this relationship is
not one of mere nature ; it is a high privilege of grace,
the result of a divine adoption, and of the impartation
of a new supernatural life.[1] Even this, however, does
not exhaust Christ's doctrine of the divine Fatherhood.
It is an indubitable part of His Gospel, on which
modern theology does well to lay stress, that there is a
divinely-related element in every human soul, even in
the worst ; that man was made in God's image, and
that it lay in his original calling and destination, even
by creation, to be a son of God.[2] That destiny he has
frustrated, has turned his back upon it, has forfeited it
through sin, and it can only be restored to him through

---

[1] Cf. John i. 12, 13.

[2] I cannot, therefore, agree with the late Dr. R. Candlish, in his book
on *The Fatherhood of God*, in holding that man's relation to God in creation
was a purely legal and servile one. It can hardly be questioned that, even
on the footing of creation, man was constituted by God for the filial relation. It was God's design for man, whether it could be immediately
realised or not, that he should grow up into that knowledge of Himself,
and that love, trust, and freedom of intercourse, which we describe as the
relation of sonship.

grace. God's fatherly heart, however, still yearns over him, and seeks to draw him to itself; and on the ground of that original destination, now re-opened to him in Christ, the veriest sinner, when he comes to himself, can return and say, " My Father." [1] Only, the grace that restores him does infinitely more than simply carry through the original purpose of his creation. It bestows on him, through Christ, a relation of privilege, dignity, and blessedness, which, on the footing of creation, he could never have attained. Thus, it seems to me, something like the fulness of Christ's teaching on the divine Father-hood is reached, and the different aspects of that doctrine are harmonised.

Leaving aside for the present the question as to whether Fatherhood in God sublates what may be called the juridical or governmental aspects of the divine character, I proceed to glance at how modern thought has affected the doctrines of *man* and *sin*. That these also have been profoundly influenced, there can be no question, and this in two rather opposite directions. On the one hand, the trend of the higher philosophy, in laying stress on the dignity of man as rational, self-conscious spirit, and on his kindredness therein to the divine, has aided theology by correcting the tendency in older speculation to hold God and man too far apart, and to regard them as wholly disparate in nature. Here also we see the tendency to break down antagonisms, and conciliate such opposites as finite and infinite, the divine and human. On the other hand, the scientific doctrine of evolution, in seeking an origin of man from lower forms, and starting him off in mental and moral equipment but one degree removed from the brutes, has, on the face of it, serious con-

[1] Cf. Luke xv. 18.

sequences for the whole scriptural doctrine of man, and
for the doctrines of sin and redemption which depend
on that.   It is not simply the Augustinian—or shall I
say, the Biblical—doctrines of a fall from original
purity, and an inherited depravity and death of the
race, which are imperilled ; but the whole Christian
conception of sin, as something abnormal, perverted,
voluntary, in man's development—something absolutely
opposed to God's holiness, and involving man in spiritual
and eternal ruin—is put in jeopardy.   Man, on the new
reading, is not a fallen being, but is in process of ascent ;
he deserves, not blame, but, on the whole, praise, that
he has done so marvellously well, considering the dis-
advantageous circumstances in which he started ; the
doctrines of redemption associated with the older view
—atonement, regeneration, justification, sanctification,
resurrection—have no longer any place, or change
their meaning.   There are those who, under the
influence of the modern spirit, cheerfully face these
consequences, and even think them a gain.   Unfortunately, the elements it is proposed to dispense
with—the sense of sin and guilt, the pain of spiritual
bondage, the war between flesh and spirit, recognised
as *evil* in the self-condemnation and shame that attend
it, the craving for atonement, the felt need of regeneration, the consciousness of forgiveness and renewal—are
not simply so interwoven with the texture of Scripture
that to part with them is virtually to give up *Christian*
theology altogether, but are parts of an actual human
experience that cannot be blotted out of existence, or
dismissed from consideration, even to suit the require-
ments of a modern scientific hypothesis.   I do not
wish unduly to dogmatise, but I must frankly confess,
after repeated and prolonged deliberation, that were I
to adopt the views in question, I should feel myself face

to face with an antinomy beyond my power to solve. But I cannot acknowledge that the state of the facts places us in any such dilemma. Evolution is a theory which, within certain limits, is supported by an accumulation of evidences that, to the modern scientific mind, makes its acceptance inevitable. But evolution has its limits ; it does not explain everything. Above all, it does not explain *origins*. It has not yet even mastered the factors which explain change. I believe I am warranted in saying that, up to the present moment, within the limits in which it has been scientifically justified, the doctrine of evolution imposes on us no obligation to think of man otherwise than as a special product of divine wisdom and power ; not that natural factors did not co-operate in his origination, or that he does not stand in genetic connection with the organic past,—everything supports that view,—but that with his advent there was a new appearance on the earth, the entrance of a rational and moral agent, who bore on his soul the print of the divine image, and who, for aught that science can adduce to the contrary, may have been as pure in nature, and have stood in as close and conscious relations with his Maker, as the most orthodox theory can require.[1] With man's appearance at the head of the organic world, a new moral and spiritual kingdom was founded. Who that believes that in the humanity thus introduced lay the " promise and potency " of the incarnation, will think it strange that a special creative act was involved in the founding of it ? I venture to assert that even in a scientific

[1] The alternative of "evolution" and "special creation," as commonly presented, is precisely another instance of those seeming oppositions which it is the merit of modern thought to enable us to reconcile ; for evolution is not incompatible with creative origins, but is studded with them all along the line—is, indeed, in constant process of bringing to light new potencies.

regard the introduction of the first human pair upon the globe is every whit as great a mystery of the laboratory of nature as before evolution was heard of.[1] In other respects the peculiar contributions of modern thought—*e.g.*, in the doctrine of heredity, and the greater stress laid on the organic constitution of the race, with the deepened sense of the evil and misery of the world which marks the close of the century, and finds philosophical expression in Pessimism—have not been unfavourable to the Christian doctrine of sin, but have furnished important corroborations and elucidations of it.

The order of thought leads me next to speak of the gains the modern age has reaped in the department of *Christology.*   Here also, as was inevitable, there has been a keen sifting of older decisions ; revivals, too, of antiquated and exploded errors, often as if they were discoveries of the newest brand ; attempts at reconstruction which have ended in failure.   But there have been rich advances as well.   From both sides we find the problem of Christ's Person approached—both from the side of the divinity and from the side of the humanity—the general object being, in consonance with the tendency to conciliation, to find a synthesis which will enable us to grasp both in a more living unity than was attainable in the old doctrine.

Germany has been the special field of attempted reconstructions of the doctrine of the Person of Christ. In the Hegelian and other speculative Christologies we

---

[1] I have not thought it necessary to enter into other anthropological questions, those, *e.g.*, connected with the antiquity of man, and fetish and other theories of the origin of religion. My views on these subjects may be seen in my *Christian View of God and the World*, the positions in which I have not seen reason to modify.

have the endeavour to construe the divinity of Christ
though the assertion of the metaphysical *identity* of the
divine and human. The true incarnation is in the race ;
Christ is the individual in whose consciousness the unity
of God and man is first religiously apprehended. This
theory of a universal incarnation can be regarded in two
ways ;—either, pantheistically, as a denial of a true
personality in God, who first attains consciousness of
Himself in the consciousness of Man ; or as the affirmation that humanity in its *essence* is grounded in God,
while unfolding itself in a world of finite personalities,
of whom Christ is one. In neither form can believing
theology accept it as a substitute for its own assertion
of a personal incarnation of the divine Word in the one
Lord Jesus, in whom "dwelleth all the fulness of the
Godhead bodily," [1]—who is (or in whom we possess)
"the true God and eternal life." [2] None the less has the
idealistic philosophy done abiding service in emphasising
that essential kinship of the divine and human which
is the basis of a sound theology of the incarnation ;
and in representing the union of Godhead and humanity
in Christ as the climax of that ever more perfect
revelation of God in the finite which we see taking
place in nature and history. With this connects itself
the Christian doctrine that the Son is the ἀρχή (origina-
tive principle) and τέλος (end) of creation—"the image
of the invisible God, the first-born of all creation"—and
that "in Him all things consist" (hold together).[3]
Schleiermacher, from another side, thought to secure "a

---

[1] Col. ii. 9.
[2] 1 John v. 20. The best scholars take "the true God" as re-
ferring to the Father ("Him that is true"), but the sense is still, in
Westcott's words, "this One who is true, who is revealed through and in
His Son, with whom we are united by His Son" ("in Him . . . even in
His Son Jesus Christ").
[3] Col. i. 15-17 : cf. John i. 3, 4 ; Rev. iii. 14.

peculiar being of God" in Christ, adequate to the
Christian verity, by recognising in Him the perfect
supremacy of that divine element (" God-consciousness ")
which is present in germinal form in every human
personality, but only in Christ attains to full strength
and rule. Christ is thus at once Son of God (in the
perfection of His sinless, filial consciousness) and
archetypal man. Manifestly, this does not take us
beyond an ideal manhood ; still it lays hold of the fact
that receptivity for the divine belongs to the true idea
of humanity, and that the entrance of God in His fulness
into humanity does not detract from its integrity or
perfection, but is the raising of it to its ideal potency.
And it is much to have it affirmed that in Christ in
some form *that* fulness was present. Even the theologians of the liberal school (*e.g.,* Biedermann, Lipsius,
Pfleiderer), with their acknowledgment that in Christ
we have the revelation of the absolute " principle " of
religion—a " principle," however, which they carefully
distinguish from the personality that is the bearer of it
—afford a striking testimony to the unique and world-
historical importance of Christ's Person, and seize a
central fact in Christ's consciousness (His knowledge of
Himself through his filial consciousness as Founder of
the Kingdom of God). More recently we have the
attempt in the Ritschlian teaching to disencumber
Christology from all " theoretic " affirmations about
Christ's Person, and to give a purely " religious " sense
to the term " Godhead " ; with the effect that the real
knot of the Christological problem is not untied, but
only evaded. No embargo of this kind can long
restrain intellect from putting its old questions as to
the real nature and rank of the being to whom it is
asked to give its " religious " confidence and homage.
But Ritschlianism has its merit in recalling men's minds

from speculative and scholastic subtleties to the historical revelation of God in Christ, by which all Christological theories must ultimately be tested, and takes high ground in its recognition of Christ as the spiritual Founder and Head of the Kingdom of God, who stands in perfect solidarity of will and purpose with God, and gives assurance of His grace.

The gain, then, from these endeavours is, that whereas the old Church doctrine approached the subject of Christology predominantly from the side of the opposite predicates of the two natures, modern theology approaches it from the side of the receptiveness of humanity for the divine ; of the natural grounding of the Spirit of Man in the divine Logos ; of a union of God with humanity which does not make humanity less human because it participates in the divine. Once started on this line, it is felt to be, not a contradiction, but a consummation of the relation of God to Man grounded in creation, that the union should become *personal* — the Eternal Son appropriating a perfect humanity to Himself, and making it the organ of His divine-human manifestation. So far, on the other hand, as these reconstructions stop short of this personal entrance of God into humanity, and leave us only with a divinely-constituted, supremely-endowed, and God-revealing Man, they have, I submit, in principle been already left behind. They do not satisfy the needs of faith, fall far short of the Apostolic Gospel, are insufficient for the ends of our redemption. They emerge in theories and schools, but as yet have not gained any footing in dogmatic formulations — are, indeed, as emphatically disavowed by the general Church consciousness as ever.

This conclusion is confirmed if we turn, next, to the

attempts that have been made to reconstruct the conception of Christ from the *historical* side. The gain
here also has been very great. There is no doubt
that a certain docetic element continued to cling to the
orthodox conception of the Person of Christ, as it came
from the hands of the Councils. The necessary stress
laid in the early controversies on the divine side of this
" mystery of godliness " tended to overshadow, and in
important respects, even, almost to suppress, the human
side. The reality and integrity of Christ's humanity
were confessed in doctrine, but were not distinctly
realised in fact. Start was made from the doctrine of
the Trinity,—from the internal relations of the Godhead,
—and from this there was descent, through the act of
incarnation, to a Person at once divine and human.
But this Person was not set in the frame of a truly
human life. Little was conceded to the growth or
development of Christ's human consciousness ; He was
conceived of as possessing, even as man, the attributes
of omniscience and omnipotence ; if He refrained from
the exercise of these attributes, it was voluntarily, from
respect to the limitations imposed on Him by His
Father's will. Christ's life, on its historical side,
accordingly, awakened, down almost to our own day,
a comparatively feeble interest. Intense pathos, indeed,
attached to His death on the Cross of shame ; and
liveliest exultation was felt at His resurrection on
the third day. But even here it was not the historical
circumstances, or inner spirit, of these sufferings, so
much as their theological significance, which arrested
attention and evoked discussion. It will not be denied
that the historical, scientific spirit of modern times has
done much to rectify this one-sidedness, and to give us
the impression of a *human* Christ, as the world has
never possessed it since the days of the first generation

of believers. The attempt, it is granted, has often resulted in an opposite one-sidedness. Putting theology aside, the frank aim of the historical spirit was, in the first instance, to see Christ with the eyes of the men and women of His own day, and to explain Him, as far as possible, out of natural factors. Discarding the "legend" of the Virgin-birth, it pictured Him as the Son of Joseph and Mary of Nazareth, as the preacher of Galilee, as the prophet of righteousness to a formal and unspiritual age. It tried to get into His consciousness; to re-think His thoughts; to set Him in the fullest light of His environment. It sought to account for Him through His surroundings, or on principles of evolution. But it has failed. "Lives" of Christ have been written from every possible point of view, but none of them has solved the enigma. The nearer men have got to Christ, the more microscopically they have studied Him, the more have they—or the age for which they wrote—been compelled to stand back with awe, and say with the centurion, "Truly this man was the Son of God"![1] His unique self-consciousness, His flawless character, His words and works of majesty and power, His entire oneness with the Father in knowledge, will, and aim, the grace and truth that dwelt in Him—a "glory as of the only-begotten of the Father"[2]—His death of voluntary surrender, the new life in which He rose, permit no other conclusion. Unbelief dashes itself against this stone in vain. The cry, "Back to the historic Christ" has corrected its own errors, or is in process of doing so.

The gain, therefore, of the whole movement has been that of faith. Christ is restored to us a more truly human Person, yet a more divine. The effect on

[1] Mark xv. 39.   [2] John i. 14.

the method of theology has been marked. Instead of starting with the Trinity—which we can only know as it grows out of the historic revelation—we begin with the earthly manifestation of Christ, and *ascend* to the Trinity as the only admissible view of the Godhead for those who believe in the Father, in the Son, and in the Holy Spirit of grace. Theology plants its feet on solid earth — " that which we have seen and heard declare we unto you "[1]—not that it may remain there, but that, with the apostle, it may mount to loftiest heights of assertion, in declaring that " the Word was God," [2] and that " the eternal life which was with the Father was manifested unto us." [3] Through this contact with historical reality, it safeguards itself against the reproach of being " metaphysical" and unreal. What are called, though erroneously, the " metaphysics " of theology can never support themselves in air. They must, to survive, be felt to be, not " metaphysics " at all, but plain, undeniable implications of the moveless facts of our redemption.

One result of this new concentration of attention on the Person of Christ is that theology in the modern age has tended to become *Christo-centric.* That is, seeing in Christ at once the centre of the revelation of God's purpose, and the goal of that purpose itself, it desires to read everything else in revelation in the light of its relation to Him—to find in Him the clue to the right knowledge of God, man, sin, duty, salvation, destiny. Christianity cannot help being Christo-centric in this sense—that it must discern in Christ's appearance the aim of all that has gone before, and the starting-point of the new creation that is to come after. Whether the Person of Christ can properly be

---

[1] 1 John i. 3.   [2] John i. 1.   [3] 1 John i. 2.

made the governing principle of a theological system
—which, as I said at the beginning, must follow the
order of the logical dependence of doctrines—is another
matter. A second consequence of the attention given
to these subjects, and specially to the conditions of
Christ's earthly life, has been the renewed and elaborate
discussion of the question of the *Kenosis*. If I do not
enter into the details of the modern Kenotic theories,[1]
it is because, as I take it, the influence of most of these
is already a thing of the past. The self-obliteration
of the Logos to the point of the surrender of His
conscious life in the Godhead (which is their salient
feature), is more than " self-emptying "—it is practically
self-extinction ; while the person that results is in no
way distinguishable from ordinary man save in His
undeveloped potencies. Thus, by a curious reversal of
stand-point, Kenoticism works round to a species of
Ebionitism. Accordingly, the tendency of the newer
Christological theories has been to dispense with the
pre-existent Logos altogether as a metaphysical figment.
This type of doctrine, therefore, is no longer influential.
The form in which the Kenotic problem now particularly presents itself is that of the limitations of Christ's
earthly knowledge. That Christ was subject to growth
and development, in wisdom as in stature, we know ;[2]
and His ignorance on one crucial point in the future
of His kingdom rests on His own testimony.[3] But on
the *extent* of this limitation of Christ's knowledge, how
far it was voluntary, in what degree it involved acceptance of current beliefs,[4] as about angels and demons,
or the age and authorship of the Scriptural books, or
what authority attaches to His teaching on such subjects,

---

[1] Professor Bruce's *Humiliation of Christ* may be consulted for these.
[2] Luke ii. 52.   [3] Mark xiii. 33.
[4] Cf. Weiss's *Teaching of Jesus.*

much controversy still exists.   Naturally, the treatment of those who proceed on purely humanitarian assumptions tends to conclusions which would, if adopted, destroy reliance on Christ's consciousness on any matters involving objective knowledge.   Those, on the other hand, who accept the postulate of the incarnation, while acknowledging the difficulty on many points of arriving at an exact settlement, can take much more positive ground, and will attribute to Christ's consciousness, not only an absolute self-certainty on all that relates to Himself and His mission to the world, but a uniqueness of vision and depth of insight into things both spiritual and natural, arising not simply from purer intuition, but from the unveiled intercourse He sustained with the Father,[1] and the elevation above ordinary conditions of knowledge resulting therefrom.

There is yet another doctrine on which I must try to let fall the light of this modern spirit—I mean the doctrine of *atonement*.   It was a great service which Schleiermacher rendered when he defined Christianity as the religion in which everything is referred back to Christ through the consciousness of redemption by Him.   This put redemption back into the heart of the Christian scheme, from which rationalism had displaced it.   But while, since Schleiermacher's day, the right of Christianity to be regarded as the religion of redemption is not seriously contested, there has admittedly been a powerful reaction against that form of conceiving of redemption which regards Christ's death as a vicarious atonement for sin.   One reason of this no doubt was that the scheme of salvation, in the forms of the covenant theology, had become too hard, mechanical, juridical, and the minds of men, in consequence, had

[1] Cf. Matt. xi. 27 ; John v. 19, 20, etc.

come to yearn for something more vital and ethical. Hence the attraction of theories like those of Maurice or Erskine of Linlathen, which placed the nerve of atonement in the surrender of Christ's holy will to the Father; of Bushnell, who sought the key to it in the power of sympathetic love; of M'Leod Campbell, which explained it as a perfect confession of the sin of humanity by Christ, which had in it all the elements of a vicarious *repentance* for sin;[1] or the simpler solution still, that God reconciles us to Himself, without atonement of any kind, by the revelation of His fatherly love and grace. It is characteristic of all these views that they set aside what was an undeniable element in the Reformation doctrine of redemption, viz., the so-called "forensic" aspect of Christ's atonement, His satisfaction to the justice of God by the endurance of sin's penalty in name and room of men. To this result also other influences have contributed; not least the evolutionary theory of man's animal origin and low primitive condition. This, from its nature, makes a view of the sin and guilt of the race, such as constitutes a presupposition for a doctrine of atonement, impossible. Christ, from the point of view of this theory, represents rather the apex of evolutionary development, an inspiration and aid to humanity in its upward striving, but in no real sense the world's *Redeemer*.

To say that these theories are inadequate is by no means to affirm that the attitude of theology towards them should be one of uncompromising rejection. On the contrary, they bring to light important elements in

[1] Dr. Campbell has found few to agree with him in his theory of a vicarious repentance. His view, however, has much deeper elements in regarding this confession of the sin of the world as a response—an Amen —from the depths of humanity to God's righteous condemnation of it. Counterparts of all these theories, including Campbell's (cf. Häring), are to be found in Continental theology.

the total work of Christ.   There is not one of them we
could afford to want : theology is richer through their
elucidations.   They help in recalling us to the perception that Christ's sufferings in our nature were no
arbitrary ordinance, but sprang naturally out of His
relation to us, His position in the world, His witness
for the Father ; [1] in showing us that His substitution
of Himself for us was no external act, but had its vital
roots in the sympathetic love which led Him to take
the sins and sorrows of the race He came to save upon
His heart ; [2] in reminding us that the value of His
sacrifice lay, not in the mere *quantum* of His suffering,
but in the ethical elements it involved—in His obedient
will, and perfect love to God and man, and spiritual
realisation of the evil of sin, and honour done to the
righteousness of God in submission to His judgment on
sin.   Not any of these, as our survey has shown,
are absolutely new thoughts ; but they are put in new
lights, with finer appreciation of the spiritual laws
involved, and are made leading thoughts in the interpretation of Christ's sacrifice.   Thus far they do not
conflict with, but enable us to understand better, Christ's
death as an atonement for sin.   Those who hold most
strictly by the judicial view may find in them elements
of assistance.   Thus it is a distinct gain to this doctrine
that modern thought should lay stress upon, and
claim to have established, the organic constitution and
solidarity of the race.   It cannot be overlooked that
the cogency of much of the criticism passed on the
doctrine of vicarious atonement rests on individualistic
presuppositions.   How can it be right that one should

---

[1] Thus Anselm.   There are, however, elements in the later sufferings
of Christ (Garden and Cross) which seem to require special explanation
from His relation to us as sin-bearer.
[2] Matt. viii. 17.

suffer for another?—that the innocent should suffer for
the guilty? But if society is considered from the
organic as well as from the individualistic point of
view, such suffering is seen to be one of the commonest
facts of life. "None of us liveth to himself, and no
man dieth to himself."[1] We do participate in the good
and evil of one another's acts. Heredity is a biological
witness to the law of solidarity. The penalties of sin
are rarely confined to the individual evil-doer. They
overflow on all connected with him—descend to his
posterity. The innocent has to bear the load and
shame of them, and often voluntarily assumes them.
This brings in the principle of substitution. Can substitution ever be right? The use of such theories as
Bushnell's is to remind us that the world is full of
substitutionary forces; that they are involved in the
very nature and ministries of love. Willingness to take
on oneself pain, labour, shame, and penalty for others
is universally regarded as the highest proof of love.
"Greater love hath no man than this, that a man lay
down his life for his friends."[2]

The problem which modern theology is concerned
with, however, is not the righteousness of the innocent
suffering for the guilty; or the sympathetic taking by
one upon himself of the pains and sorrows, and even
the *cost* in penalty, of another's transgressions. The
law of vicarious suffering—the obligation, in Bushnell's
phrase, of "making cost" for others—is recognised in
all theories. Altruism has substitution in its heart.
The question which presses is that of the *expiatory* or
satisfactory character of these sufferings—their power
to *atone* for the guilt of others. Is there need for such
expiation and satisfaction as the old theory required? If

[1] Rom. xiv. 7.   [2] John xv. 13.

needed, is it thinkable that one should be able to render it for others?   It cannot be denied, as I have said, that there is a widespread recoil from this idea, though as yet no creed has ventured to exclude it (probably could not succeed in doing so), and there are many signs that earnest thought is feeling its way back to it.[1]   With many it is held as an axiom that the modern recognition of the Fatherhood of God excludes anything of a "judicial" or "forensic" character in the dealings of God with men.   This I believe to be a profound mistake, carrying with it the overthrow of much else than a doctrine of atonement—even of those pillars of righteousness on which the stability of the moral universe depends.

There are, in my judgment, two considerations which make it indispensable that the relation to *law* and *guilt* in the atonement of Christ should be retained.   The first is that it is an indubitable element of the doctrine of Scripture [2]—interwoven with its deepest teachings regarding God, sin, and the conditions of forgiveness of sin.   The second is that it alone meets the needs of conscience in its testimony to the reality of moral law, and of the evil and condemnableness of sin.   The modern age owes not a little to Kant for the decision with which he upheld those great primary convictions of the moral consciousness on which the demand for atonement of sin rests [3] (though he does not make this particular application of his principles).   The question of a "forensic" aspect

---

[1] This both in Germany and in our own country.

[2] See summaries of the Scripture testimony in Dale, Crawford, Cave (on Sacrifice), etc.

[3] Ritschl very fully recognises this in his first vol. on *Justif. and Recon.*   But he considerably alters his positions in the second and third volumes.

of the atonement is simply, reduced to its ultimate, as it seems to me, the question of the reality of moral law for God as well as for man. If there is moral law, grounded, not in the will, but in the nature, of God, —such law as conscience reveals, and as is implicitly recognised in the daily moral judgments of men,[1]— then the relations of God to men *must* have in one aspect a "forensic" character. Our relation to God in conscience, *e.g.*, is "forensic," and can be nothing else. Fatherhood cannot—though so much higher and more tender—sublate this still more fundamental aspect of God's relation to His world.[2] We call on the Father, who is also the Judge.[3] Father and Law-giver, in other words, are in no way opposites. A universe without law would be chaos. A God for whom moral law was not as sacred as it is, or ought to be, to the consciences of His creatures would not be a God we could revere. It is easy to say, "Love is above law, and can freely remit sin." But love is not above law in the sense that it can set aside law at pleasure. There are things which even God cannot do, and one is to say that His holiness shall not react against sin in condemnation and punishment. We read that God is merciful and gracious, forgiving iniquity, transgression, and sin ; but the same Scripture declares with no less emphasis that He will " by no means clear the guilty." [4] This does not mean that God cannot forgive sin, for it has just been affirmed that He can. But it does mean that he can never call sin aught but what it is ; can never tamper

---

[1] Rom. ii. 1.

[2] More fundamental in the same sense that the so-called metaphysical determination of God's being and thought precede in idea the moral. The general moral relations in like manner precede in thought and fact the free loving relations of Fatherhood.

[3] 1 Pet. i. 17.　　　　　　　　[4] Exod. xxxiv. 6, 7.

with the condemning testimony of His law against it ; cannot forgive it even, without seeing that, in the very act of forgiveness, the interests of holiness are conserved.[1]

This, then, is the reason why I cannot consent to part with the idea of satisfaction to law in Christ's atonement. A complete theory of atonement, that is to say, must take account of the judicial and punitive aspect of God's character, and Christ's work must be shown to have a relation to that aspect as to every other. It is of the nature of conscience—which, as remarked above, knows God in his "forensic" character, and no other—that it craves that sin shall not be simply forgiven, but that, in the very forgiving of it, the law shall be upheld. It was the answer, based on God's word in Scripture, it made to this demand, which, as I formerly showed, gave the Reformation its strength as a religious movement.[2] It is the same answer the Church must give still if, under the disquieting sense of guilt, a stable basis is to be found for peace with God. I do not fear, then, but that theology will come back to this aspect of the atonement as an imperative necessity of a full Gospel. Yet the way in which even this side of the atonement will be apprehended and presented will, I conceive, differ somewhat from the older mode. Less stress will be laid on federal conceptions, and more on the organic and vital relations of Christ with believers. Substitution will be interpreted through representation—the old idea of the Head suffering for the members, and through the priestly qualification of sympathy.[3] The ethical elements that entered into Christ's sacrifice will

---

[1] Mr. Lidgett in his work on the Atonement puts all this into the Fatherhood. I can hardly follow him here.

[2] Cf. above, Lecture V.III.   [3] Heb. ii. 10-17 ; iv. 14-16.

receive more prominence, and be used as motives to win the heart.[1]   Christ's sufferings will be seen to spring from His vocation, and His endurance of penal evils, death included, to be a consequence of His identification of Himself with sinners in their *whole* lot as under the curse.   It will be felt how naturally, standing in this intimate relation to us, and knowing Himself appointed thereto, Christ should constitute Himself our sin-bearer, honouring God's law by submission alike to its precept and penalty, glorifying the righteousness of God, and, under the full realisation of the doom which sin had brought upon our race, rendering to God from the depths of our humanity that "Amen" which M'Leod Campbell speaks of, which had in it, if anything could have, the virtue of atonement. For it is again to be repeated, that it was not the mere endurance of the judgment of God against sin, but the way in which Christ met that judgment, in which the atonement for sin lay.   This work of Christ, apprehended by faith, is our justifying righteousness before God—that in which we stand absolved and accepted before Him.   Seeing in that perfection of our Redeemer all we would wish to be, but are not, God graciously counts it ours, and sets it before us as our life-task to grow up into Him who is our Head in all things, till the likeness is complete.

III. I have left myself but little space for the last topic I have to touch on—that which brings these lectures to a close—the relation of our modern age to *Eschatology.*   I pointed out in previous references to the subject[2] that there has never been an epoch for eschatology as for other doctrines.   So far as the early

---

[1] Cf. an interesting chapter in Sartorius, *Divine Love*, pp. 147 ff. (E.T.). Cf. Lectures I., IX.

Church had a doctrine of the last things, it was prevailingly chiliastic, *i.e.*, millenarian.[1]   In the Fathers who succeeded we have already the beginnings of all the tendencies which have since been developed more fully. In Origen, *e.g.*, in the first half of the third century, we have the doctrine of final restitution ; as in his predecessor Clement, we have a theory of what would now be called second probation.   Origen was followed in his restoration theories by Gregory of Nyssa (fourth century), Theodore of Mopsuestia (fifth century), and others. Neither his views nor Clement's, however, obtained general currency in the early Church, still less were favoured in the Mediæval Church.   Attempts have repeatedly been made to identify the apologists and early Fathers with what is known as the doctrine of conditional immortality, *i.e.*, the theory of the natural mortality of man, soul as well as body, and of the annihilation of the wicked—immortality being viewed as a gift of grace.   But there is here a misapprehension. These Fathers do, indeed, frequently speak of immortality as depending on the will of God ; but this only in opposition to the Platonic doctrine of an inherent immortality of souls (subsisting both before and after birth), and not with the intention of throwing doubt on the immortality of souls *de facto*.   The usual theory in the Church was that of an eternal punishment for the wicked and eternal reward for the good.   The traces of the cruder view are few, and in ill-instructed writers.[2] Very early, on the other hand, we come on germs of what afterwards ripened into the doctrine of purgatory, *i.e.*, an intermediate state for the purification by suffering of the imperfectly sanctified, or of expiation of sins not sufficiently satisfied for here.   Hermas in his *Shepherd*

---

[1] Thus, *e.g.*, Papias, Justin, Irenæus.
[2] *E.g.*, Hermas (second century), Arnobius (end of third century).

(second century) has already the germ of such a belief, and prayers for the dead from an early date imply it. Still with Augustine (fifth century) purgatorial suffering is still only a perhaps, and not till the end of the sixth century does the doctrine receive formal shape at the hands of Pope Gregory the Great. Thereafter eschatology enters on what may be called its mythological phase in the Middle Ages. The invisible world is divided into Heaven, Hell, and Purgatory, and imagination revels in descriptions of the topography, arrangements, and experiences of each region. The Reformation swept away these creations of terror and fancy, and reverted to the severe antithesis of Heaven and Hell. Both abodes are conceived of as entered at death, though the final reception to blessedness or banishment to woe is after the resurrection and final judgment. Thus the matter stood, and very awful were the liberties which the holiest of men permitted themselves in picturing the irreversible condition and terrible torments of the lost. There is hardly anything in literature more appalling, for example, than the sermon of Jonathan Edwards on this subject, nor is it easy to explain how so spiritual and gracious a man—one so penetrated by the thought of the love of God—could allow himself to write as he did of the dealings of the Almighty even with the condemned. So with Boston and other divines.

All this of necessity provoked a reaction. We see already a decided weakening of the doctrine in Arminians like Limborch. Deism and the easy-going theology of the illuminist period, with their lighter views of sin, protested against the orthodox view. Then the stronger intellect and conscience of the nineteenth century took up the opposition. The general enlargement of knowledge, the better acquaintance with other civilisations and religions, reflection on the unnumbered millions of the heathen world who had never heard of Christ, the stronger feeling of the complexity of the problem of responsibility awakened by discussions on heredity, operated in the same direction of fostering doubt and provoking inquiry.   The theological doctrine itself was plainly inconsequent in its sharply-exclusive division into Heaven and Hell, while acknowledging that neither condition is complete in the interval of disembodied existence.   Is it to be supposed that beings, after spending ages of happiness or misery in these abodes, are brought forth from them at the resurrection to be judged, only to be sent back to the same conditions after the final sentence?   I formerly hinted, as a contributing cause to this deeper interest in eschatological questions, at the sense of exhaustion and sadness—the somewhat pessimistic temper—in which the century closes, as if human affairs were drawing to some final crisis.

The effect of the influences I have enumerated has been to engender a far profounder sense of the complexity and difficulty of the eschatological problem than existed a generation or two ago.   People are less inclined to dogmatise in a region where so much is necessarily obscure; are less disposed to lift the veil which it is felt God has wisely left on large portions of the future; and would not for the world take upon their lips the kind of language about the hereafter of the majority of mankind which godly men freely employed in last century.   We can observe a more tender tone in the utterances even of the most orthodox in their allusions to the fates of men.   On the other hand, not content with this laudable caution, many boldly plunge into speculations and dogmatisms of an opposite kind.

Older theories are revived and defended with learning and ability; "larger hopes" blossom into dogmatic universalisms; the Fatherhood of God is made the ground of inference that none of the Father's children can be allowed to perish; others seek to solve the problem of final obduracy by annihilation; with many a favourite view is that of continued, or second, probation,—this lasting till, as they say, every soul has been brought into the full light of the knowledge of Christ, and led to definitive acceptance or rejection of Him.

I realise—I can even to some extent sympathise with—the motives which prompt these various theories. The one thing I feel compelled to say about them is, that they seem to me to rest on no solid basis in Scripture; have, in truth, in nearly every instance, very explicit Scriptural statements against them; further, that even if Scripture be put aside, the arguments in their support drawn from reason, or general considerations of the divine character, are largely illusory. A thoughtful mind, surveying the constitution of the actual world, will be extremely hesitant about *à priori* constructions of what *must* follow from a doctrine of the love or Fatherhood of God. If we elect to abide by Scripture the basis of the new theories is even more precarious. Take the hypothesis of the *restitutionist.* I think I am justified in saying that fair exegesis of Scripture does not warrant such hopes of a final universal restoration of the race as the theorist of this class indulges in.[1]   Scripture divides men at the judgment; and so far as its light carries us—so far as the force of the term αἰώνιος extends, or language that bears the weightiest stamp of finality affords any clue —it *leaves* them divided, a universe apart in destiny.

[1] Cf. Note on "Alleged Pauline Universalism" in my *Christian View of God and the World*, Lect. IX.

The ancient prophets knew how to hold out to Israel hopes of an earthly restoration after all their sorrows, and Jesus and His apostles could have spoken as explicitly of a final gathering home of all souls to God. But the impressive fact is that *they did not.* I would not press the silences of Scripture too far ; but he will be a bold man who, in face of these silences, will draw aside the veil, and venture to give the assurance that every soul, whatever its moral state or attitude to light here, will infallibly be saved hereafter—if not now, in some remote age of the future. What can any man conceivably know of the beyond to warrant such an assurance? He knows nothing of the conditions of that future life ; he knows not whether conversion, or new decision, is possible there at all ; whether eternity may not be the *fixing* of a man's essential character, without possibility of radical change.[1] Yet he presumes, in name of God's love, to give an assurance to every soul, however negligent of opportunity here, that it will be well with it in the life that is to be ! This he is not entitled to do.

As little is the theory which solves the problem of sin by the *coup de grâce* of annihilation in fortunate case as respects scriptural warrant. It has in modern times important names in its favour—those, *e.g.*, of Rothe and Ritschl—but it is a hypothesis based on metaphors, or on *à priori* considerations which have no sufficient justification. The ordinary conditional immortality doctrine has additional difficulties. It builds on such words as "destruction," "perishing"; but whereas, according to Scripture, this destruction falls on men at the judgment, the theory in question, for its own ends, not only revives the (naturally-mortal) soul after death, but prolongs its existence for an

---

[1] "Once to die, and after this judgment" (Heb. ix. 27).

indefinite period beyond the day of doom. It pleads the words " life " and " death " ; but has itself to give a deeper connotation to these words than is implied in bare existence, or its opposite, extinction. The condemned soul continues to exist for a longer or shorter time after judgment, but has not, in the Scriptural sense, " life."

Finally, plausible as the theory of a second or prolonged probation may seem to be—indispensable in some form, as one may think, if the range of opportunity is to be extended to those who may be without the knowledge of Christ, or proper means of acquaintance with Him, here—it has also little to say for itself, beyond the ambiguous passages in 1 Peter,[1] in the way of positive support from Scripture. The latter texts are enough to keep us from dogmatising in an opposite direction ; but the general strain of Scripture is not such as to encourage these hopes, or to hold out hope at all to those who have been wilfully disobedient to light on earth. Appeal and promise are concentrated on the present ; the consequences of unbelief now are represented as fatal. The judgment itself proceeds on the deeds done in the body ;[2] these alone, apparently, determine the character and measure of award. There is no hint of a possible change from the one side to the other at, or prior to, the judgment seat. The great problem, therefore, remains unrelieved by any solution afforded us by positive revelation. Factors, indeed, of some kind unknown to us there may, and even must be ; for we feel instinctively that the last word has not been spoken in respect of the winding up of the affairs of a world involving the destinies of incalculable multitudes of immortal spirits. Probably

---

[1] 1 Peter iii. 18-20 ; iv. 5, 6.
[2] Cf. Matt. xxv. 31-46 ; 2 Cor. v. 10, etc.

with our present faculties we could not understand it if it were. As I have expressed it elsewhere, we have not a calculus adequate to deal with the difficulties and relations of this infinitely complicated subject.[1] God is the judge. Enough for us, while seeing to it that we do not ourselves fail to enter into the rest of God through unbelief,[2] to be assured, that whatever love can do and righteousness permits, with the infinite grace that streams from Christ's cross behind, will not be left undone.

I trust, that, as the result of this survey in which we have been engaged, I have succeeded in some degree in making it apparent that there is a true meaning and progress in the history of dogma, and that some glimpse even has been obtained into the law of that progress. I close by reiterating my conviction that the outlook in theology, if not all bright, is assuredly not all dark. There are, indeed, not wanting signs that we are on the eve of new conflicts, in which new solvents will be applied to Christian doctrines, and which may prove anxious and testing to many who do not realise that Christian faith in every age must be a battle. That battle will have to be fought, if I mistake not, in the first instance, round the fortress of the worth and authority of Holy Scripture. A doctrine of Scripture adapted to the needs of the hour in harmonising the demands at once of science and of faith, is perhaps the most clamant want at present in theology. But the whole conception of Christianity will get drawn in, and many of the old controversies

---

[1] *Christian View of God and the World*, Lect. IX. On remaining eschatological questions of the Advent, Resurrection, Judgment, I must refer to this larger work.

[2] Heb. iii. 7 ; iv. 1.

will be revived in new forms. On the other hand I see many things yielding encouragement—the serious attention being given to the problems of religion ; the recognition of Christ as Master and Lord even by those who do not admit to the full His supernatural Person and claims ; the earnest temper of the age, and its desire to reach the truth in all departments of inquiry ; the searching light cast on documents and institutions, which can only result in that which is of abiding value receiving suitable acknowledgment. A constructive period may confidently be expected to follow the present season of criticism and testing of foundations, and then will be witnessed the rearing of a grander and stronger edifice of theology than the ages have yet seen. If, however, I were asked in what I think the distinctive peculiarity of twentieth-century Christianity will lie, I should answer that it is not in any new or overwhelmingly brilliant discovery in theology that I look for it. The lines of essential doctrine are by this time well and surely established. But the Church has another and yet more difficult task before it, if it is to retain its ascendency over the minds of men. That task is to bring Christianity to bear as an applied power on the life and conditions of society ; to set itself as it has never yet done to master the meaning of " the mind of Christ," and to achieve the translation of that mind into the whole practical life of the age—into laws, institutions, commerce, literature, art ; into domestic, civic, social, and political relations ; into national and international doings—in this sense to bring in the Kingdom of God among men. I look to the twentieth century to be an era of Christian Ethic even more than of Christian Theology. With God on our side, history behind us, and the unchanging needs of the human heart to appeal to, we need tremble for the future of neither. " All flesh is as grass, and all the glory thereof as the flower of the grass. The grass withereth, and the flower falleth ; but the word of the Lord abideth for ever. And this is the word of good tidings which was preached unto you." [1]

[1] I Pet. i. 24, 25.

APPENDIX

APPENDIX

THE following paragraphs from an Introduction contributed by the author to a work of Dr. B. B. Warfield's of Princeton, N.J., on *The Right of Systematic Theology*, will further illustrate the statements in Lect. I. :—

" Systematic Theology has fallen on evil days. To her may be applied with scarcely a change of a word, what Kant in the Preface to his famous *Critique* says of Metaphysics :—' Time was when she was the queen of all the sciences, and if we take the will for the deed, she certainly deserves, so far as regards the high importance of her object-matter, this title of honour. Now it is the fashion of the time to heap contempt and scorn upon her, and the matron mourns, forlorn and forsaken, like Hecuba—

> Modo maxima rerum,
> Tot generis, natisque potens . . .
> Nunc trahor exul, inops.'[1]

" But a subsequent sentence also of this great thinker may be applied to theology : ' For it is in reality vain,' he says, ' to profess indifference in regard to such inquiries, the object of which cannot be indifferent to humanity. Besides, these pretended indifferents, how-

---

[1] "So lately the greatest woman in the world, powerful in so many sons-in-law and children . . . Now I am dragged away an exile, destitute."

ever much they may try to disguise themselves by the assumption of a popular style and by changes on the language of the schools, undoubtedly fall into [theological] declarations and propositions, which they profess to regard with so much contempt.'

"The grounds on which a denial of the right of Systematic Theology to exist is based are various, but they may at bottom all be reduced to one—the denial of the existence of an adequate foundation on which such a structure can be reared. Whether it be that the human faculties are held to be constitutionally incompetent to such a true knowledge of God and His ways as is presupposed in theology; or that the nature of religion, as lying in sentiment or emotion, is thought to preclude the element of knowledge,—otherwise, indeed, than as the poetic vesture in which religious emotions transiently clothe themselves; or that there is lacking in reason or revelation a reliable source from which the desiderated knowledge may be obtained; or that the *data* in Scripture or religious facts on which theology has hitherto been supposed to rest have been rendered insecure or swept away by modern doubt and criticism—the result is the same, that theology has not a trustworthy foundation on which to build, and that, in consequence, it is an illegitimate pretender to the name of science. For it will be conceded that this last and highest branch of theological discipline proposes nothing less to itself than the systematic exhibition and scientific grounding of what true knowledge we possess of God and His character and His ways of dealing with the world and men; and if no such knowledge really exists,—if what men have is at best vague yearnings, intuitions, aspirations, guesses, imaginings, hypotheses, about God, assuming this name to be itself anything more than a symbol of the dim feeling of the mystery at the root of the universe,—if these emotional states and the conceptions to which they give rise are ever changing with men's changeful fancies and the varying stages of culture,—then it is as vain to attempt to construct a science of theology out of such materials as it would be to weave a solid tissue out of sunbeams, or erect a temple out of the changing shapes and hues of cloud-land. A 'Science of Religions' might still exist to investigate the psychological laws involved in religious phenomena and their mocking illusions, and 'Dogmatics' might remain as a study and criticism of the Church's historical creeds ; but an independent 'Science of Theology,' as a body of natural and revealed truth about God, and His purposes and dealings, would no more have any place. . . .

"Divested of irrelevancies, the issue resolves itself ultimately into the one question of the fact, nature, and verifiableness of the historical Christian (Biblical) revelation. The time is past when men's minds were captivated by the idea of a 'Natural Religion' consisting of a few simple articles drawn from, and capable of proof by, reason apart from supernatural revelation —that favourite dream of the Deists and eighteenth-century illuminists ; and while the 'speculative' theory which would render theology independent of history by resolving its essential doctrines into metaphysical ideas has still its advocates, its sceptre is long broken in the domain of really serious theology. There remains as a source of theological knowledge the positive revealing and redeeming acts and words of God which constitute the subject-matter of historical revelation, though it may be contended that these stand in no antagonism to the conclusions of sound reason reflecting on the structure of the universe, or pondering the deeper questions of origin and destiny, but rather are in truest consonance with the latter, and furnish reason with a light to help it on its way. The chief danger, accordingly, in which theology at present stands, arises from the mode in which these historical foundations of revelation are being critically and sceptically assailed, —a process which has already gone to sufficient lengths with respect to the Old Testament, and is now being applied to subvert faith in such vital facts as the Resurrection of our Lord, and the miraculous context of the life of Christ generally, in the New. It is in this part of the apologetic field, probably, that a new and decisive battle will have to be fought in the interests of the possibility of theology ; and it is satisfactory to observe that one result of the critical movement itself has been to impress on many minds the impossibility of eliminating the supernatural factor from the explanation of the history either of Israel or of Christ."

INDEX

Abelard, 136; theory of atonement, 28, 229 ff. ; opposed by Bernard, 230-231

Adoptionist controversy, 206 ; Harnack's use of term, 76-78, 90

Agnosticism, 321-322

Alogi, 90

Alexandria, school of, 82-84; 106-107 ; 182 ; 188 ff.

Allen, Dr., 6, 136

Amyraldism, 299

Anselm, 136, 162 ; epoch-making, 210 ; his *Cur Deus Homo*, 28, 211, 215, 220 ; theory of satisfaction, 221 ff. ; contrast with Abelard, 230 ; 232-233, 236-237, 255

Anthropology, 26 ; in Western Church, 135 ff. ; bearing of evolution on, 328-330

Antioch, school of, 106-107 ; 182-183 ; representatives, 183, 187 ; theology of Theodore, 183 ff.

Antonines, age of, 36

Apollinaris, 179 ; his doctrine, 179 ff. ; condemned, 181

Apologists, early, 37 ; Harnack's criticism of, 25, 48 ff. ; their Logos doctrine, 53, 78 ff. ; on the Spirit, 125

Apology, early, 24, 35 ; rise and range of, 36-37 ; Justin, 37-39, 47, 52-53 ; complexity of, 39, 54 ; aims of, 44 ff. ; Harnack on, 48 ff.

— eighteenth century, 306

— modern, comprehensiveness of, 319-320 ; relation to Christian system, 322

Apostolic Fathers, Christology of, 75 ff. ; on the Spirit, 125 ; on redemption, 242 ff. ; on eschatology, 346

Aquinas, on atonement, 28, 231 ; on will of God, 232 ; on justification, 255

Arian controversy, 25 ; origin, 108 ; importance, 109 ; parties in, 112 ff. ; Arian doctrine, 113 ; logical bearings, 115 ff. ; Council of Nicæa, 117 ff. ; after-history, 170 ff. ; Council of Constantinople, 123 ; Arian doctrine of Spirit, 127, 130

Aristides, 37, 48

Arius, his character, 108 ; doctrine, 113 ; death, 122 ; 136

Arminianism, reaction against Calvinism, 295 ; views of Arminius, 296 ; of Remonstrants, 297 ; condemned at Dort, 298 ; later history, 199-200

Artemonites, 74, 91

Athanasius, 95-96 ; in Arian controversy, 112 ff. ; persecutions and character, 120-121 ; relation to Hellenism, 123 ; on Spirit, 127 ; on redemption, 112, 174, 180, 215 ff.

Athenagoras, 37, 80, 125

Atonement, in early church, 211 ff. ; Apostolic Fathers on, 212 ff. ; Irenæus on, 70, 213 ff. ; Origen on, 215 ; Athanasius on, 215 ff. ; ransom to Satan theory, 214-215, 217-218, 222, 229-30 ; Western view, 218 ; theory of Anselm, 220 ff. ; of Abelard, 229 ff. ; of Bernard, 230-231 ; of Aquinas, 231 ff. ; connection with justification, 234, 255 ; Reformation doctrine, 235 ff. ; modern views — Schleiermacher, 338 ; Maurice, 339 ; Bushnell, 339, 341 ; M'Leod Campbell, 339, 345 ; ethical elements in, 218, 227, 229,

213-214, 217 ; on justification, 234, 272 ; on Methodism, 300
Dort, Synod of, its Calvinistic decisions, 298-299
Duns Scotus, 232, 235
Dyothelitism, 199 ff.

Ebionites, 75
Election. *See* Predestination
Ephesus, Council of (431 A.D.), 188
Epiphanius, on Spirit, 127
Episcopate, early views of, 68
Episcopius, 297, 299
Eschatology, 29 ; interest of modern age in, 29, 280, 348 ; in early church, 346 ; Mediæval, 29, 347 ; Reformation view, 29, 347 ; influence of modern spirit, 347 ff. ; difficulty of problem, 348 ; modern theories—universalism, etc., 349 ff.
Eunomians (Arians), 113
Eutyches, his doctrine, 27, 190 ff. ; condemned at Constantinople, 190 ; at Chalcedon, 191-192
Evolution and man's origin, 327-330 ; and sin, 328

Fatherhood of God, 166, 239, 324-325, 343 ; Christ's doctrine of, 325-326
" Filioque " clause, 130-131
Formula of concord, 270, 288
Francke, 289

Germany, influence of, on theology, 315
Gnosticism, 24, 35 ; Harnack's view of, 55, 63 ; gravity of crisis, 55 ; rationale of, 57 ; Gnostic systems, 58 ff. ; leading features, 60 ; decline of, 61 ; effects on Church, 62 ff., 87
God, doctrine of, 74 ff. ; early Trinitarian views, 74-87 ; Monarchianism, 87 ff. ; Arianism, 108 ff. ; Macedonianism, 124 ff. ; Augustine on God, 135, 145-146, 152, 163-164 ; Anselm on God, 222 ff. ; love of God the cause of redemption, 218-219 ; 233, 238, 275, 293-295, 324 ; Fatherhood of God, 166, 239, 324-327, 343 ; judicial character of God, 224, 227, 233,

236-237, 239, 301, 342-344 ; immanence of, 323-324
Grace, doctrine of, in Eastern Church, 26, 153 ; Augustine on, 149 ff. ; Pelagian view of, 158-159 ; Semi-Pelagian view of, 160 ff.
Gregory Nazianzen, 106, 128 ; on atonement, 217
Gregory of Nyssa, 106 ; on atonement, 217
Grotius, his "governmental" theory, 300 ff.

Harnack, Professor, Greek origin of dogma (*See* Dogma) ; on Sabatier, 10-11 ; on apologists, 25, 48 ff., 78 ff. ; on early Christology, 76-78 ; on Arianism, 109 ; on Augustine, 136, 138, 140, 142, 146, 164 ; his *History of Dogma*, 6, 12, 22, 26, 49-53, 55-56, 59, 61-65, 69, 75-76, 78, 81-82, 90-91, 112, 113, 127, 138, 140, 142-143, 175-177, 189, 191, 193, 210, 218, 219 ; on Origen's view of atonement, 215 ; on close of development, 279
Hatch, Dr., 51, 55, 64
Hegel, 12, 22, 59 ; his philosophy, 313 ; on religion, 321
Hermas, *Shepherd* of, 71 ; his Christology, 77
Hippolytus, 59, 74, 91
Honorius, Pope, 201

" Illuminism " in Germany, 307 ; counteracting influences, 307-308
Impersonality of Christ's humanity, 215
Infallibility, Papal, 93, 160, 200, 279
Irenæus, 64, 66-68 ; his theology, 70, 74 ; on Trinity, 81 ff. ; on Spirit, 125 ; on atonement, 213-214

Justification by faith, in Augustine, 143, 253-255 ; importance of doctrine, 244-245 ; relation to pre-Reformation views, 246, 248 ff. ; influence of sacramental principle, 248 ff. ; harmony with earlier piety, 250 ff., 253 ff. ; " self-estimate " of godly men, 251 ff. ;

9 781573 831611